FOR ORGANS, PIANOS & ELECTRONIC KEYBOARDS

E-Z PLAY ® TODAY

233

SONGS OF THE 70's

THE DECADE SERIES

Y0-BBY-050

E-Z Play TODAY chord notation is designed for playing **standard chord positions** or single key chords on all **major brand organs** and **electronic keyboards.**

HL Hal Leonard Publishing Corporation

7777 West Bluemound Road P.O. Box 13819 Milwaukee, WI 53213

SONGS OF THE 70's
THE DECADE SERIES

Contents

good

Pop and rock music, which had almost blended into one form in the 60's, took divergent directions again in the 70's. Pop songs became more melodic, and the lyric mellowed — not always reflecting social significance, new spiritual leanings or open rebellion. The beginning of the 70's was a high point for rock music because the public was open to a great deal of music experimentation.

The space program that sent the Apollo Expeditions to the moon in the early 70's influenced and ultimately changed the music of the decade. The music industry drew from the experience of NASA and the computer industry to turn their transistors (a novelty in portable radios in the 60's) into "integrated circuits" (devices that combine many different transistors into single "chips"). These integrated circuits became commonplace in recording studio equipment and synthesizers.

With integrated circuits and advances in tape manufacturing, recording technology advanced further in the 70's than in all previous years combined. Recording went from two tracks to 32 tracks and beyond! One hundred million stereo cassette tape decks were in American hands by the end of the 70's — a fact that foretold a change in the public's buying habits from records to cassette tapes. Synthesizers went from monophonic behemoths, for which setting the patches (sounds) was a long and laborious process, to polyphonic wonders with an almost infinite variety of preset sounds.

Because of new sound and musical instrument technology, music that was heavy with the sound of electric guitars, synthesizers, and maximum amplification ("heavy metal") found its form in rock in the 70's and grew into its own style musically, as well as in appearance. This technology was also a major influence on the explosive rise of disco in the mid-70's, a trend that radically affected many record companies and the motion picture soundtrack concept.

The technology of synthesis formed the backbone of the disco sound in the late 70's. Electronic keyboards played the melodic lines and guitars had electronic "effects," but it was the automatic, repetitive electronic drums and rhythm instruments that had the most profound effect on the disco sound. Dance music needed a very steady intense rhythm, which these instruments so precisely provided.

In some respects, the 1970's began with endings. The Beatles disbanded in 1970 with Paul McCartney's announcement on April 10 that he was leaving the group. Many music critics view this event as the close of one of the most productive, innovative periods of pop music by the absolute trendsetters of an era.

pop music — the protest song. The rebellion of the 60's, was in a sense, quelled by the reality of students graduating from college and beginning their careers, joining the military, or being drafted. In 1973 a cease-fire was signed, and the Vietnam war had finally come to an end.

U.S. Opens 3rd Cambodia Drive

 RACING ENTRIES

San Francisco Times.
THE CITY'S ONLY HOME-OWNED NEWSPAPER

VOL. LXXXIX SEVEN PARTS—PART ONE   TUESDAY MORNING, MAY 5, 1970   108 PAGES   DAILY 10c

4 STUDENTS SLAIN

Troops Open Fire on Ohio Campus

KENT, Ohio (UPI)—Four students were shot to death on the Kent State University campus Monday when national guardsmen, believing a sniper had attacked them, fired into a crowd of rioting antiwar protesters. At least 11 persons were wounded, three critically, before order was restored. The university was shut down for at least a week.

The town of 18,000 was sealed off and a judge ordered the university's 20,000 students to leave the campus by noon Tuesday. By late Monday night only 300 students, most of them foreign students, remained as 800 guardsmen patrolled in convoys of jeeps and personnel carriers armed with .50-caliber machine guns.

Students and National Guard officials gave different versions of what triggered the gunfire, but the guard admitted no warning was given that the troops would begin firing their M-1 semiautomatic rifles.

The battle was the most violent campus confrontation since the antiwar movement began. The trouble started when about 1,000 demonstrators, defying an order not to assemble, rallied on the commons at the center of the tree-lined campus. Guardsmen moved in and fired tear gas grenades at the mob, which

IN KENT, OHIO—National guardsmen advance during clash in which four students were killed.

WAR SITUATION AT A GLANCE

The stock market took a heavy beating Monday, reacting to concern over U.S. action in Cambodia. The Dow Jones industrial average dropped 19.07. Part 3, Page 9.

The Vietnam peace talks in Paris hung in the balance as the result of the U.S. Cambodia action. Page 18.

Another split occurred with Simon and Garfunkel. And two of the greatest legends in rock and roll, Janis Joplin and Jimi Hendrix, died of drug overdoses in that same year, (as did the King of Rock — Elvis Presley, in 1976).

Anti-Vietnam War protests reached their peak in 1970, with many colleges and universities holding mass protests. At Kent State University in Ohio, four students were killed by National Guardsmen during anti-war demonstrations. The death of these students marked the end of another influential aspect of

The fact that the world and U.S. events seemed increasingly hostile and disappointing may have contributed to the change in pop music in the 70's. In 1972, the Watergate scandal burst wide open with the arrest of five men for breaking into the Democratic Party Headquarters in Washington, D.C. By early 1973, the Watergate investigations revealed the involvement of Nixon's aides. Hearings began in the House, and Nixon faced possible impeachment. Meanwhile, Vice-President Agnew resigned amid income-tax evasion charges, and minority leader of the House of Representatives, Gerald Ford took his place. Watergate indictments were brought, and President Nixon resigned in 1974 — the first U.S president to do so. Ford became President and Nelson Rockefeller was later chosen as his Vice President.

The recording industry was drastically affected by the 70's oil embargo in the Middle East. The cost

of gasoline and fuel oil had quadrupled, and the cost of vinyl for recording skyrocketed. The drop of the public's purchasing power, coupled with the high costs of manufacturing, produced a profound effect on the record business. Record companies made radical cuts in recording artists' "perqs," slashed their roster of artists, and slowed the development of new talent.

The Times

VOL. CXXIII...No. 42,406   NEW YORK, SATURDAY, MARCH 2, 1974   15 CENTS

FEDERAL GRAND JURY INDICTS 7 NIXON AIDES ON CHARGES OF CONSPIRACY ON WATERGATE; HALDEMAN, EHRLICHMAN, MITCHELL ON LIST

Just at this time, a "second wave" of the British sound was happening in the U.S. in the form of a group called The Bee Gees. British-born Aussies Robin, Maurice, and Barry Gibb appeared on the U.S. music scene in the late 60's and initially took their influences from the Beatles. But by the 70's, the soul sound of rhythm and blues found its way into their music. In the early 70's, their songs were full of rich harmonies with lush orchestrations, combined with deeply emotional lyric (i.e. "How Can You Mend A Broken Heart"). In the middle of the decade, they switched to their own brand of soul/disco and had four platinum records in a row. The epitome of their disco sound was the soundtrack for *Saturday Night Fever* which included the number one hits "Night Fever" and "Stayin' Alive." The popularity of this music

Wings, had great success throughout the decade, including "My Love" in 1973 and one of the top songs of the year 1976 — "Silly Love Songs."

Two "piano men/singers/songwriters," Elton John and Billy Joel, found their niche with keyboard-based song construction and harmonies that resulted in quite divergent styles. The British Elton John started out his career as a songwriter with lyricist Bernie Taupin. As a performer, he put on colorful shows with outrageous costumes, fabulous sets and crazy antics. His music was finely crafted and highly memorable, with such 70's hits as "Don't Let The Sun Go Down On Me," "Goodbye Yellow Brick Road," and "Your Song."

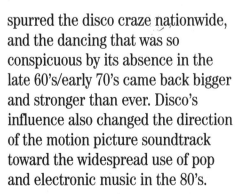

spurred the disco craze nationwide, and the dancing that was so conspicuous by its absence in the late 60's/early 70's came back bigger and stronger than ever. Disco's influence also changed the direction of the motion picture soundtrack toward the widespread use of pop and electronic music in the 80's.

After the breakup of the Beatles, we began to watch each member of the group emerge an individual artist. One of John Lennon's biggest hits with the Plastic Ono Band was his memorable ballad "Imagine." Paul McCartney, with his new group

Still another "piano man," Barry Manilow first hit the charts in the 70's after a number of years as a jingle writer ("You Deserve A Break Today" for McDonalds), as well as musical director/pianist/opening act for Bette Midler. His first #1 single ir 1975, "Mandy," paved the way for a string of hits including "Can't Smile Without You." Manilow's appeal was international and, like both Elton John and Billy Joel, covered a wide spectrum of ages; he was able to cross over from the Middle of the Road (MOR) charts to the Pop and even Jazz charts. He also proved to be one of the rare musical entertainers who was able to sustain network television music specials in the 70's.

Although classically trained, Billy Joel's roots were those of the New York lounge singer ("Piano Man"), and his early songs had that "blue smoke aura" evoking images of dimly lit restaurants and lonely people. His lyric explored the deepest feelings and the ballad "Just The Way You Are" has become one of the most performed standards. With songs touching rock, jazz, and pop styles, Joel became wildly popular with a large following representing a wide age range.

Neil Sedaka, also a pianist of the first order, had written a string of hit songs performed by himself and by other artists in the 60's, but by the 70's wasn't finding much success as a performer. So, 1975's "Laughter In The Rain" was really his first hit in ten years! Among the hits that followed, was Captain and Tennille's smash "Love Will Keep Us Together," the #1 song of 1975.

Another accomplished 60's songwriter, Neil Diamond, entered the 70's with major hits and kept on going. A highly versatile artist, Diamond reached out and touched a variety of different musical styles and concepts. As a writer, he composed a number of hits in the 60's recorded by popular groups including the Monkees and Jay and the Americans. However, he cracked the pop charts in 1970 as a performer with his song "Cracklin' Rosie," and continued throughout the 70's in turning out hit recordings of his own songs, including "Song Sung Blue" in 1972 and "You Don't Bring Me Flowers" in 1978 — a duet with Barbra Streisand.

Janis Joplin was the personification of the 60's drug culture and hippie era — an era that was rapidly changing in the 70's. Few will forget

her immortal rendition of Kris Kristofferson's classic "Me and Bobby McGee," a recording that was released just after her death in 1970. The popularity of that song gave a boost to Kristofferson's songwriting career, followed by his popularity as a singer and actor.

Kristofferson and other country music songwriters had a profound effect on Nashville in the 70's, taking the "western" out of what was previously referred to as "country/ western" music by bringing a new depth of feeling to the lyric and introducing a contemporary structure to the music. Many country hits of the 70's also found their way onto the Adult Contemporary and Pop charts. Anne Murray's recording of "You Needed Me" in 1978 was one such hit.

The 70's were a quiet period for Broadway show music, although what may have been lacking in mass appeal and memorable music was made up for in new production values — different formats, a wider range of musical styles, new stage technologies — all of which exemplified the influence of radio, television, motion pictures, and rock music on Broadway. Of the shows that did make an impact were two Andrew Lloyd Webber/Tim Rice spectaculars, *Jesus Christ Superstar* and *Evita. Superstar,* with its timely release at the beginning of the "Jesus rock" era, spawned several hits, most notably, "I Don't Know How To Love Him." *Evita's* most successful hit was "Don't Cry For Me Argentina." The songs of this young new team had appeal to both the theatre-going public and to young adult ears that were previously more geared to rock than Broadway.

Stephen Sondheim had several diverse and uniquely crafted musicals on Broadway in the 70's. One of his most haunting tunes, "Send In The Clowns" from *A Little Night Music,* has since permeated nearly every level of musical recording, to the extent that the song has probably been licensed for use in more music boxes than any other song in history.

Marvin Hamlisch was successful in several levels of music in the 70's — motion pictures, Broadway shows, and pop tunes. His Broadway smash *A Chorus Line* was a seamless show — a celebration of the unsung chorus dancers, presenting a group of dancers auditioning for a forthcoming musical — and produced the showstopping ballad "What I Did For Love."

Leave it to Broadway to build a hit around a favorite comic strip! The 1977 production of *Annie* was the inspiration of the show's lyricist director, Martin Charnin, and portrayed in music and dance the story of everyone's favorite waif, Little Orphan Annie. One of the longest-running musicals of the 70's, the show gave us a modern-day song of hope and optimism, "Tomorrow."

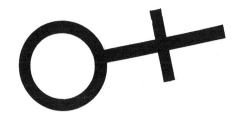

Although the 70's did not see many new civil rights laws, the laws that were implemented in the 60's began to take hold and become accepted parts of our lives, especially to a new generation. The Women's Rights movement grew stronger, and several songs, including Gloria Gaynor's "I Will Survive" (as well as Helen Reddy's "I Am Woman"), became anthems of the movement.

On the music charts, there were more crossovers from the Black charts to other charts than ever before. Earth Wind & Fire crossed over with continual hits that had a richly harmonized and orchestrated sound. Their music had an air of spirituality and a stress on sister and brotherhood in their lyric. Many Black female artists, especially Gladys Knight and Roberta Flack, also had enormous crossover hits.

One very special time for the U.S. in the 70's that became a special celebration of music as well was the commemoration of our nation's Bicentennial. Fireworks, parades and celebrations, including a Fourth of July extravaganza from New York with a fleet of tall ships from 31 countries sailing past the Statue of Liberty — none of these celebrations would have had the same impact without MUSIC! From patriotic marching bands to rock and roll, from full symphony orchestras to surfing songs, American music of every variety was heard and celebrated.

As the decade of the 70's drew to a close, it heralded new beginnings. On a musical level, the age of "digital synthesis" was born and "new age" music was embryonic. In health, the emphasis on fitness and nutrition was becoming a national trend. In space, Pioneer 11 gave us our first closeup views of Jupiter and Saturn. In world affairs, Egyptian President

Anwar Sadat and Israeli Prime Minister Menachem Begin signed a peace treaty for which they were awarded the Nobel Peace Prize in 1978. Ironically, President Jimmy Carter's role in securing this treaty would be overshadowed by his failure to secure the release of the American hostages in Iran, and foreshadowed the passing on the Presidency to a Republican who would change the course of the country in the 80's . . . .

JOINED IN PEACE—Egypt's Anwar Sadat, President Carter and Israel's Menachem Begin just after the White House treaty signing.

After The Love Has Gone

Registration 4
Rhythm: Rock

Words and Music by David Foster,
Jay Graydon, and Bill Champlin

13

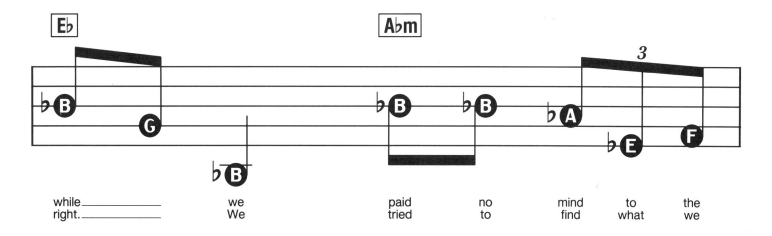

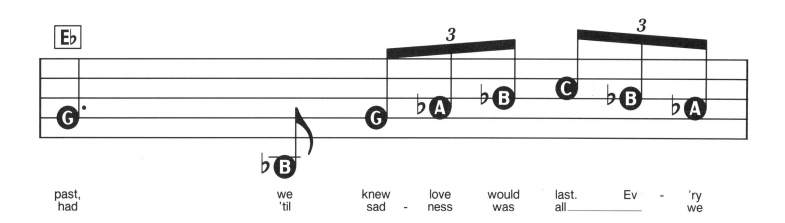

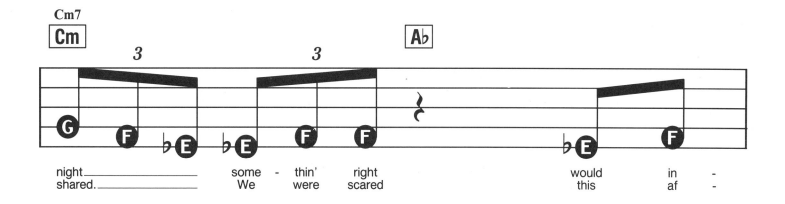

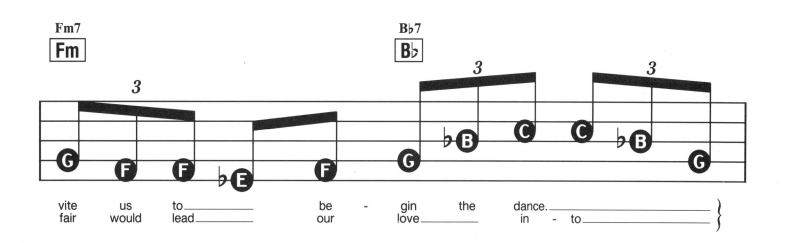

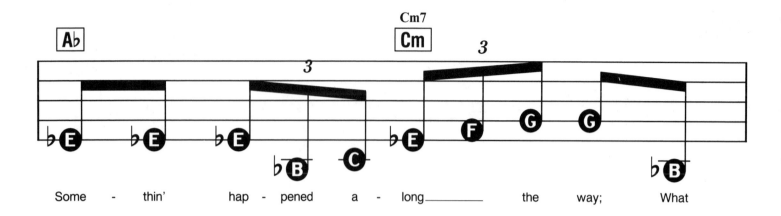

Some - thin' hap - pened a - long———— the way; What

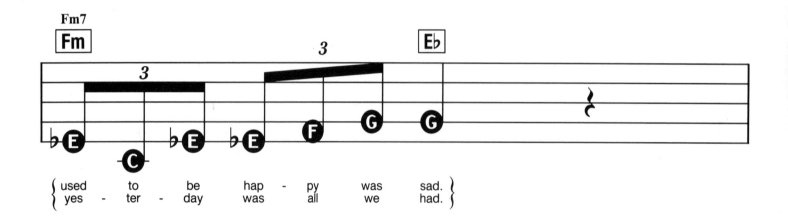

{ used to be hap - py was sad. }
{ yes - ter - day was all we had. }

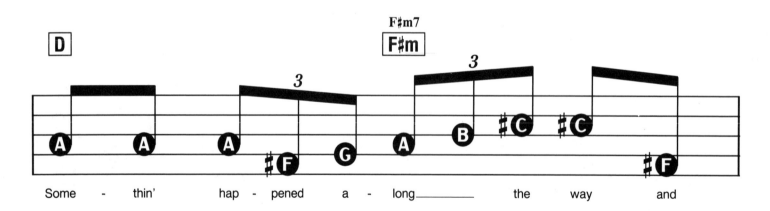

Some - thin' hap - pened a - long———— the way and

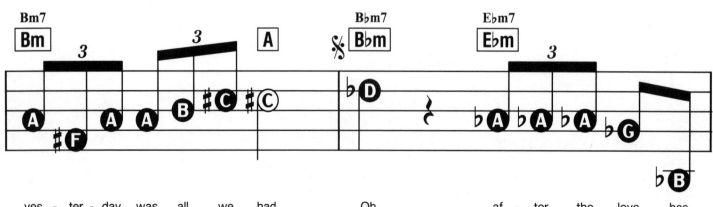

yes - ter - day was all we had. Oh, af - ter the love has

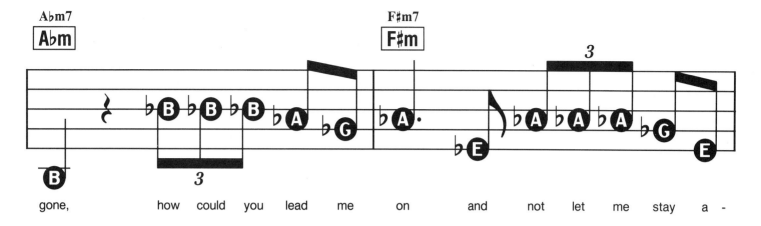

gone, how could you lead me on and not let me stay a -

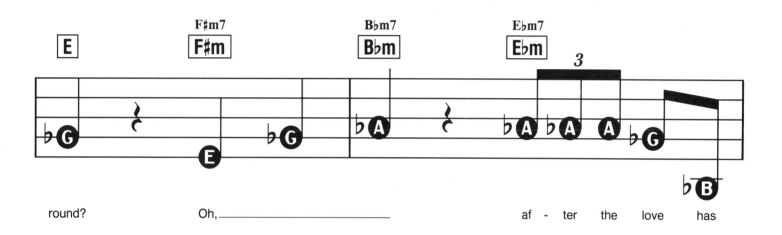

round? Oh,_____ af - ter the love has

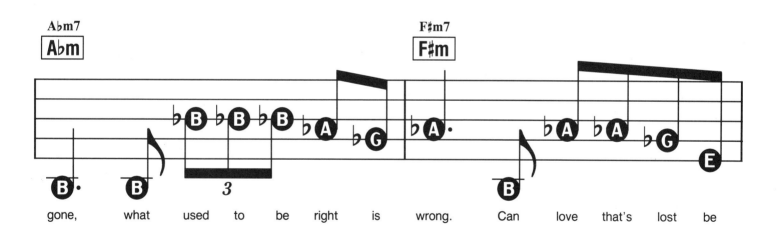

gone, what used to be right is wrong. Can love that's lost be

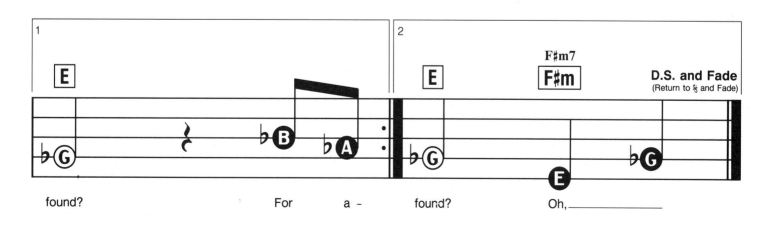

found? For a - found? Oh,_____

Can't Smile Without You

Registration 3
Rhythm: Fox Trot or Swing

Words and Music by Chris Arnold,
David Martin and Geoff Morrow

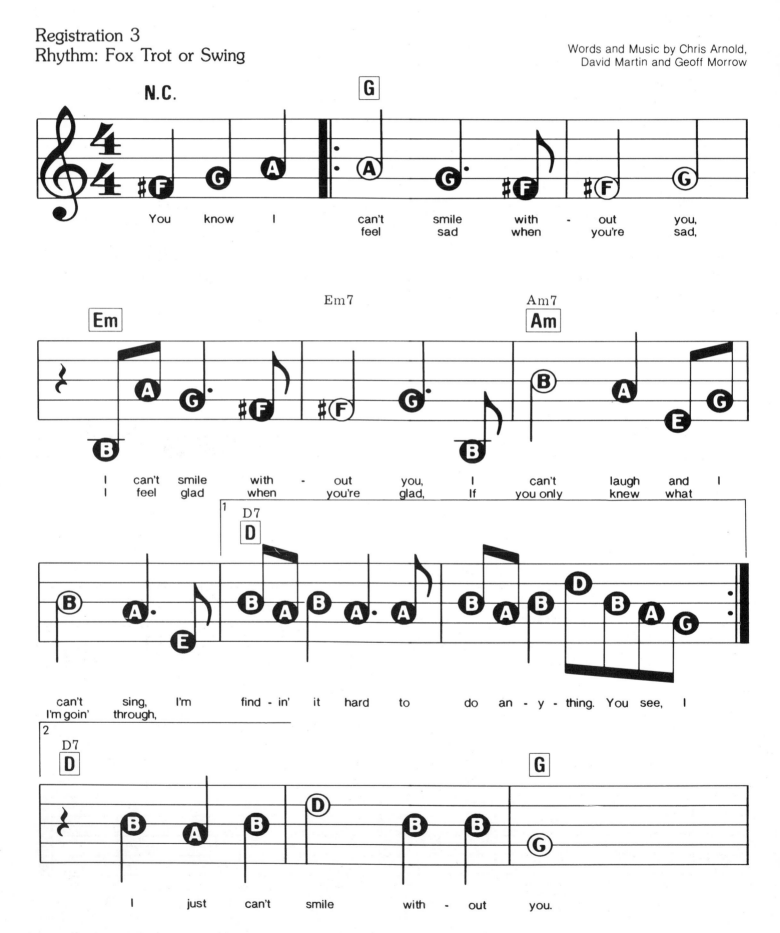

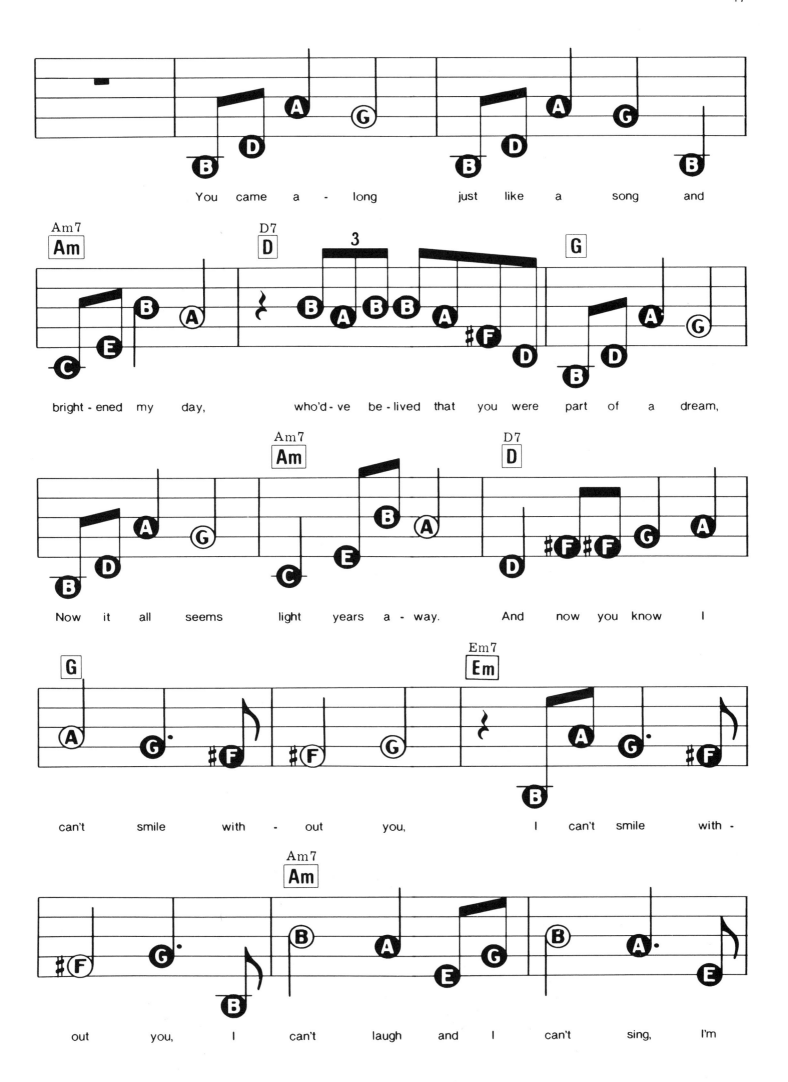

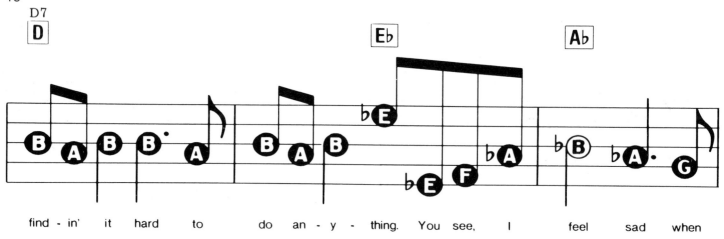

find - in' it hard to do an - y - thing. You see, I feel sad when

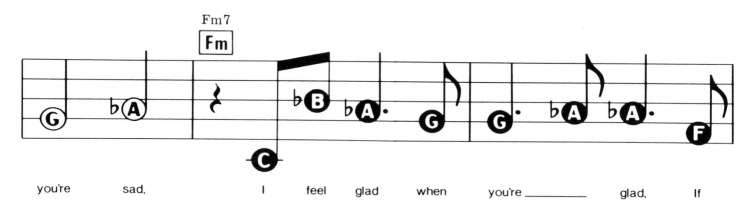

you're sad, I feel glad when you're _____ glad, If

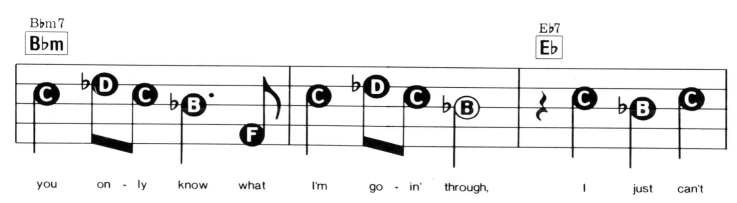

you on - ly know what I'm go - in' through, I just can't

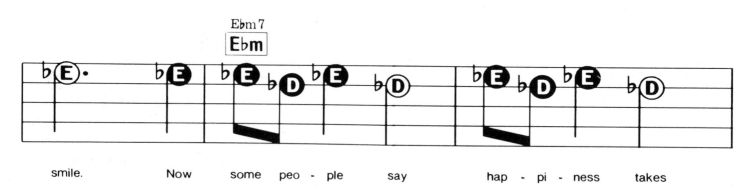

smile. Now some peo - ple say hap - pi - ness takes

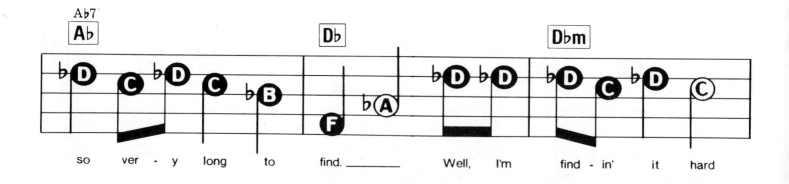

so ver - y long to find. _____ Well, I'm find - in' it hard

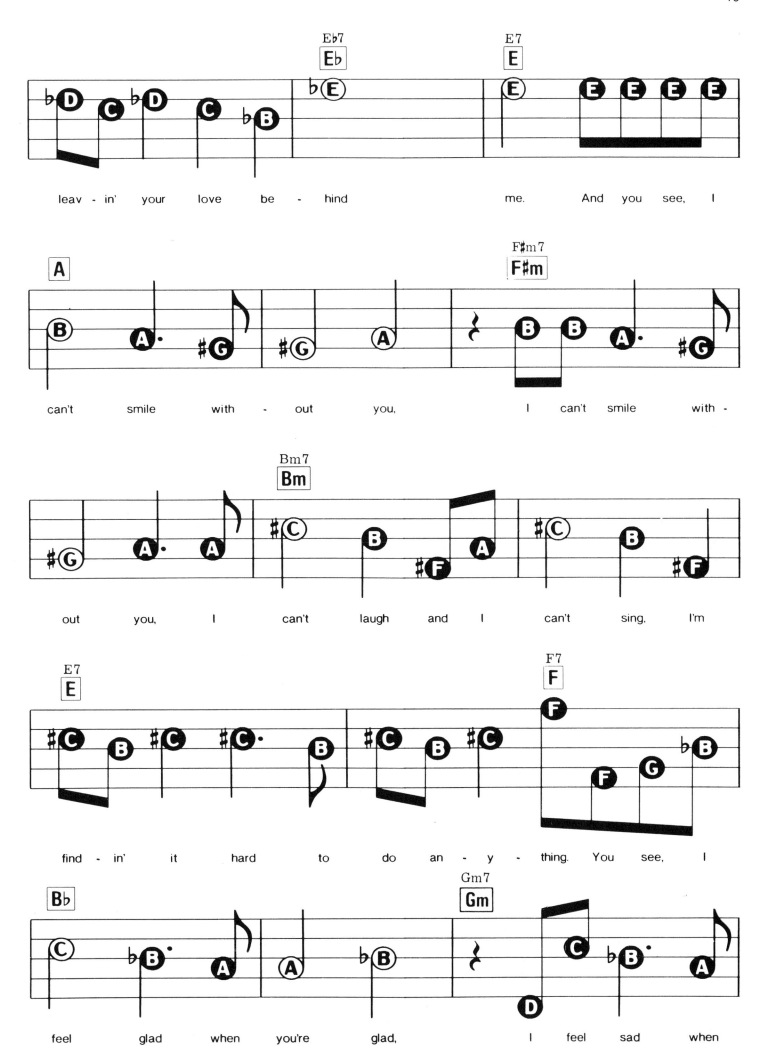

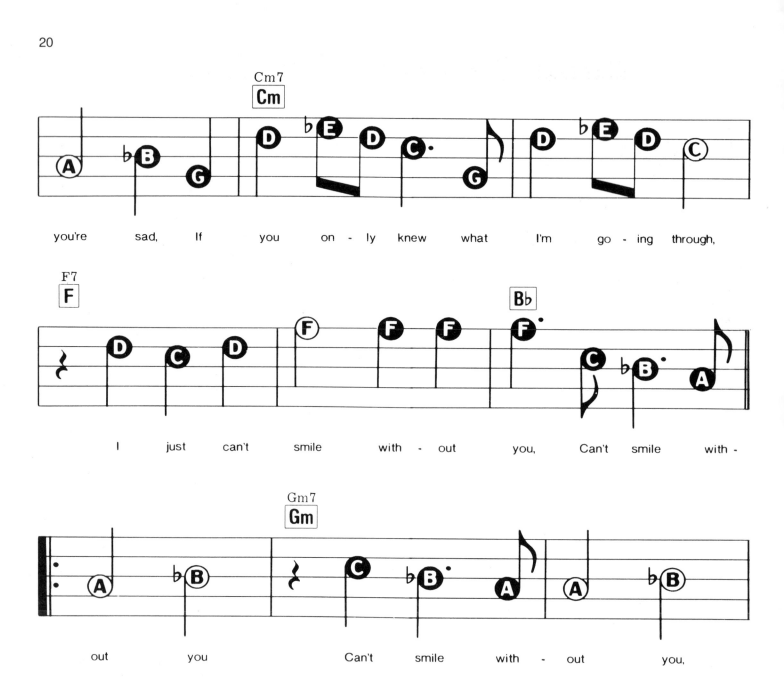

you're sad, If you on - ly knew what I'm go - ing through,

I just can't smile with - out you, Can't smile with -

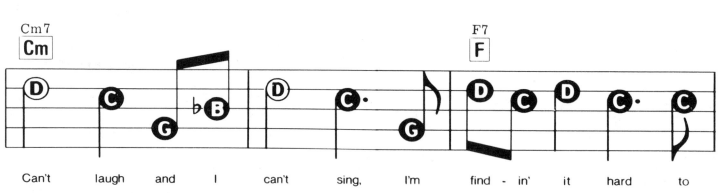

out you Can't smile with - out you,

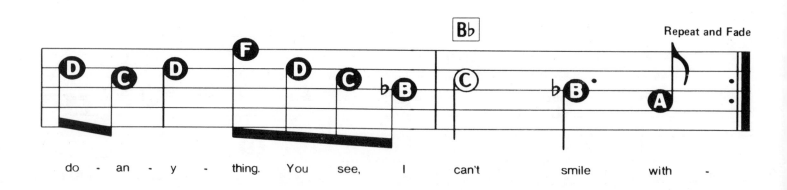

Can't laugh and I can't sing, I'm find - in' it hard to

do - an - y - thing. You see, I can't smile with -

Come In From The Rain

Ballade
Bright Pop

Registration 10
Rhythm: Ballad

Words and Music by
Melissa Manchester and Carole Bayer Sager

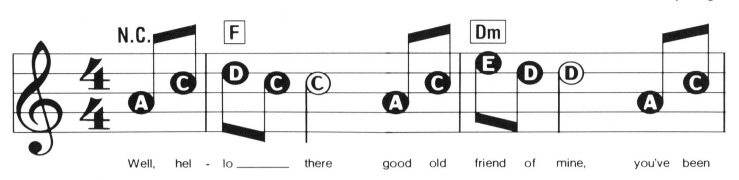

Well, hel - lo _____ there good old friend of mine, you've been

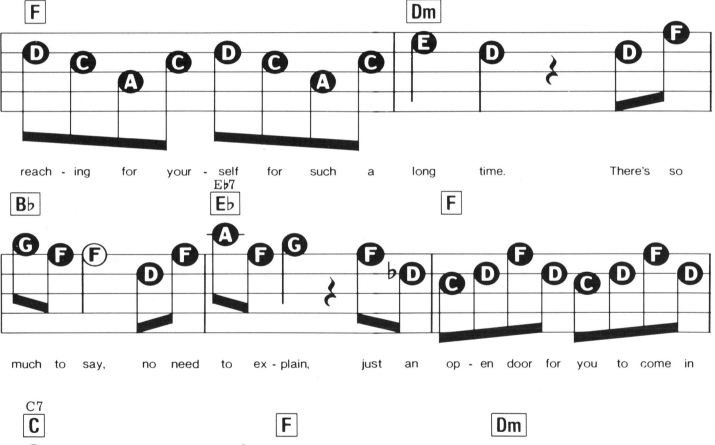

reach - ing for your - self for such a long time. There's so

much to say, no need to ex - plain, just an op - en door for you to come in

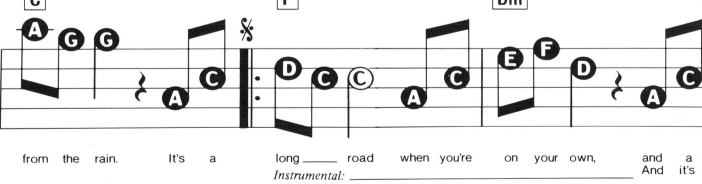

from the rain. It's a long _____ road when you're on your own, and a

Instrumental: _____ And it's

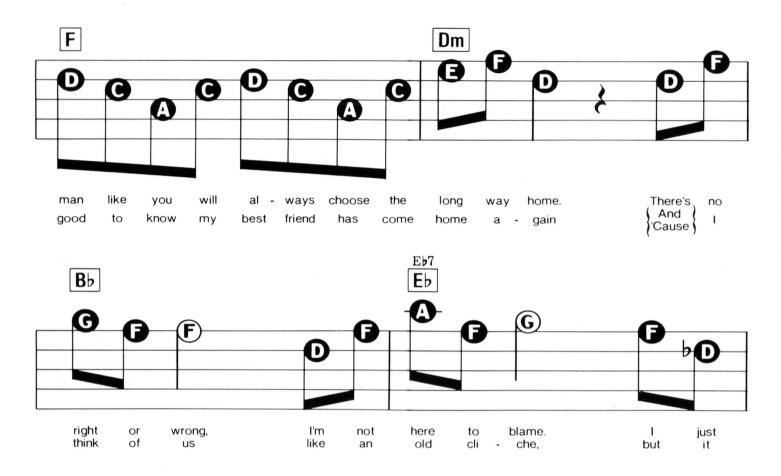

man   like   you   will   al - ways   choose   the   long   way   home.   There's   no
good   to   know   my   best   friend   has   come   home   a - gain   { And   } I
                                                                                                       { 'Cause }

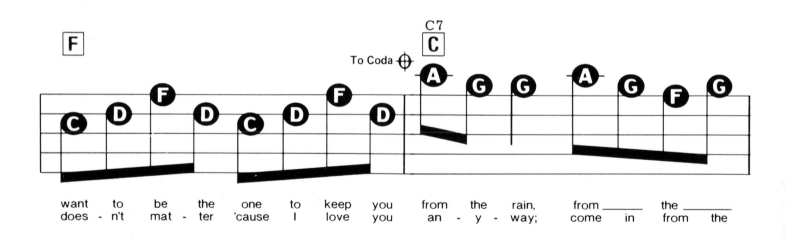

right   or   wrong,   I'm   not   here   to   blame.   I   just
think   of   us   like   an   old   cli - che,   but   it

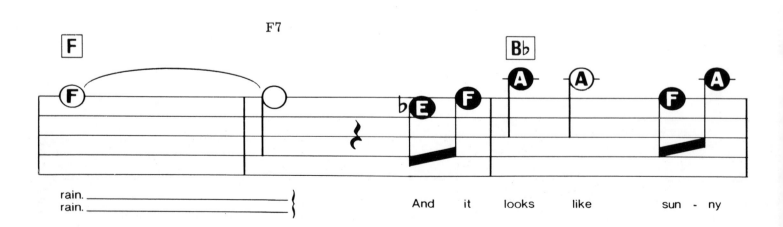

want   to   be   the   one   to   keep   you   from   the   rain,   from _____ the _____
does - n't   mat - ter   'cause   I   love   you   an - y - way;   come   in   from   the

rain. _____ }
rain. _____ }   And   it   looks   like   sun - ny

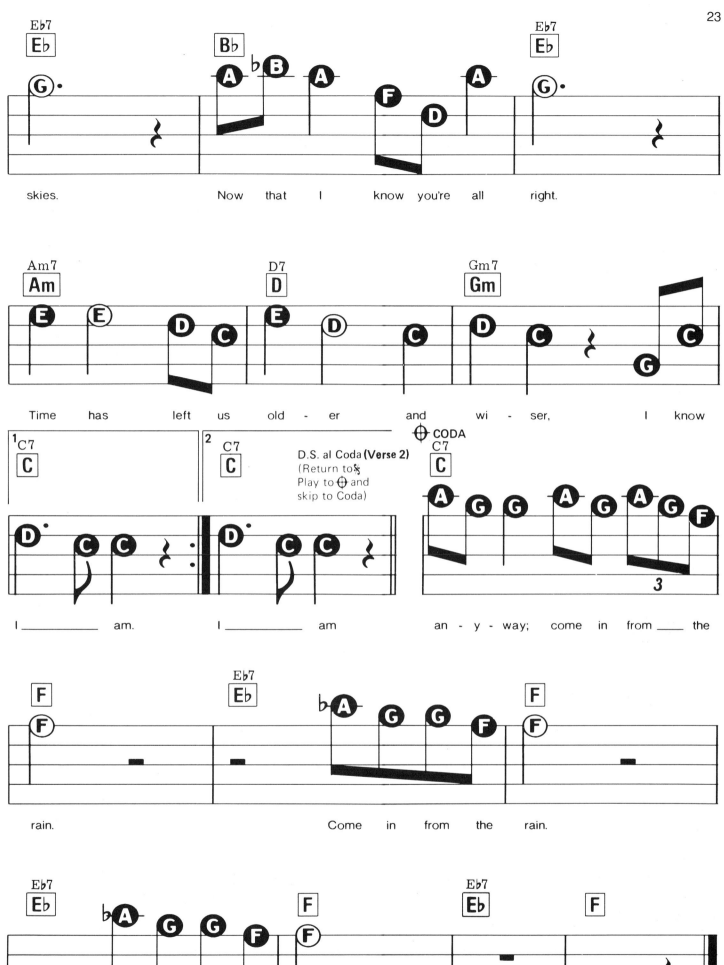

Cracklin' Rosie

Registration 5
Rhythm: Fox Trot or Ballad

Words and Music by
Neil Diamond

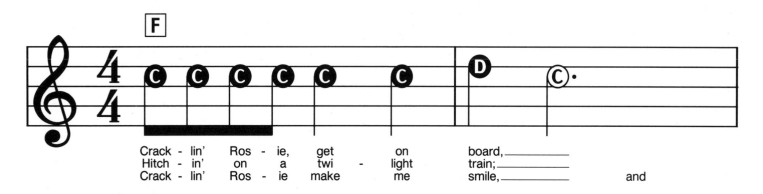

Crack - lin' Ros - ie, get on board,
Hitch - in' on a twi - light train;
Crack - lin' Ros - ie make me smile, and

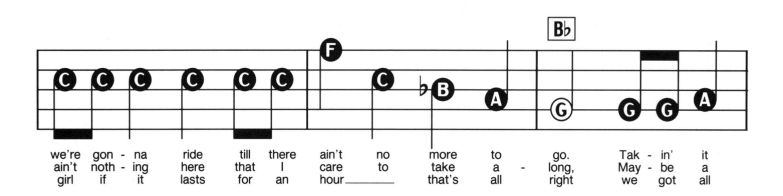

we're gon - na ride till there ain't no more to go. Tak - in' it
ain't noth - ing here that I care to take a - long, May - be a
girl if it lasts for an hour that's all right we got all

slow, And Lord don't you know. I'll
song to sing when I want. Don't
night to set the world right.

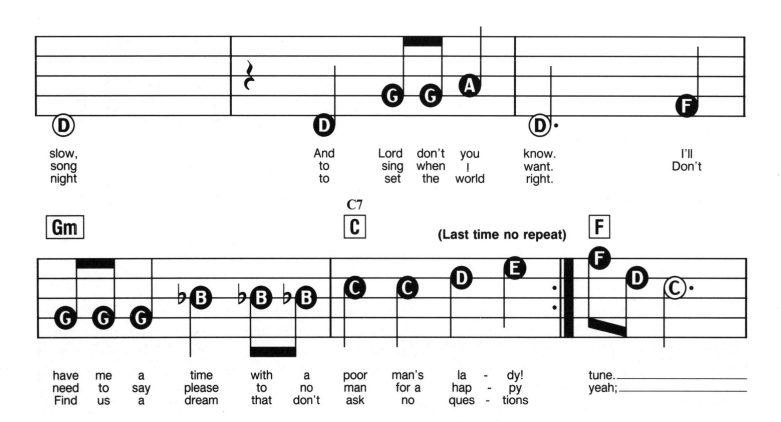

have me a time with a poor man's la - dy! tune.
need to say please with to no man for a hap - py yeah;
Find us a dream that don't ask no ques - tions

(Last time no repeat)

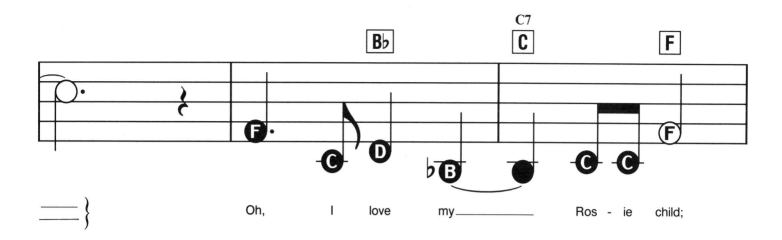

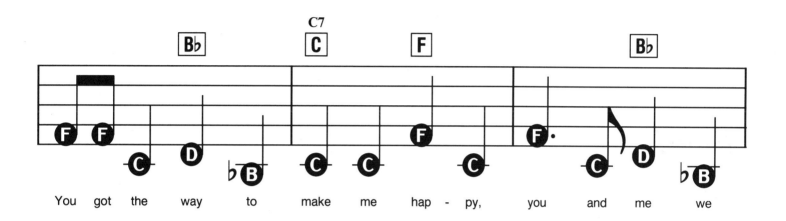

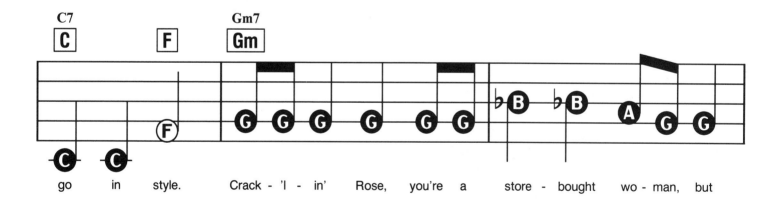

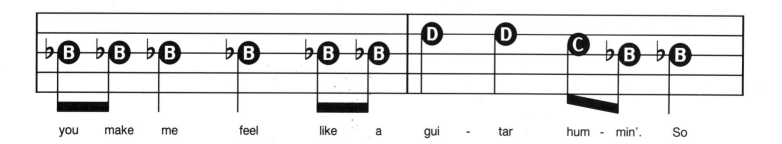

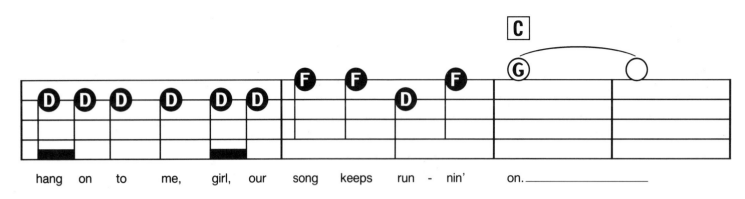

hang on to me, girl, our song keeps run - nin' on.____

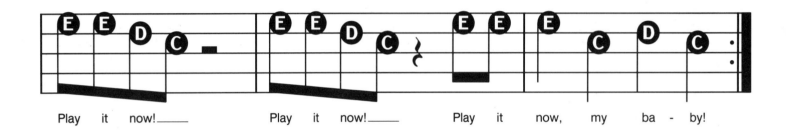

Play it now!____ Play it now!____ Play it now, my ba - by!

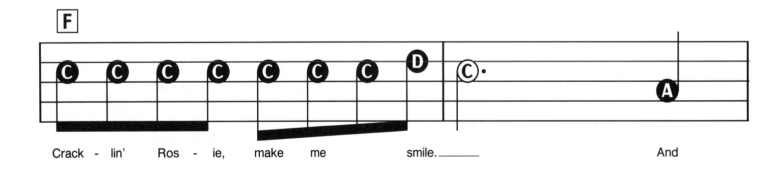

Crack - lin' Ros - ie, make me smile.____ And

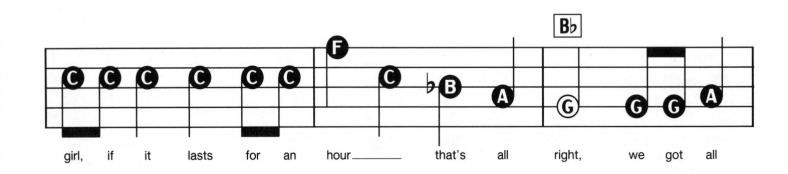

girl, if it lasts for an hour____ that's all right, we got all

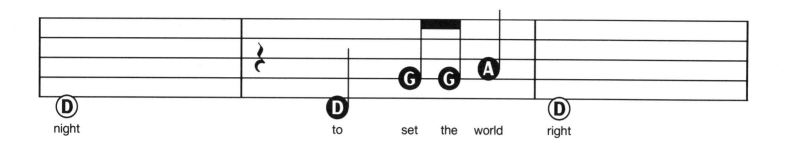

night   to   set   the   world   right

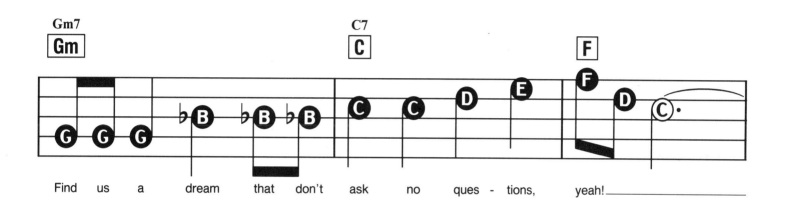

Find   us   a   dream   that   don't   ask   no   ques - tions,   yeah!_____

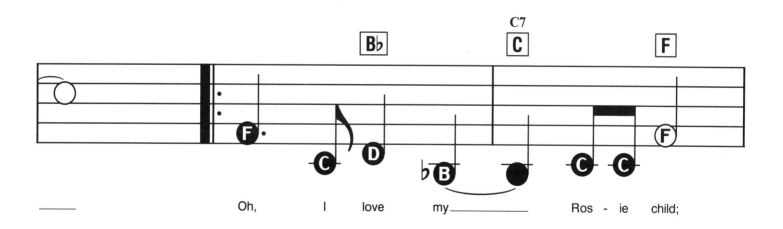

_____   Oh,   I   love   my_____   Ros - ie   child;

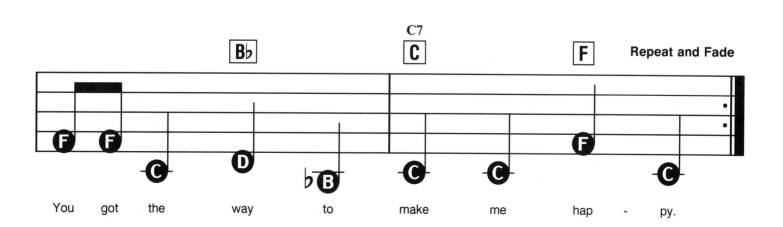

You   got   the   way   to   make   me   hap - py.

Daniel

Registration 2
Rhythm: Latin or Rock

Words and Music by Elton John
and Bernie Taupin

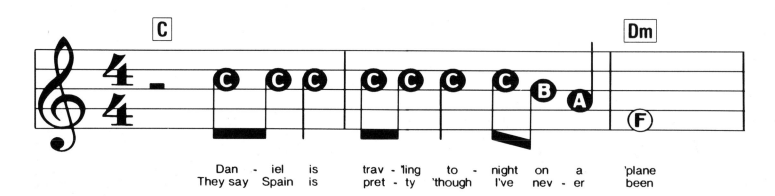

Dan - iel is trav - 'ling to - night on a 'plane
They say Spain is pret - ty 'though I've nev - er been

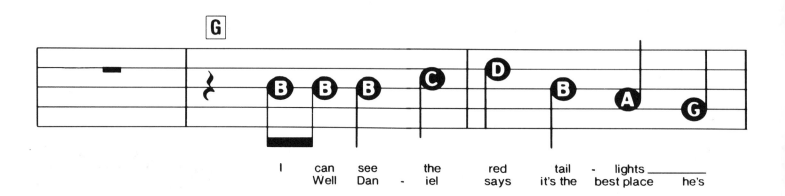

I can see the red tail - lights _____
Well Dan - iel says it's the best place he's

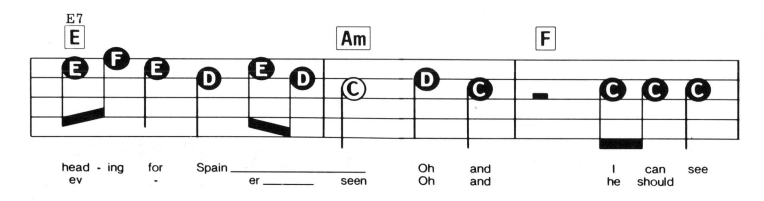

head - ing for Spain _____ Oh and I can see
ev - er _____ seen Oh and he should

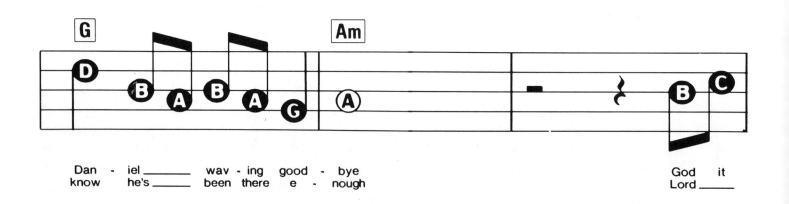

Dan - iel _____ wav - ing good - bye God it
know he's _____ been there e - nough Lord _____

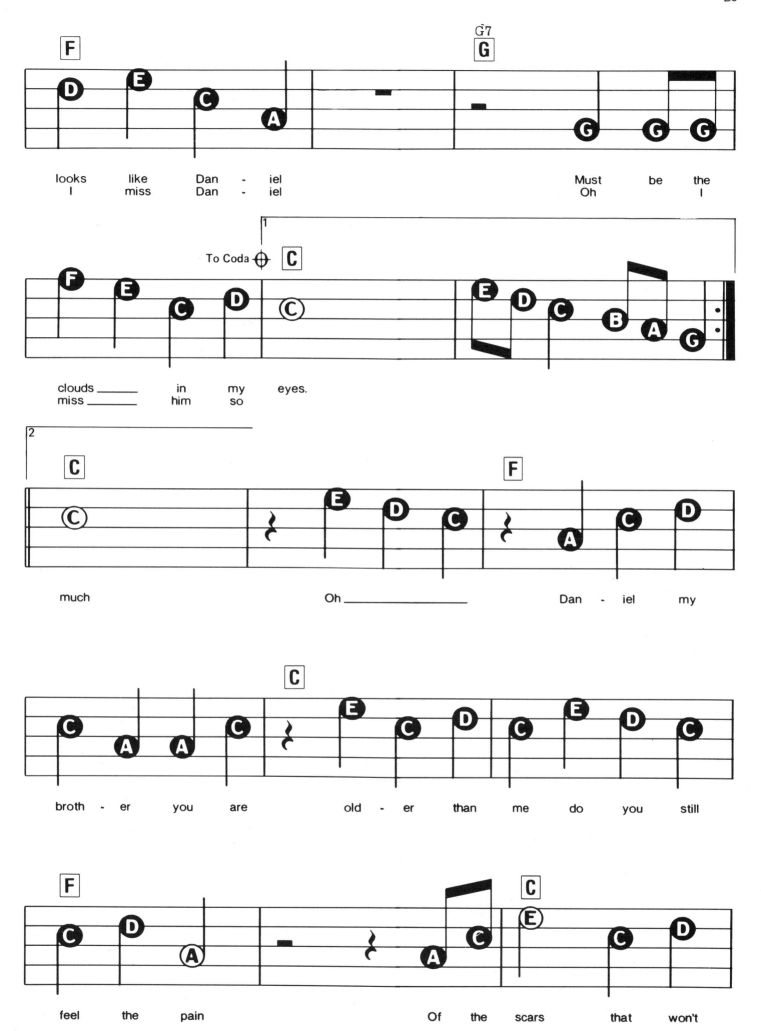

30

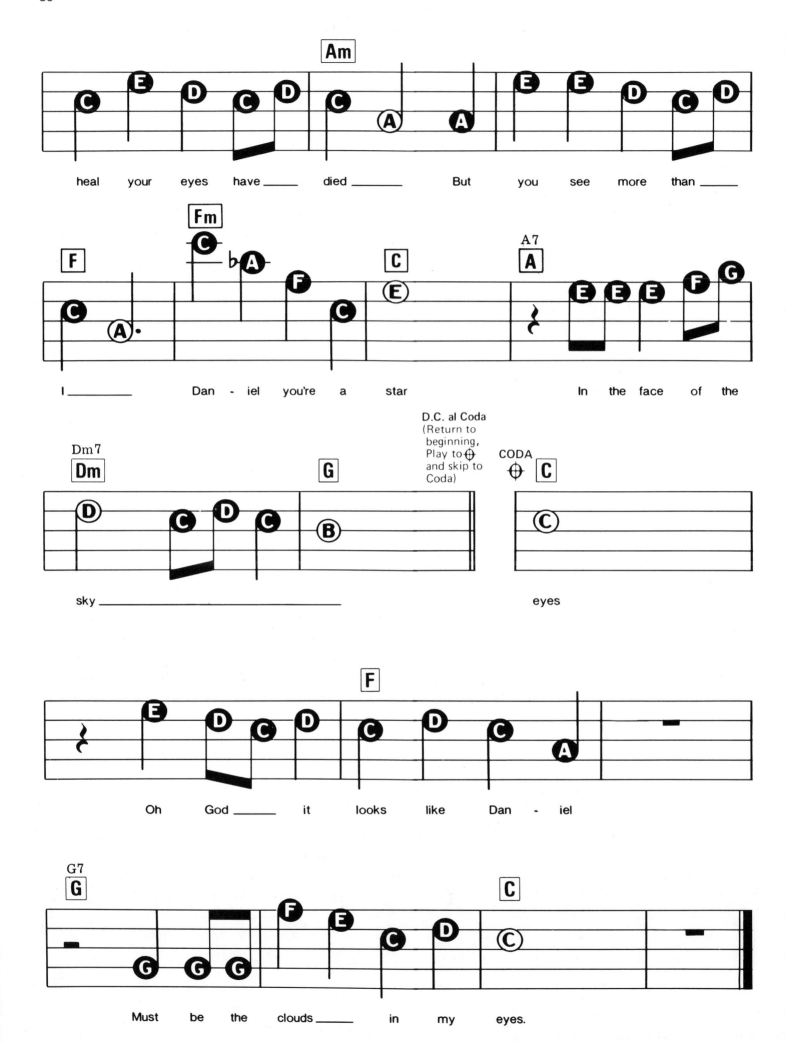

Fire And Rain

Registration 2
Rhythm: Rock

Words and Music by
James Taylor

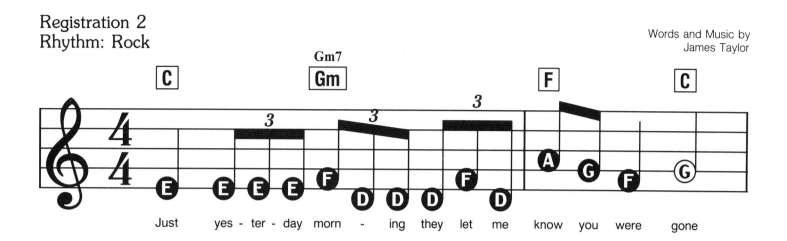

Just yes-ter-day morn - ing they let me know you were gone

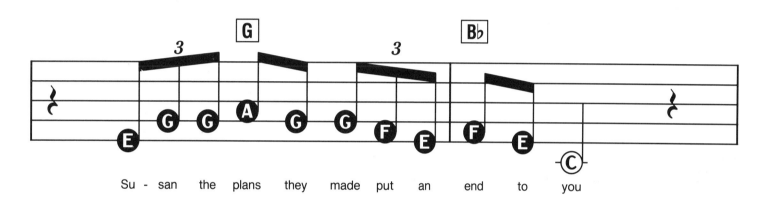

Su - san the plans they made put an end to you

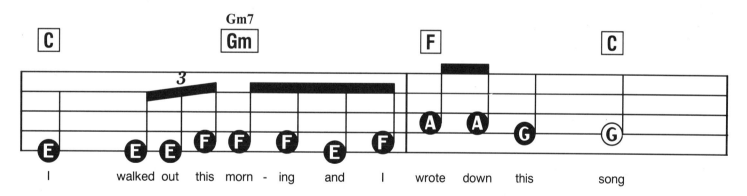

I walked out this morn - ing and I wrote down this song

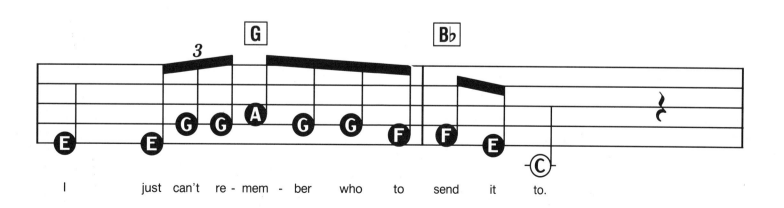

I just can't re-mem - ber who to send it to.

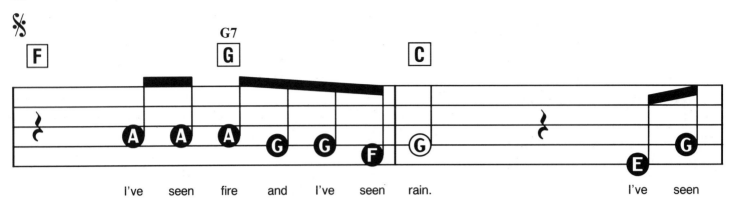

I've seen fire and I've seen rain. I've seen

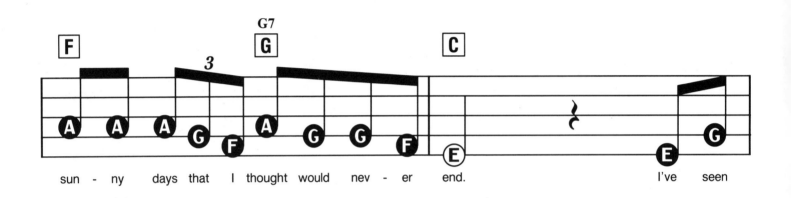

sun - ny days that I thought would nev - er end. I've seen

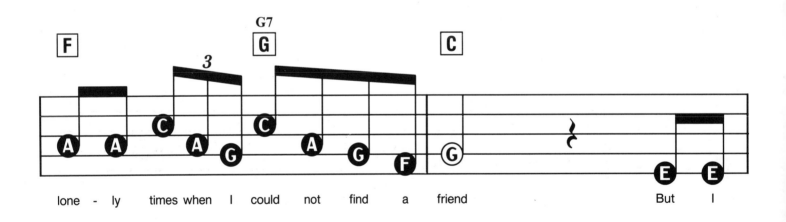

lone - ly times when I could not find a friend But I

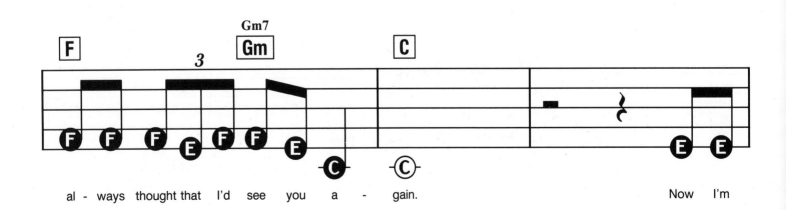

al - ways thought that I'd see you a - gain. Now I'm

33

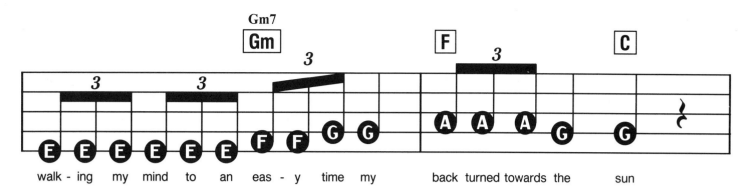

walk - ing my mind to an eas - y time my back turned towards the sun

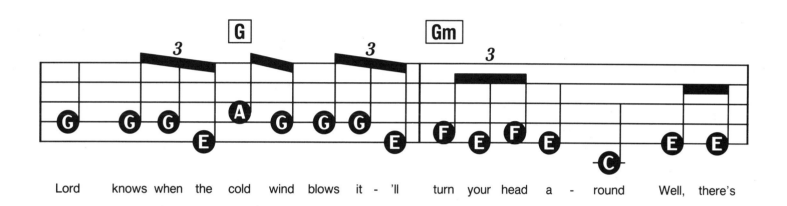

Lord knows when the cold wind blows it - 'll turn your head a - round Well, there's

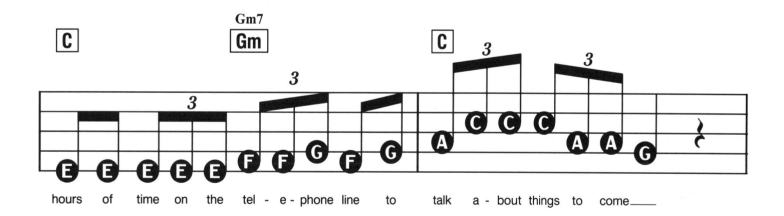

hours of time on the tel - e - phone line to talk a - bout things to come

D.S. and Fade
(Return to % and Fade)

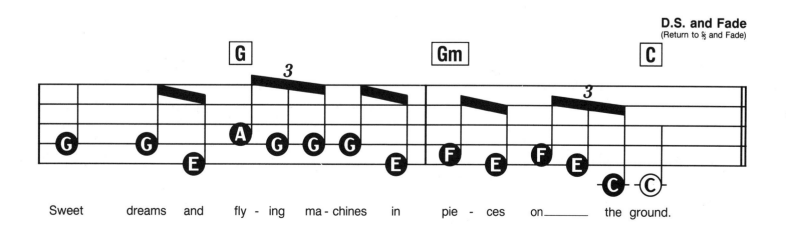

Sweet dreams and fly - ing ma - chines in pie - ces on the ground.

Don't Cry For Me Argentina

Registration 9
Rhythm: Tango or Latin

Lryic by Tim Rice
Music by Andrew Lloyd Webber

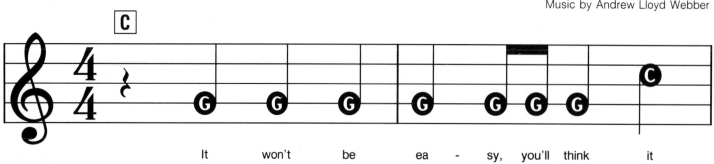

It won't be ea - sy, you'll think it

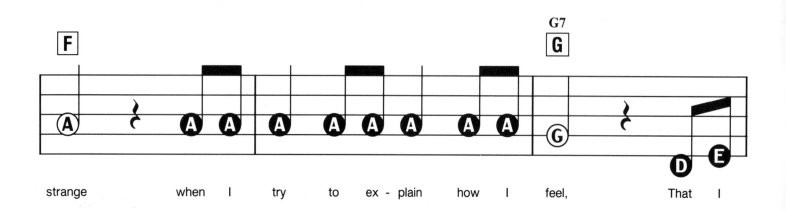

strange when I try to ex - plain how I feel, That I

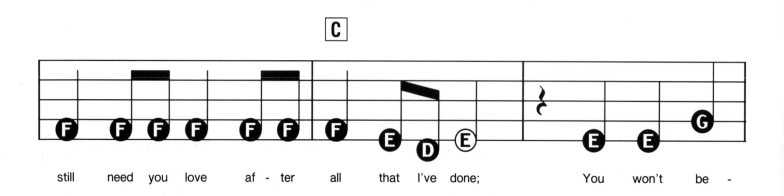

still need you love af - ter all that I've done; You won't be -

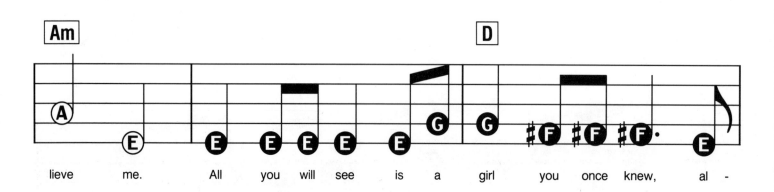

lieve me. All you will see is a girl you once knew, al -

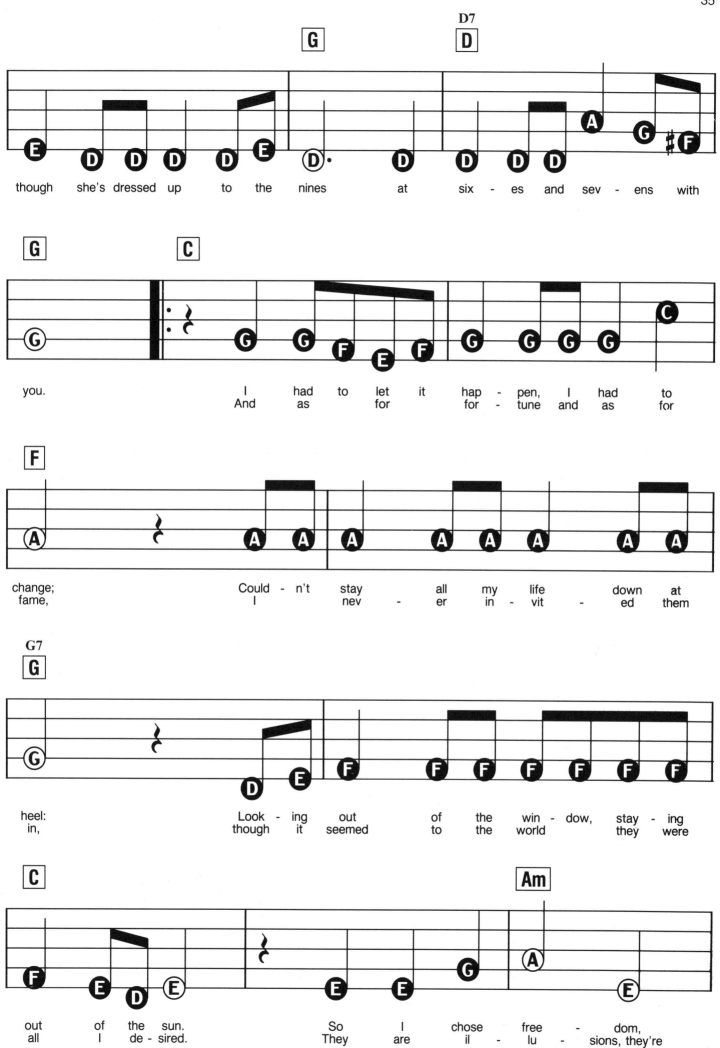

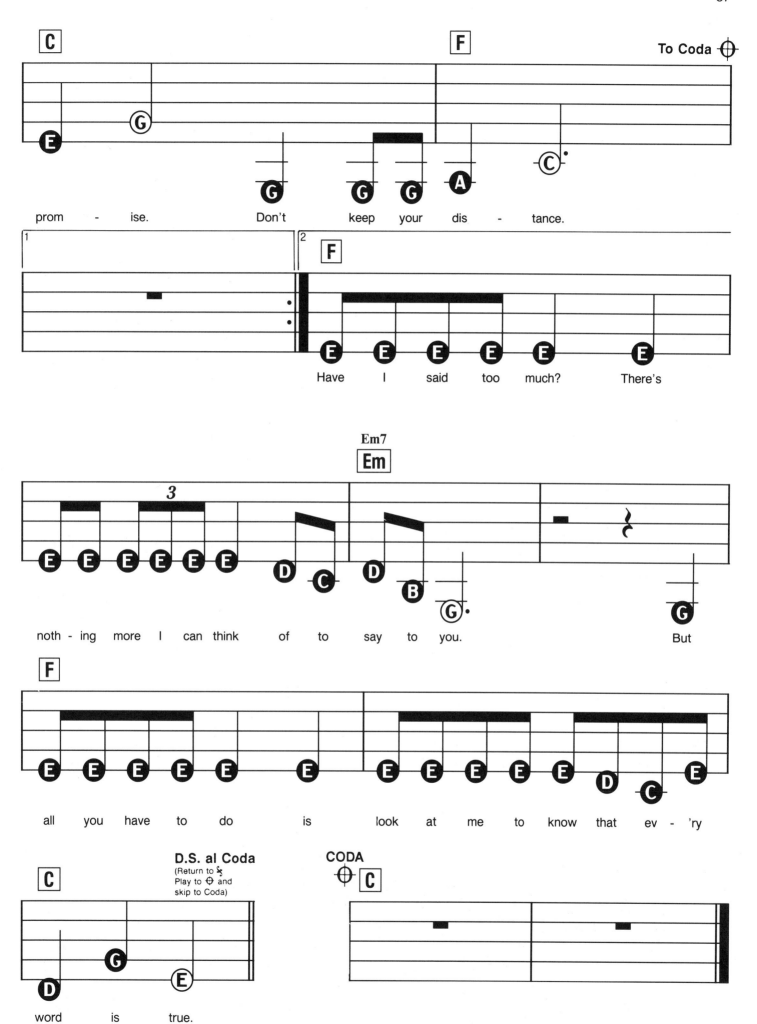

Don't Let The Sun Go Down On Me

Registration 4
Rhythm: Rock

Words and Music by Elton John
and Bernie Taupin

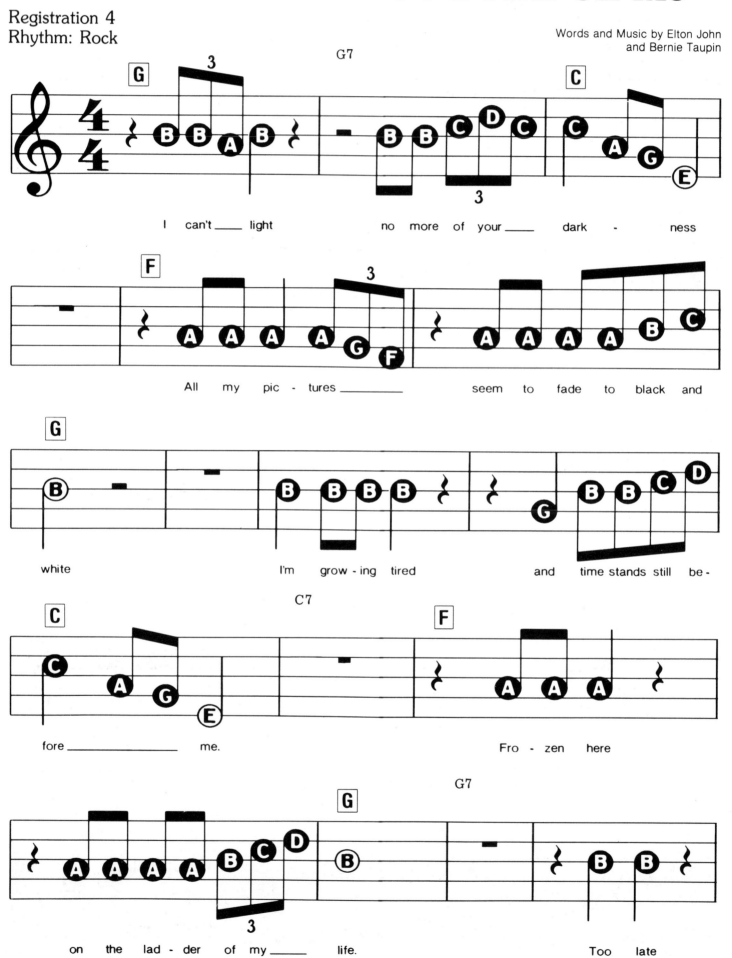

I can't___ light no more of your___ dark - ness

All my pic - tures ___ seem to fade to black and

white I'm grow - ing tired and time stands still be -

fore ___ me. Fro - zen here

on the lad - der of my ___ life. Too late

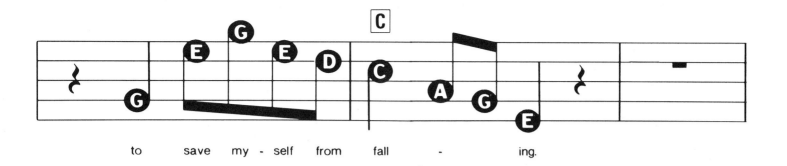

to save my-self from fall - ing.

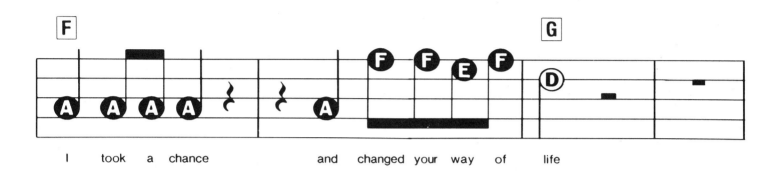

I took a chance and changed your way of life

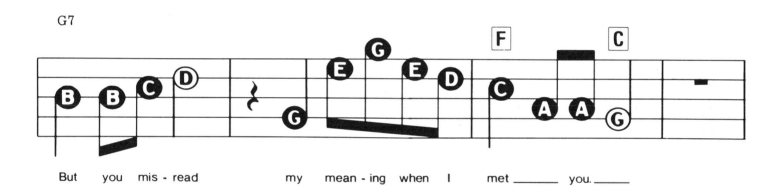

But you mis-read my mean-ing when I met _____ you. _____

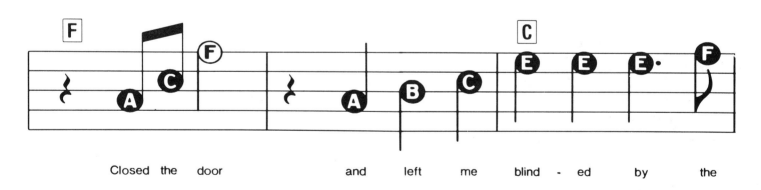

Closed the door and left me blind-ed by the

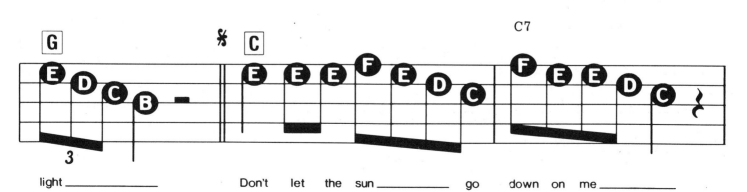

light _____ Don't let the sun _____ go down on me _____

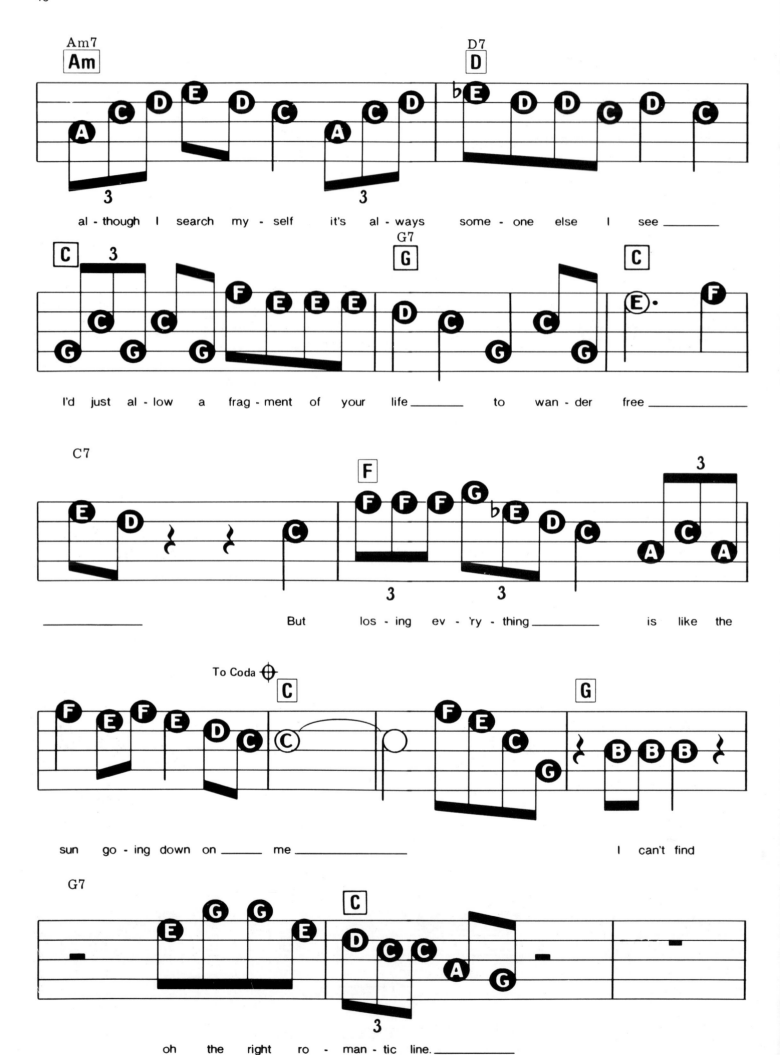

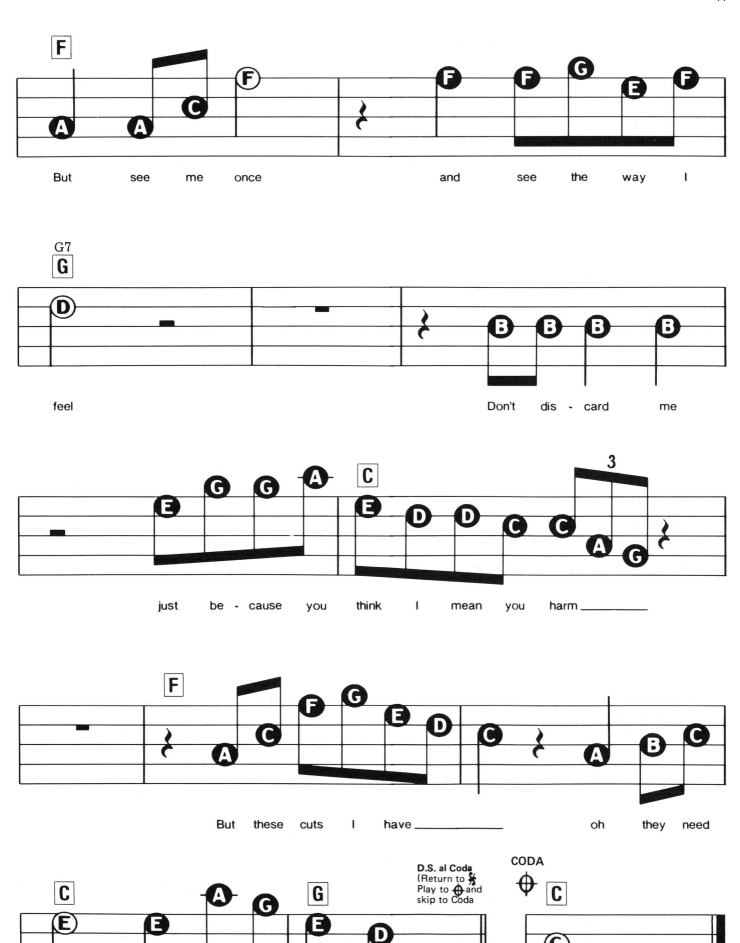

Dust In The Wind

Registration 10
Rhythm: Rock

Words and Music by
Kerry Livgren

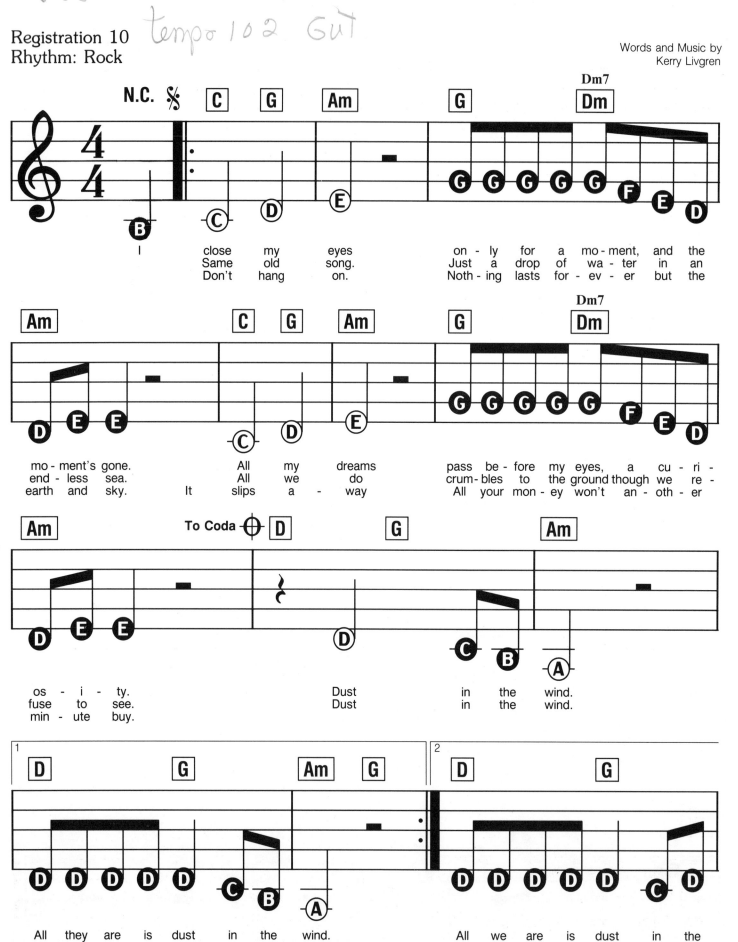

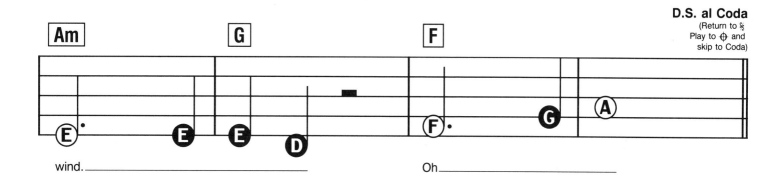

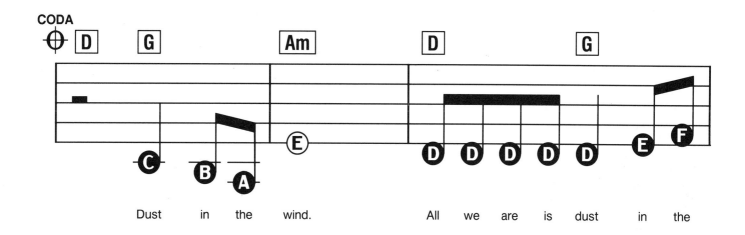

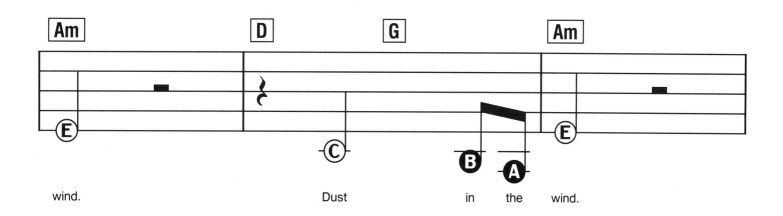

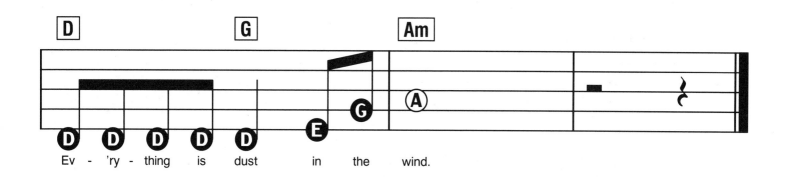

Everything Is Beautiful

Registration 8
Rhythm: Rock or Jazz Rock

Words and Music by
Ray Stevens

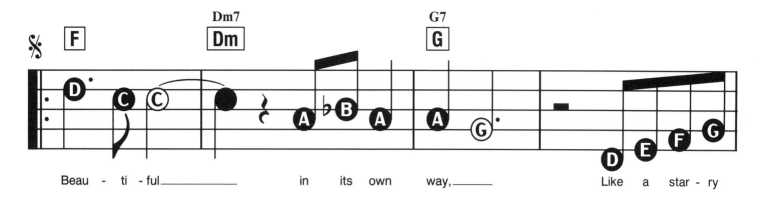

Beau - ti -ful_____ in its own way,_____ Like a star - ry

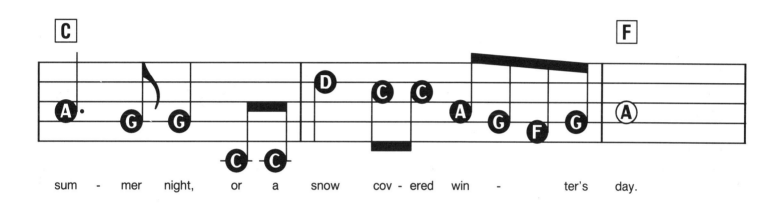

sum - mer night, or a snow cov - ered win - ter's day.

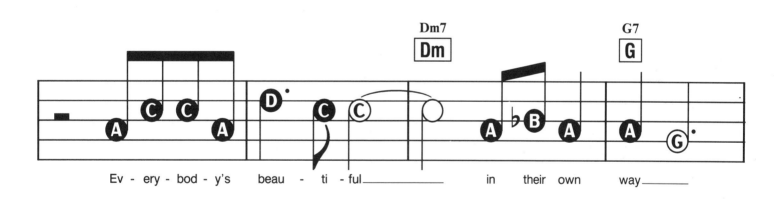

Ev - ery - bod - y's beau - ti -ful_____ in their own way_____

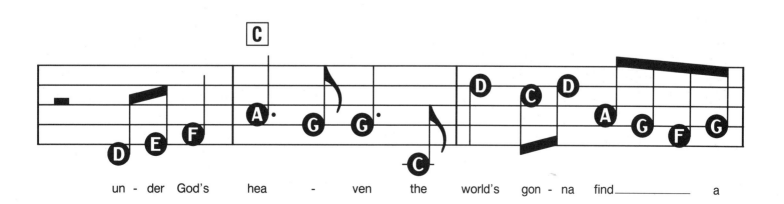

un - der God's hea - ven the world's gon - na find_____ a

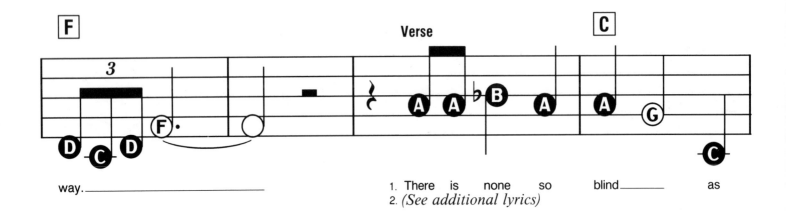

way._____

Verse

1. There is none so blind_____ as
2. *(See additional lyrics)*

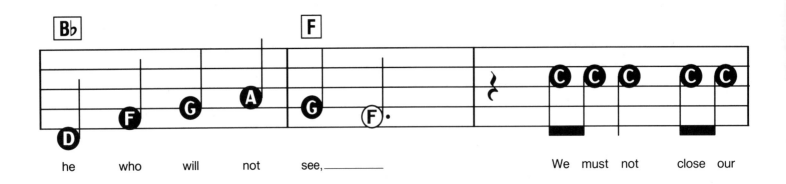

he who will not see,_____ We must not close our

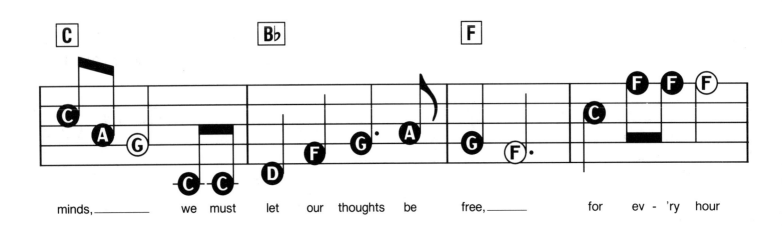

minds,_____ we must let our thoughts be free,_____ for ev - 'ry hour

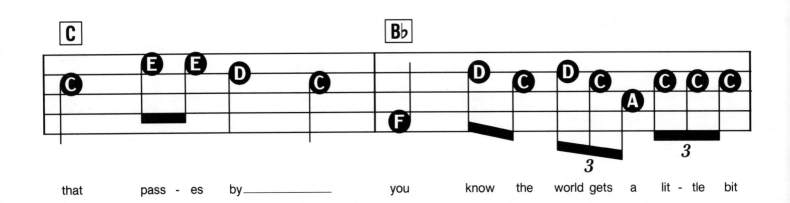

that pass - es by_____ you know the world gets a lit - tle bit

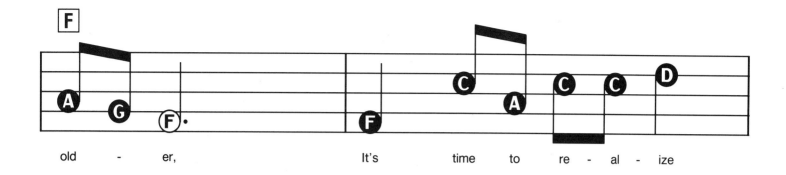

old - er, It's time to re - al - ize

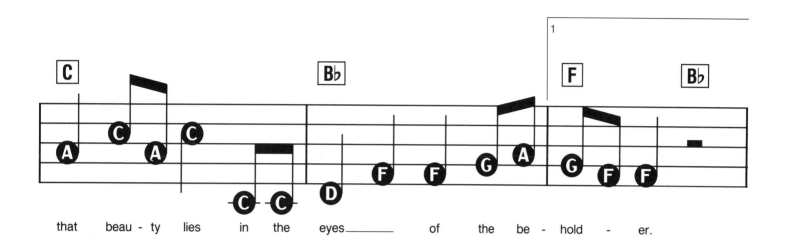

that beau - ty lies in the eyes_____ of the be - hold - er.

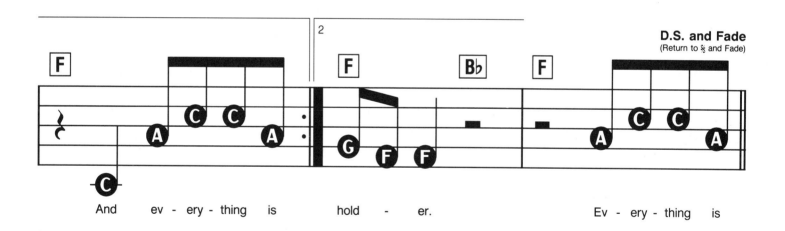

And ev - ery - thing is hold - er. Ev - ery - thing is

Additional Lyrics

2. We shouldn't care about the length of his hair or the color of his skin,
   Don't worry about what shows from without but the love that lives within,
   We gonna get it all together now and everything gonna work out fine,
   Just take a little time to look on the good side my friend and straighten it out in your mind.

Feelings
(¿Dime?)

English Words and Music by Morris Albert
Spanish Lyric by Thomas Fundora

Registration 5
Rhythm: Slow Rock

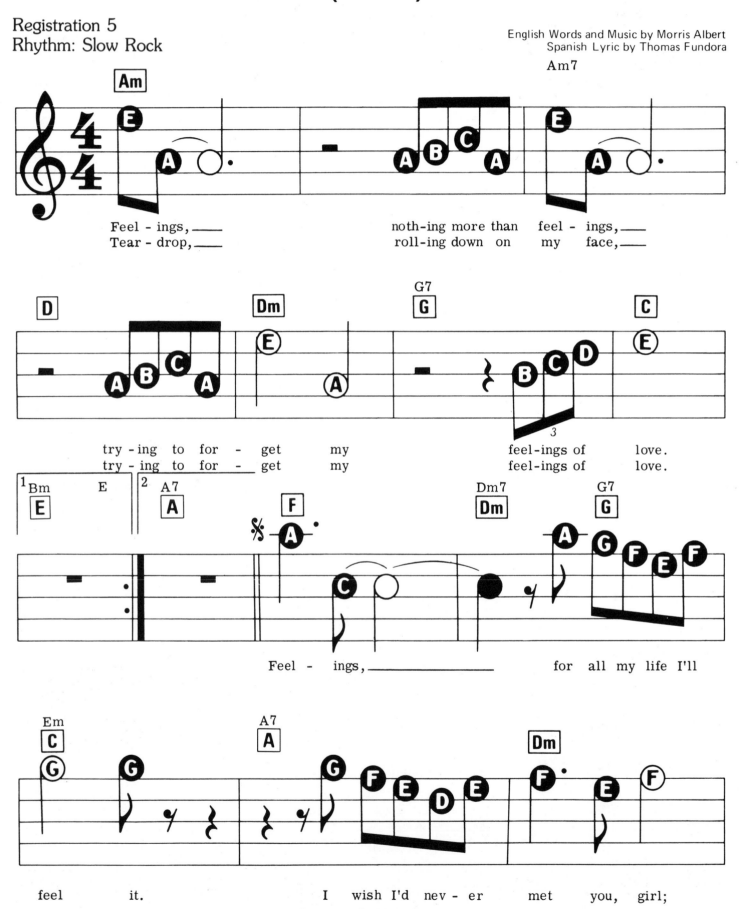

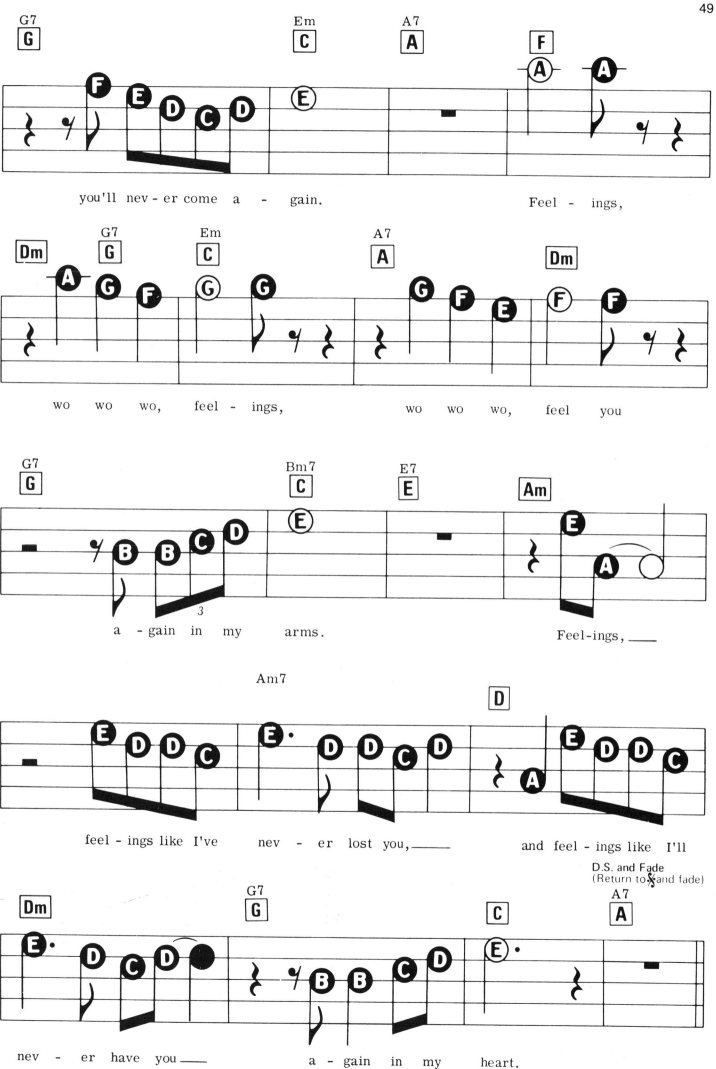

The First Time Ever I Saw Your Face

Registration 9
Rhythm: Ballad

Words & Music by Ewan MacColl

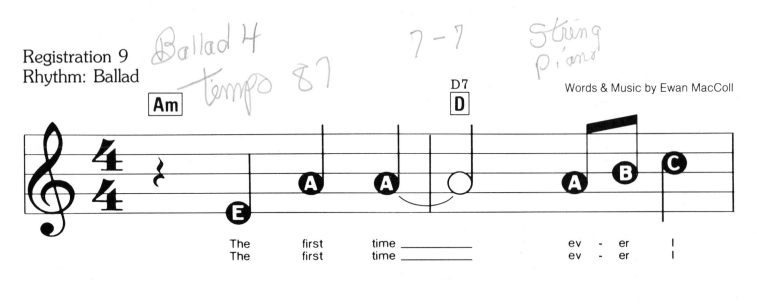

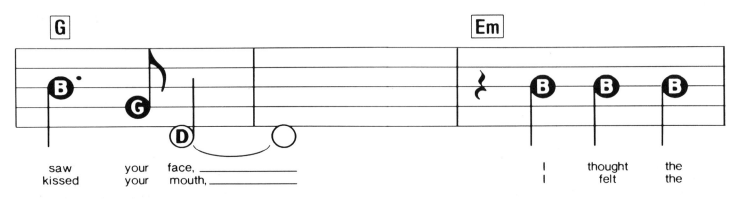

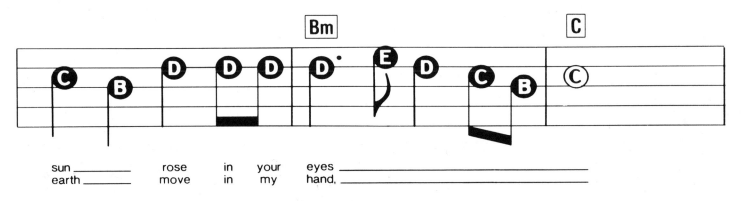

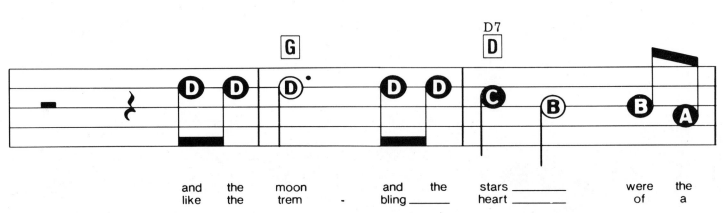

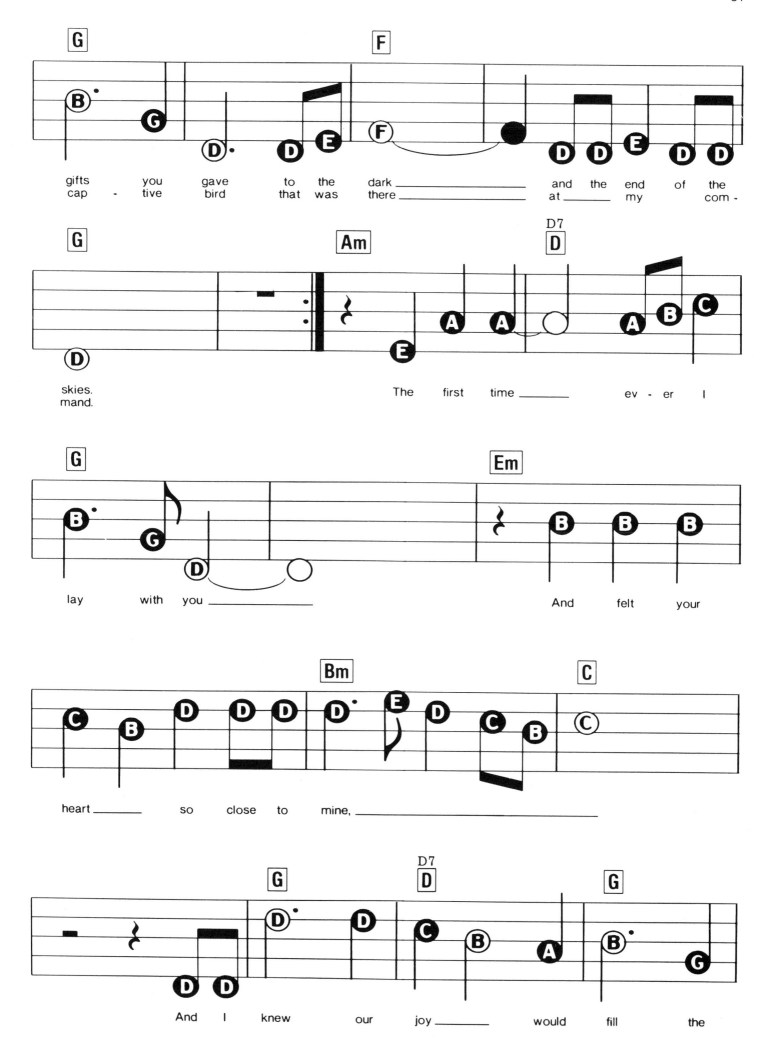

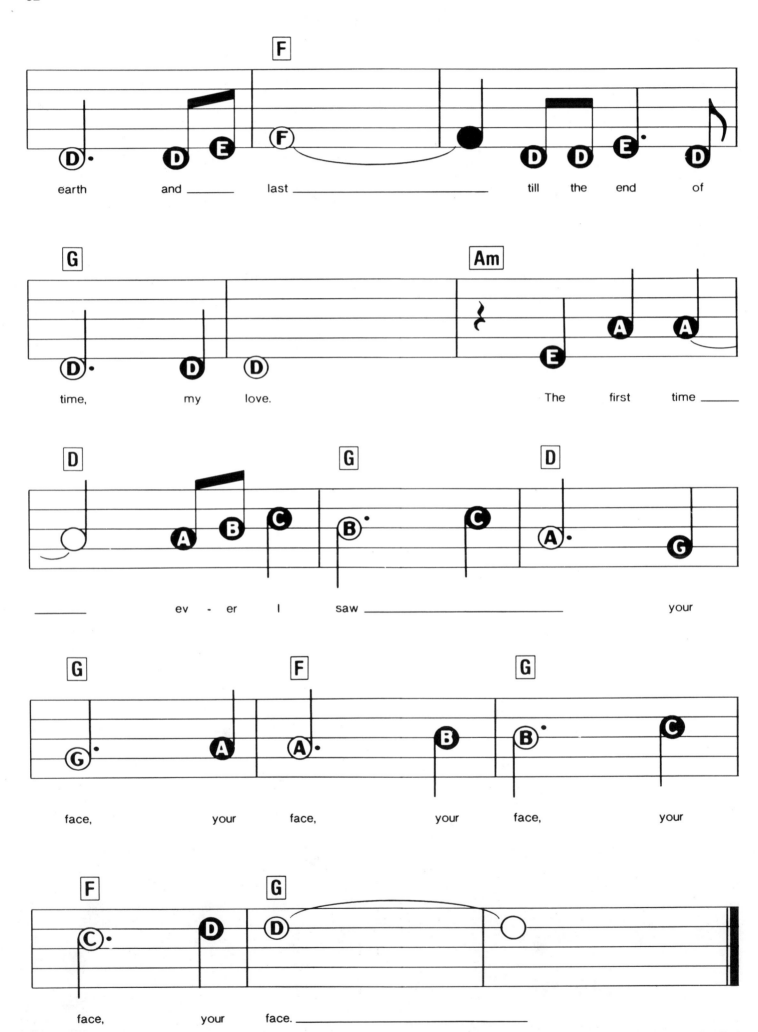

Free Bird

Registration 2
Rhythm: Slow Rock or 12 Beat

Words and Music by
Allen Collins and Ronnie Van Zant

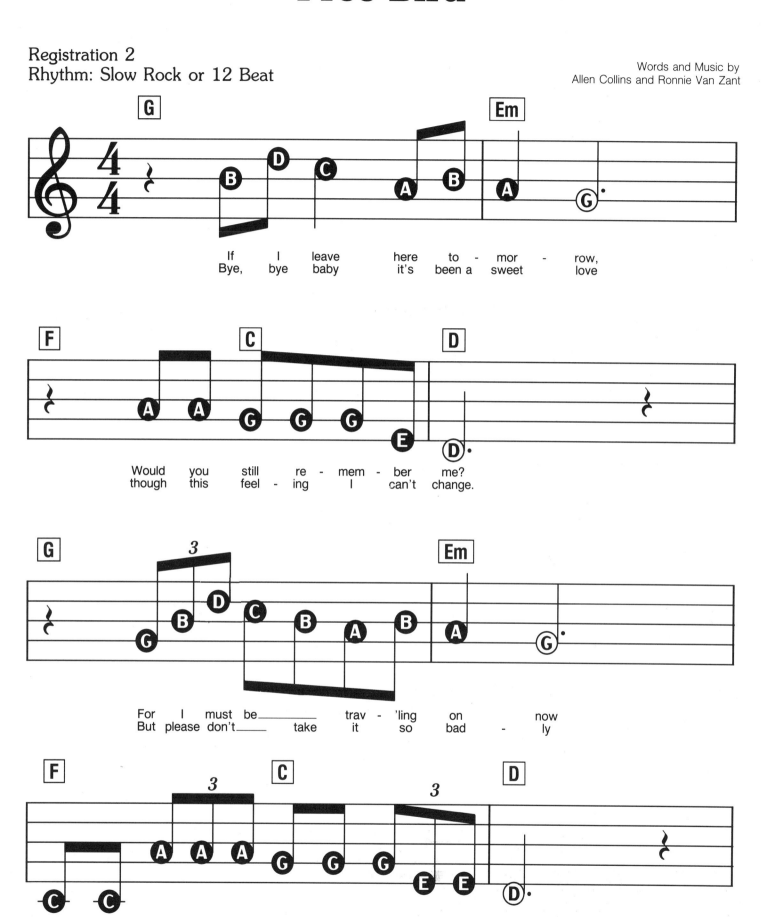

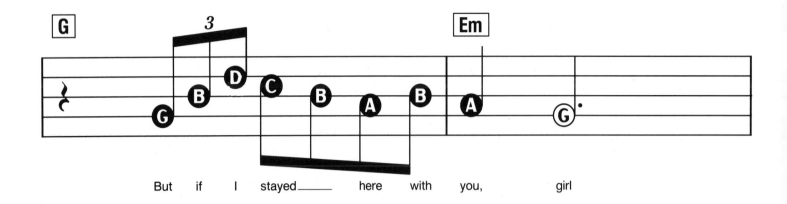

But if I stayed____ here with you, girl

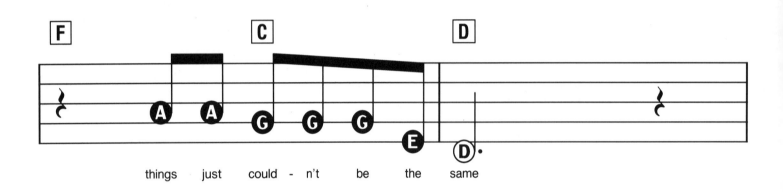

things just could - n't be the same

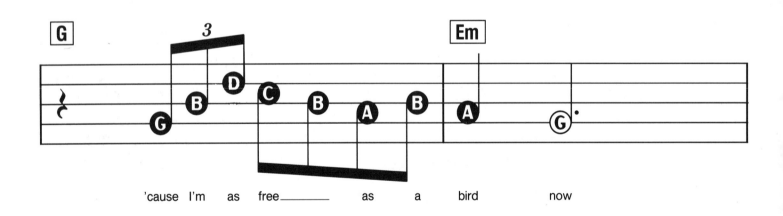

'cause I'm as free____ as a bird now

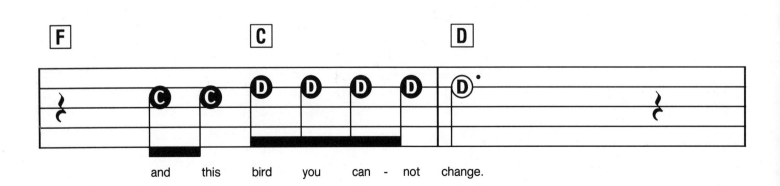

and this bird you can - not change.

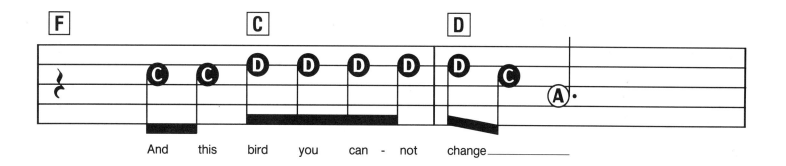

And this bird you can - not change_____

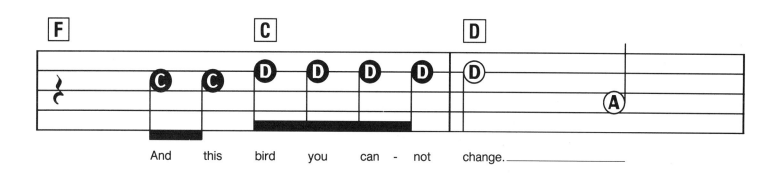

And this bird you can - not change._____

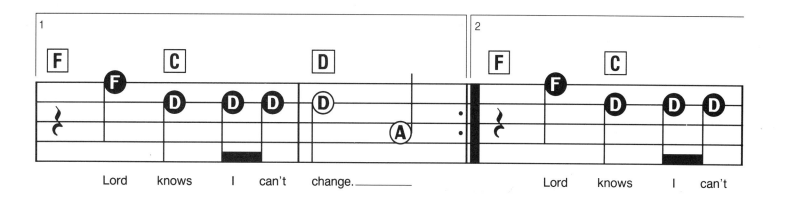

Lord knows I can't change._____ Lord knows I can't

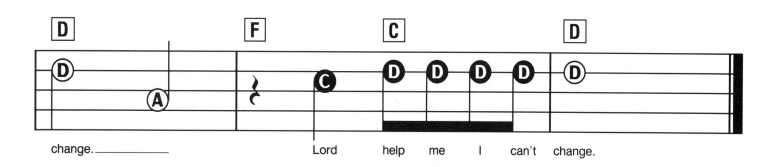

change._____ Lord help me I can't change.

For All We Know
(From the Motion Picture "LOVERS AND OTHER STRANGERS")

Words by Robb Wilson and James Griffin
Music by Fred Karlin

Registration 3
Rhythm: Rock or Ballad

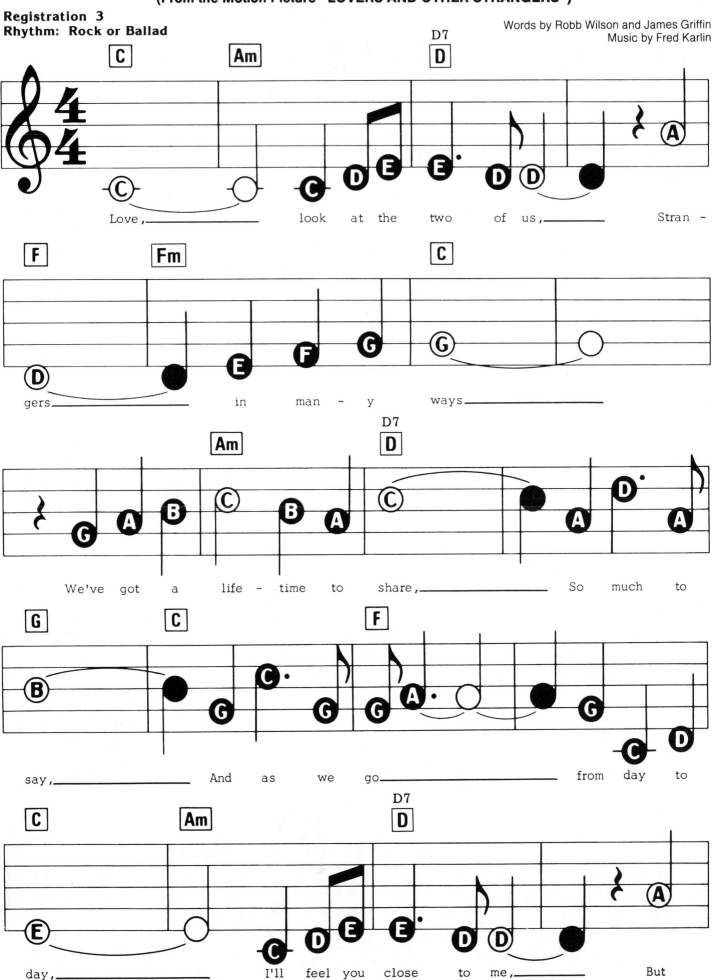

MCA MUSIC PUBLISHING

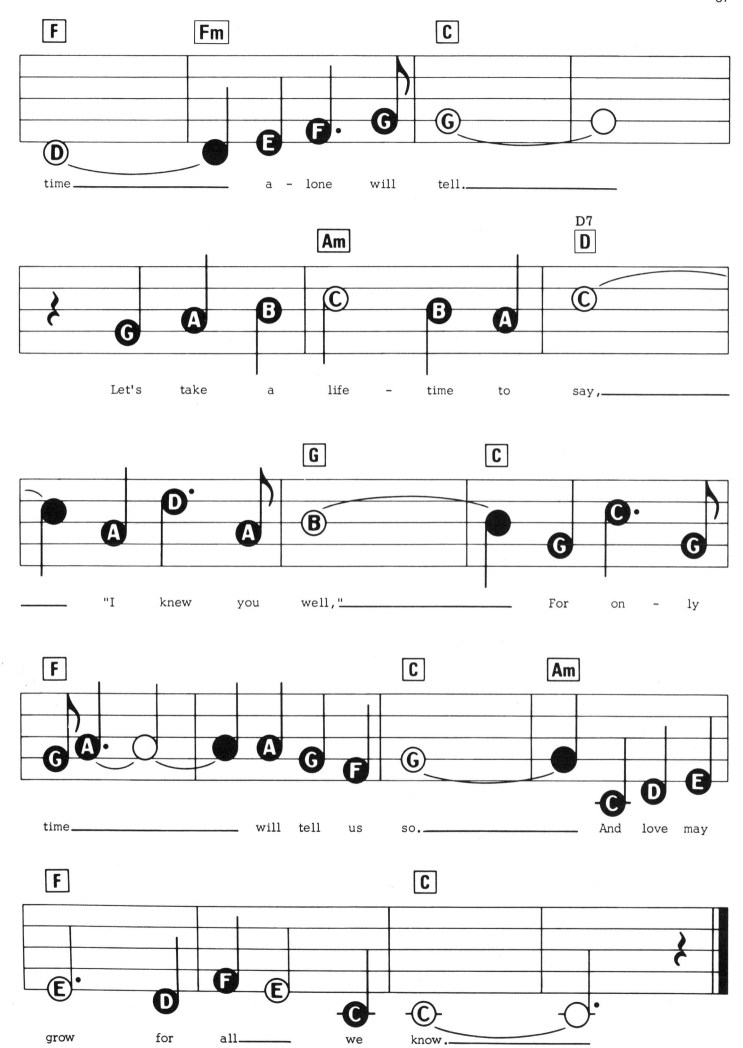

Goodbye Yellow Brick Road

Registration 5
Rhythm: Slow Rock

Words and Music by
Elton John and Bernie Taupin

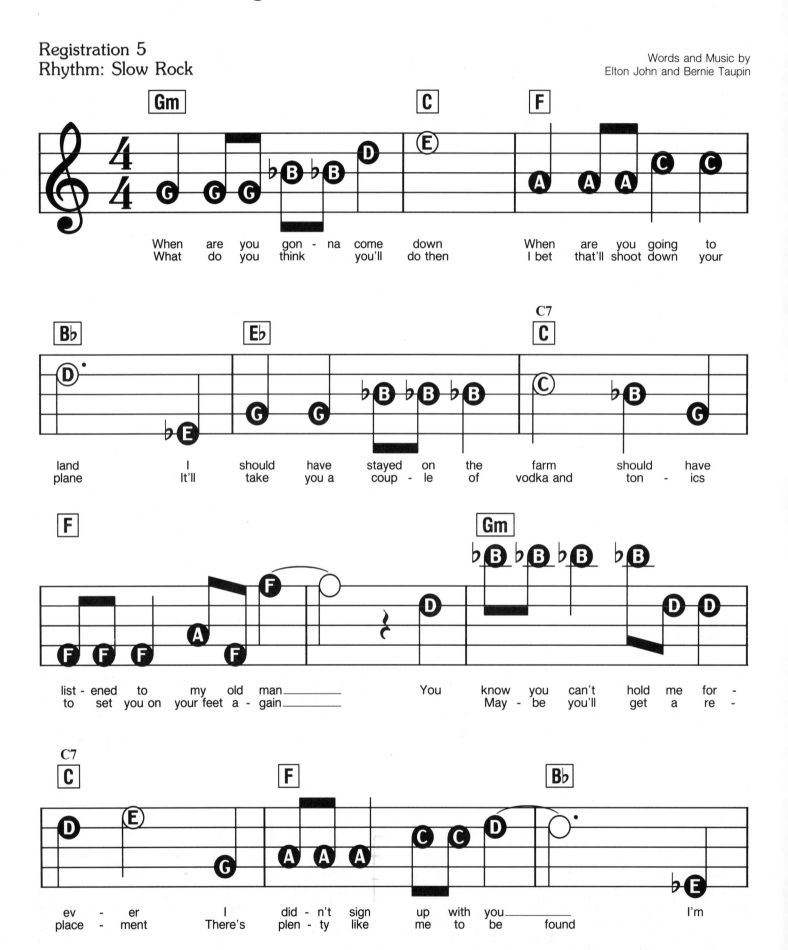

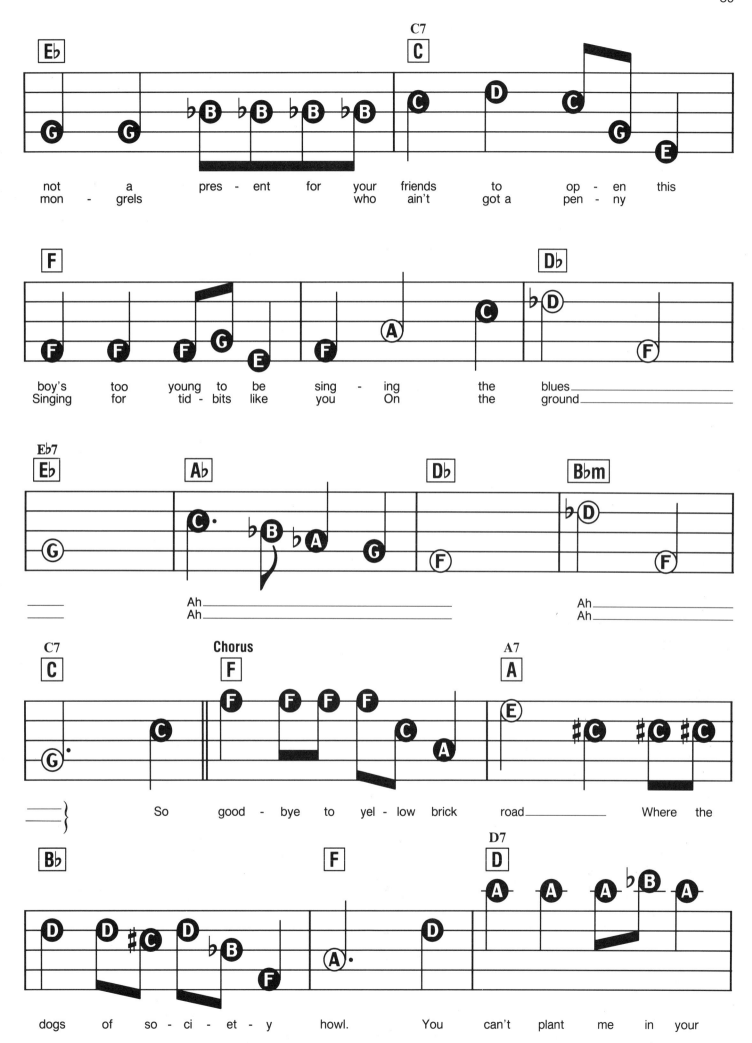

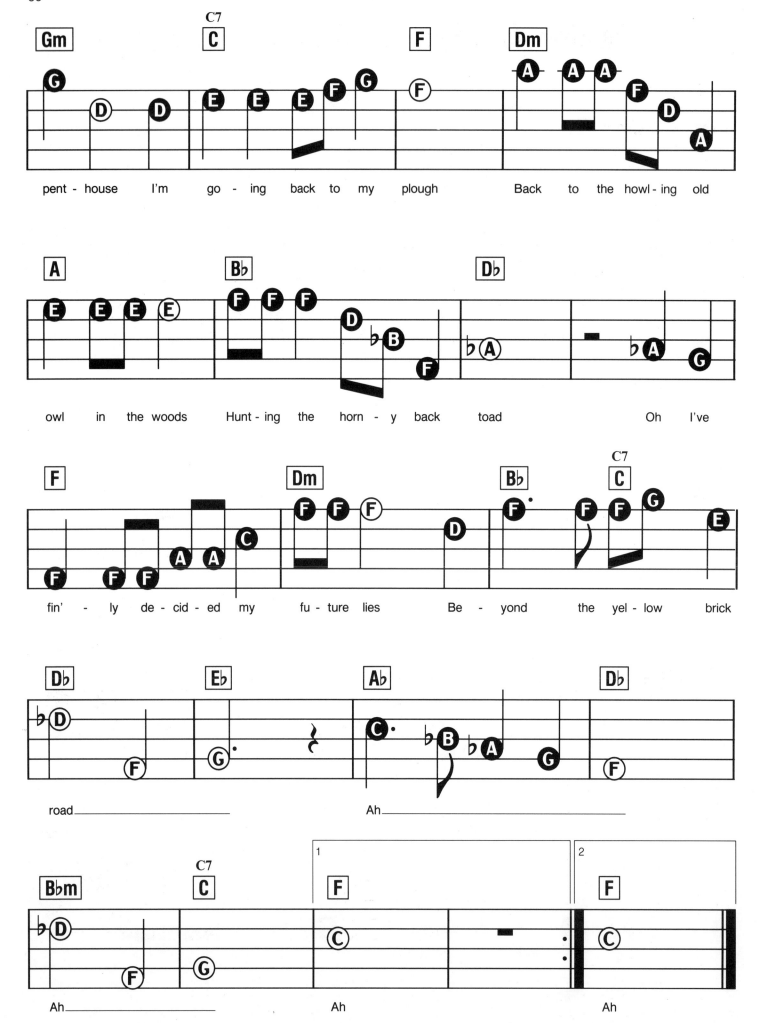

How Deep Is Your Love

Registration 4
Rhythm: Rock or Disco

Words and Music by Barry Gibb
Robin Gibb and Maurice Gibb

I know your eyes in the morn - ing sun. I feel you
me I be - lieve in you. You know the

touch me in the pour - ing rain. And the mo - ment that you won - der
door to my ver - y soul. You're the light in my deep - est,

far from me, I wan - na feel you in my arms a - gain. And you
dark - est hour; you're my sav - ior when I fall. And you

come to me on a sum - mer breeze; keep me warm in your love, then you
may not think I _____ care for you when you know down in - side that I

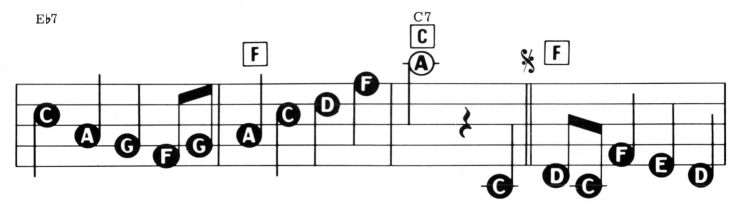

soft · ly leave.
real · ly do. And it's me you need to show: How deep is your love? How

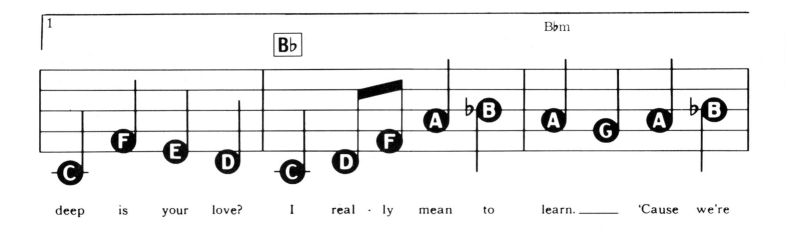

deep is your love? I real · ly mean to learn. _____ 'Cause we're

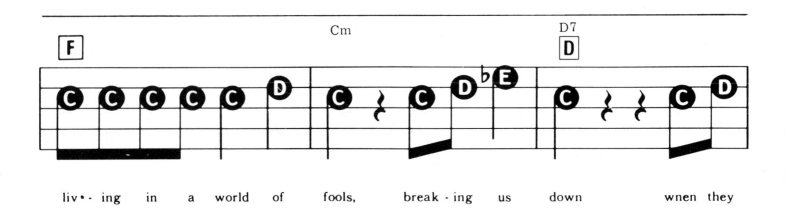

liv· · ing in a world of fools, break · ing us down wnen they

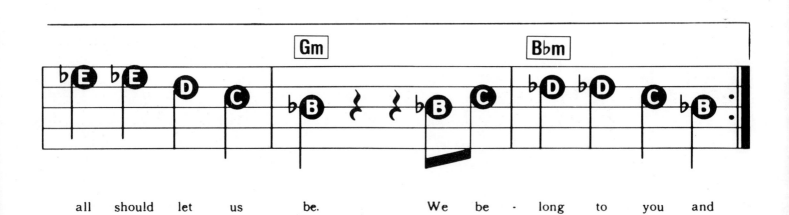

all should let us be. We be · long to you and

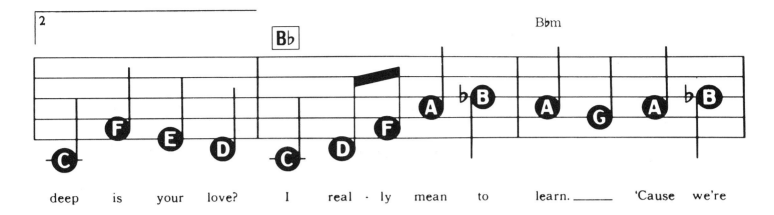

deep is your love? I real · ly mean to learn.____ 'Cause we're

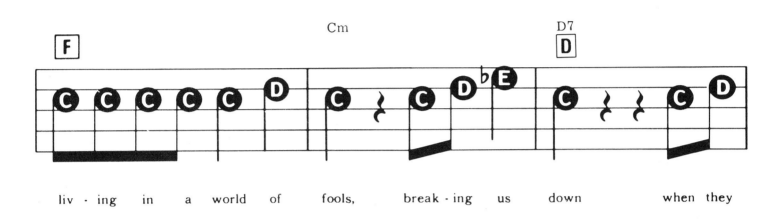

liv · ing in a world of fools, break · ing us down when they

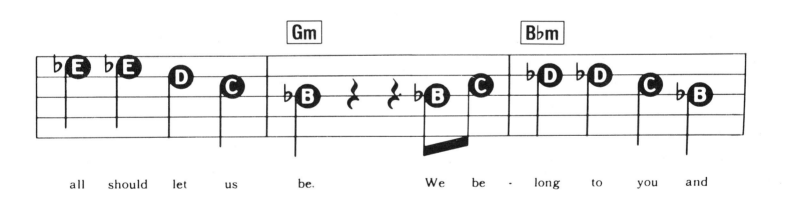

all should let us be. We be · long to you and

D.S. and Fade
(Return to 𝄋
and fade)

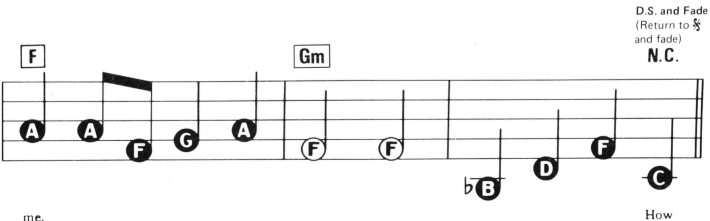

me. How

Help Me Make It Through The Night

Registration 2
Rhythm: Country or Fox Trot

Words and Music by
Kris Kristofferson

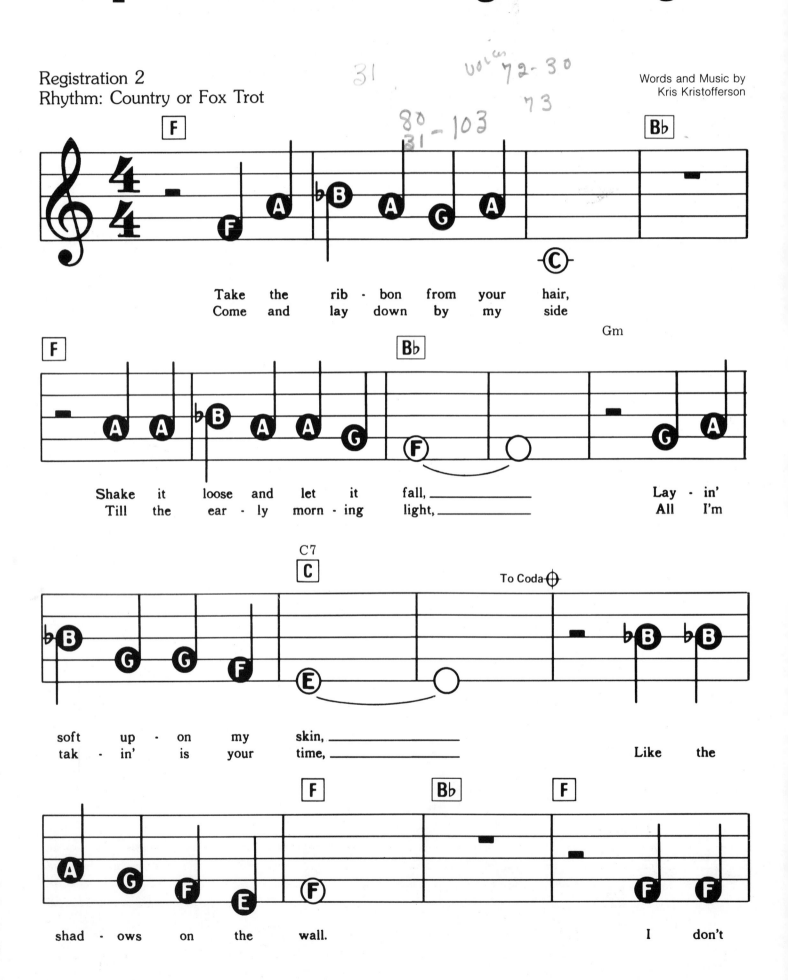

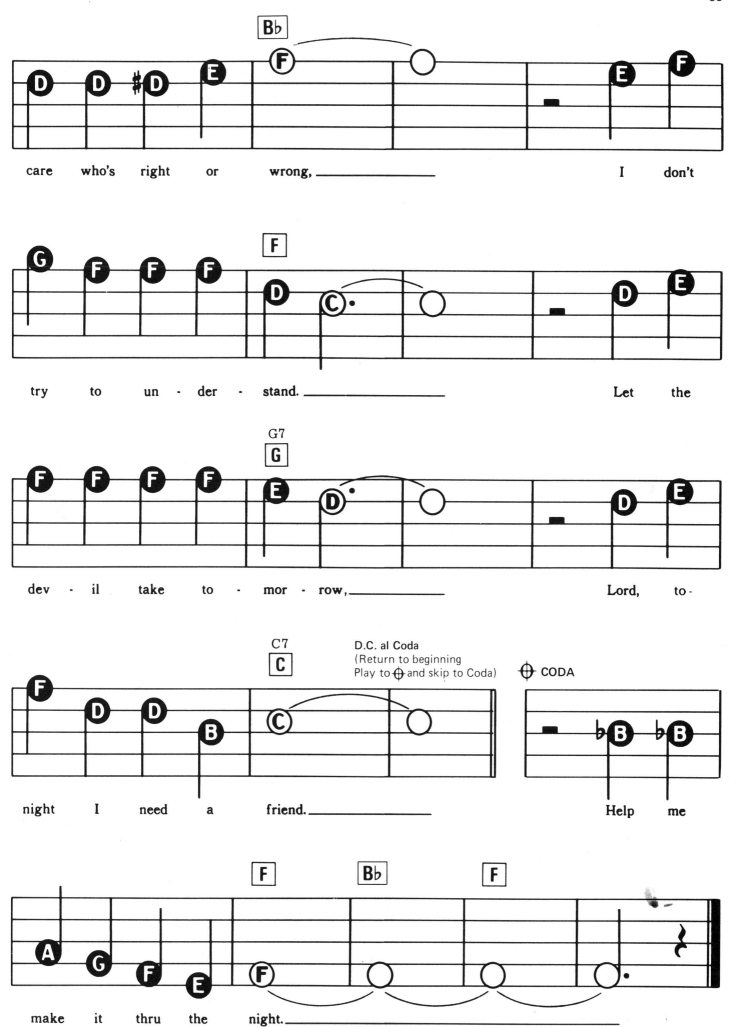

How Can You Mend A Broken Heart

Registration 5
Rhythm: Rock

Words and Music by
Barry Gibb and Robin Gibb

I can think of young - er days when liv - ing for my life was
I can still feel the breeze that rust - les through the trees and

ev - 'ry - thing a man could want to do. I could nev - er see to -
mis - ty mem - o - ries of days gone by. We could nev - er see to -

mor - row but I was nev - er told a -
mor - row, no one said a word a -

bout the sor - row. And how can you mend
bout the sor - row.

bro - ken heart? How can you stop the rain from fall - ing down?

67

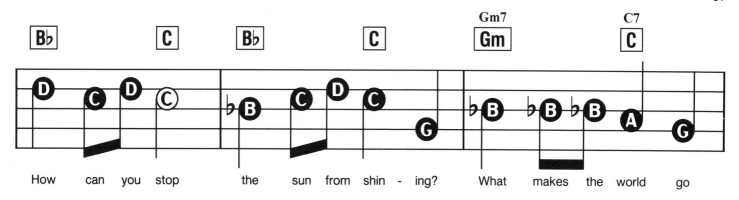

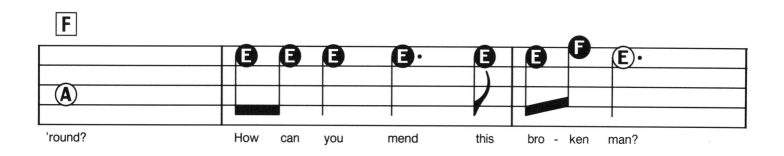

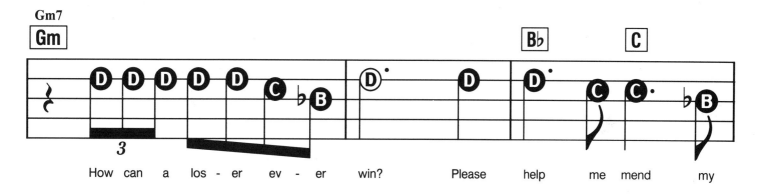

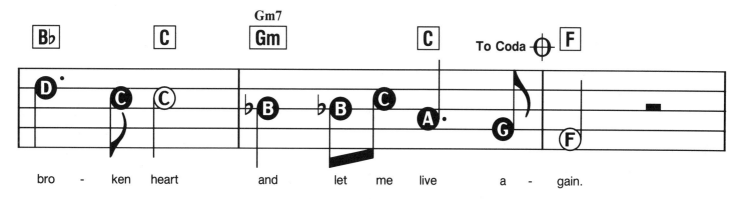

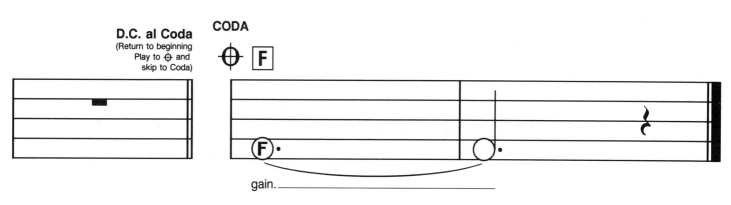

I Don't Know How To Love Him
(From "JESUS CHRIST SUPERSTAR")

Registration 1
Rhythm: Rock

Words by Tim Rice
Music by Andrew Lloyd Webber

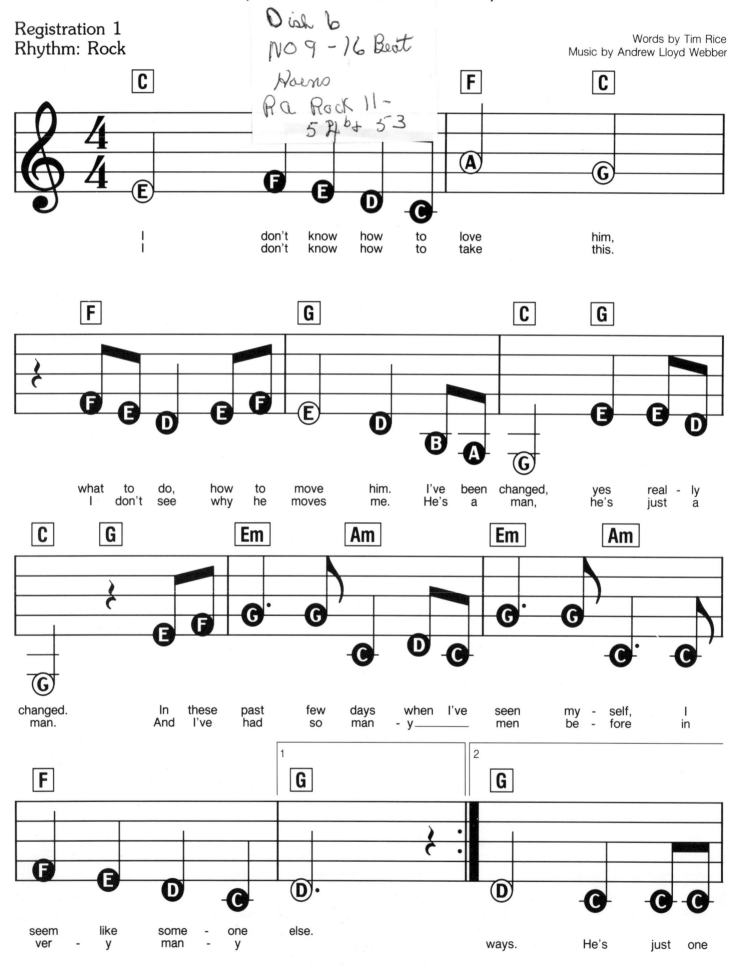

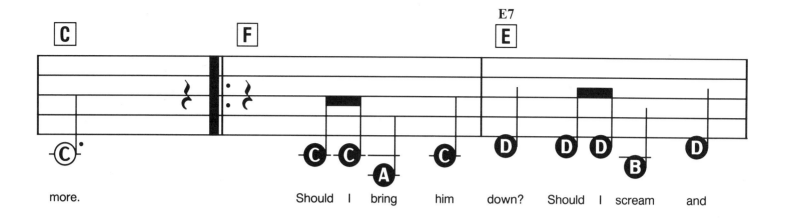

more. Should I bring him down? Should I scream and

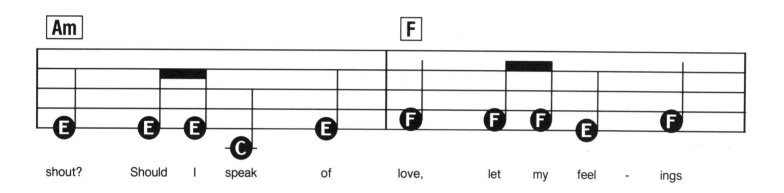

shout? Should I speak of love, let my feel - ings

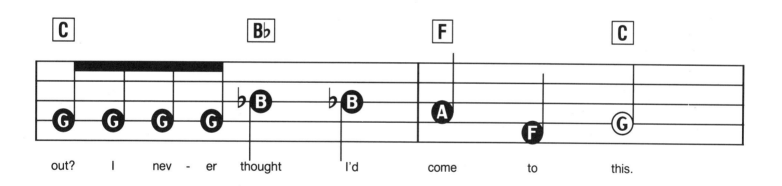

out? I nev - er thought I'd come to this.

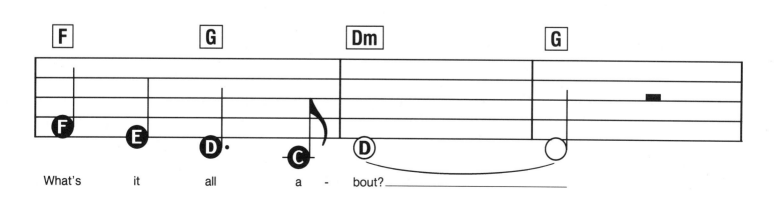

What's it all a - bout?

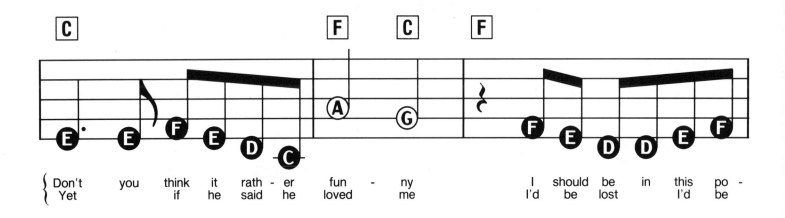

Don't you think it rath - er fun - ny | I should be in this po -
Yet if he said he loved me | I'd be lost I'd be

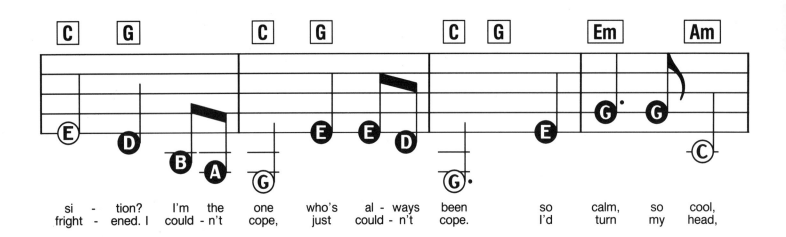

si - tion? I'm the one who's al - ways been so calm, so cool,
fright - ened. I could - n't cope, just could - n't cope. I'd turn my head,

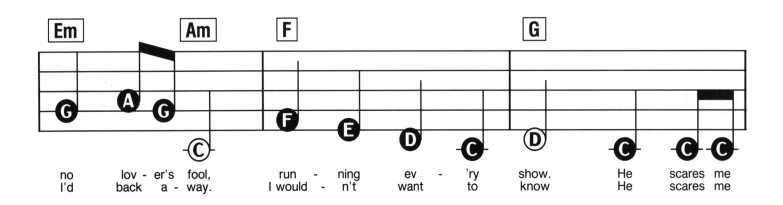

no lov - er's fool, run - ning ev - 'ry show. He scares me
I'd back a - way. I would - n't want to know He scares me

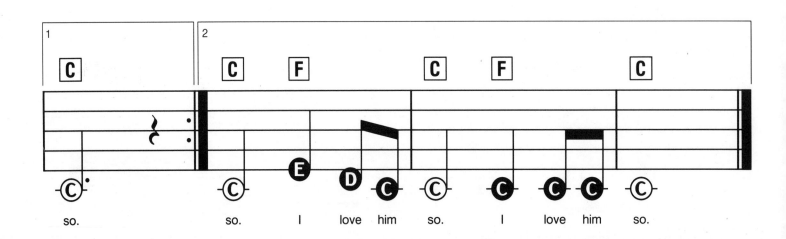

so.
so. I love him so. I love him so.

Imagine

Registration 8
Rhythm: Rock or Slow Rock

POP ROCK
US Grove

Words and Music by
John Lennon

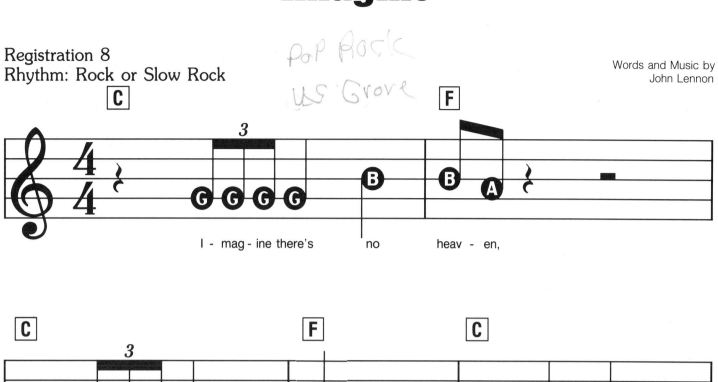

I - mag - ine there's no heav - en,

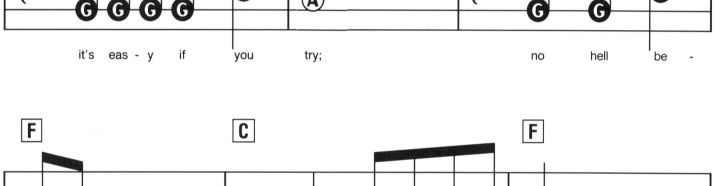

it's eas - y if you try; no hell be -

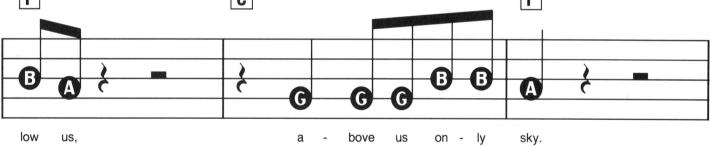

low us, a - bove us on - ly sky.

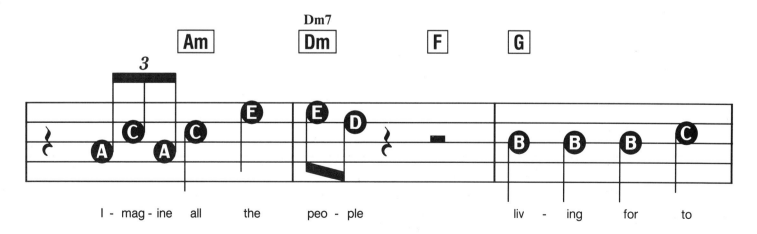

I - mag - ine all the peo - ple liv - ing for to

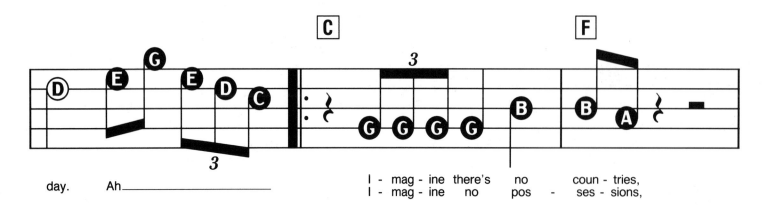

day.   Ah_____

I - mag - ine there's   no   coun - tries,
I - mag - ine   no   pos - ses - sions,

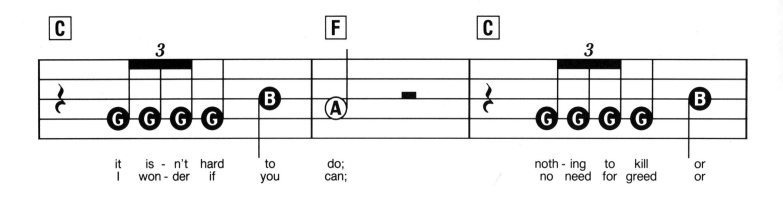

it   is - n't hard   to   do;
I   won - der if   you   can;

noth - ing   to kill   or
no   need for greed   or

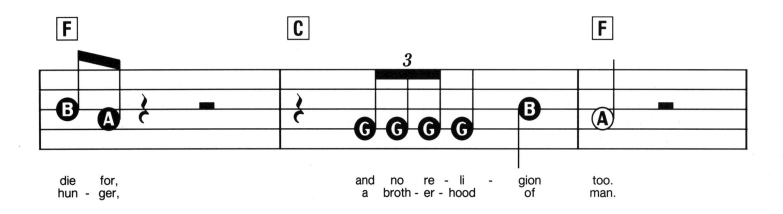

die for,
hun - ger,

and no re - li - gion   too.
a broth - er - hood   of   man.

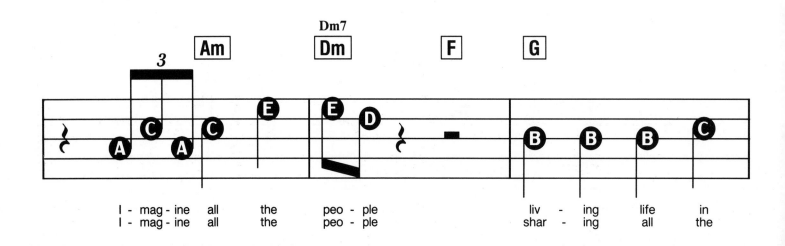

I - mag - ine all   the   peo - ple
I - mag - ine all   the   peo - ple

liv - ing life   in
shar - ing all   the

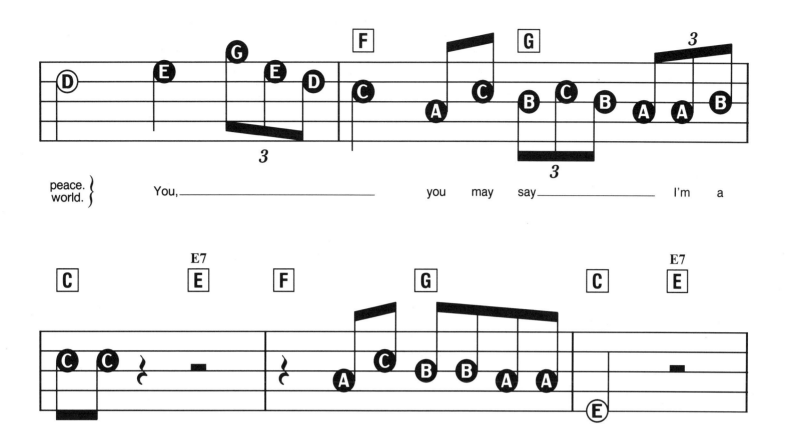

peace.
world.
You,_____ you may say_____ I'm a

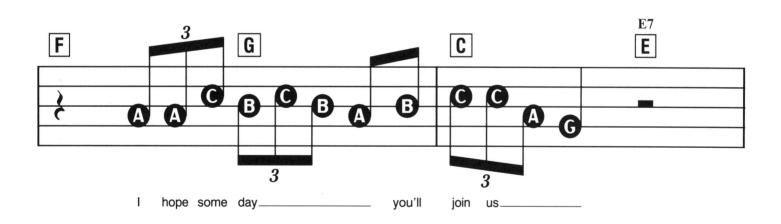

dream - er, but I'm not the on - ly one.

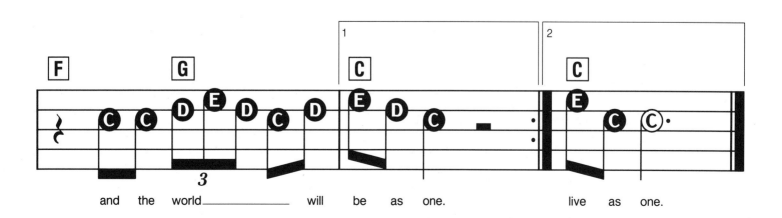

I hope some day_____ you'll join us_____

and the world_____ will be as one. live as one.

I Will Survive

Registration 5
Rhythm: Rock or Disco

Words and Music by
Dino Fekaris and Freddie Perren

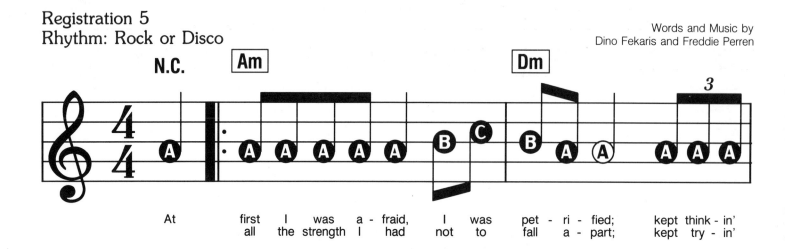

At first I was a-fraid, I was pet-ri-fied; kept think-in'
all the strength I had not to fall a-part; kept try-in'

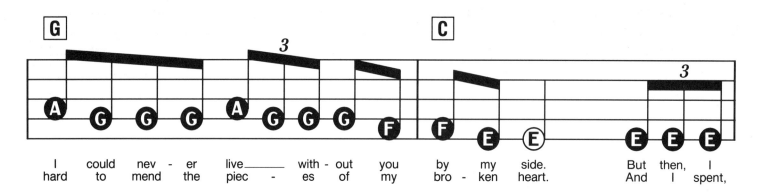

I could nev-er live____ with-out you by my side. But then, I
hard to mend the piec-es of my bro-ken heart. And I spent,

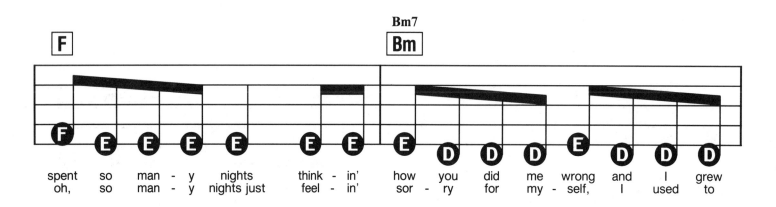

spent so man-y nights think-in' how you did me wrong and I grew
oh, so man-y nights just feel-in' sor-ry for my-self, I used to

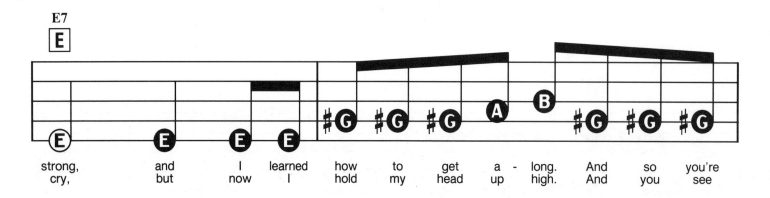

strong, and I learned how to get a-long. And so you're
cry, but now I hold my head up high. And you see

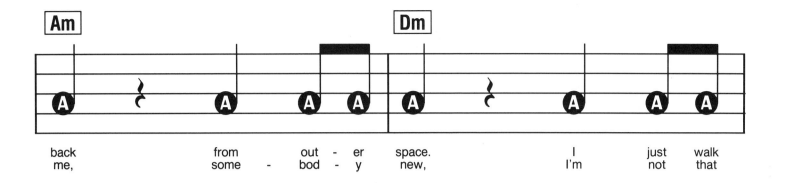

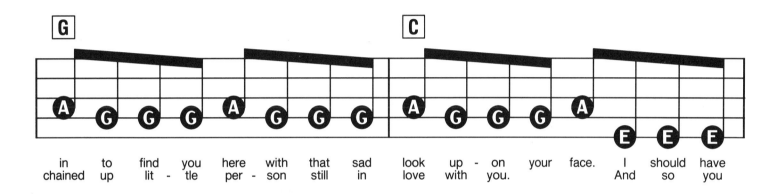

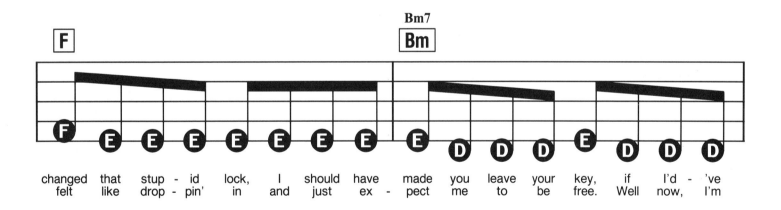

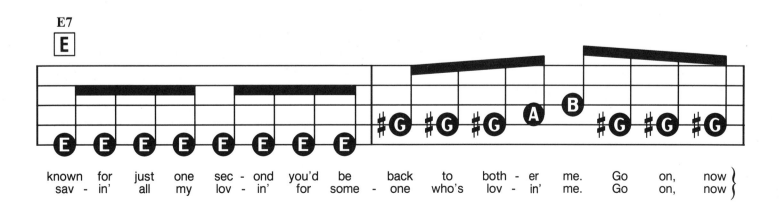

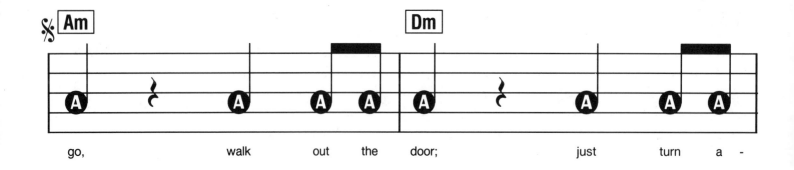

go, walk out the door; just turn a-

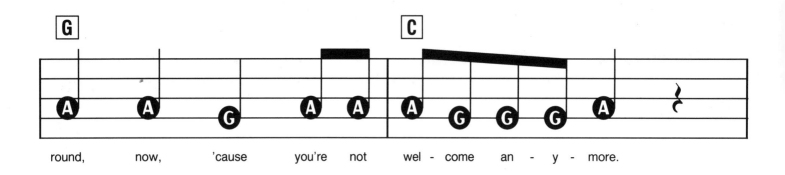

round, now, 'cause you're not wel - come an - y - more.

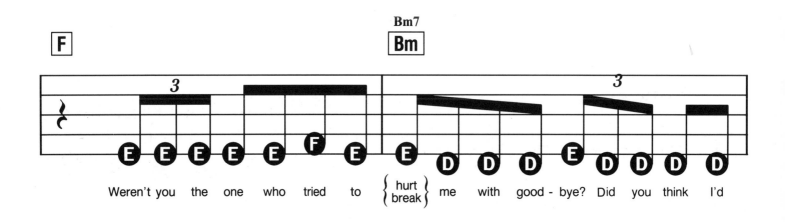

Weren't you the one who tried to {hurt/break} me with good - bye? Did you think I'd

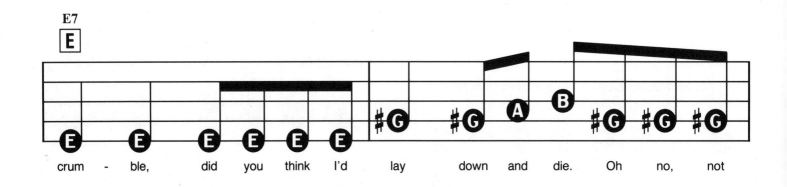

crum - ble, did you think I'd lay down and die. Oh no, not

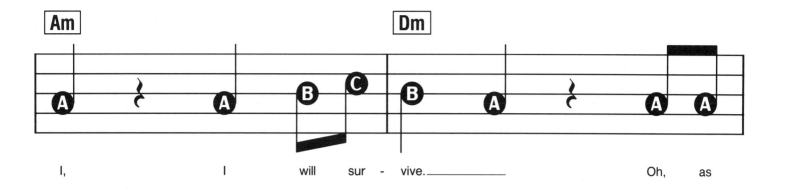

I, I will sur - vive._____ Oh, as

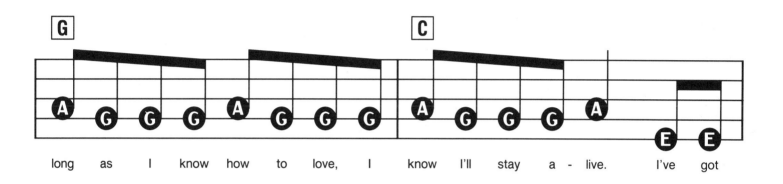

long as I know how to love, I know I'll stay a - live. I've got

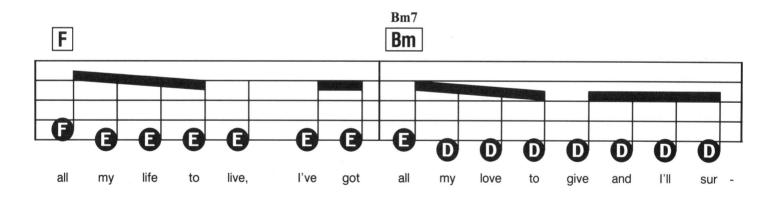

all my life to live, I've got all my love to give and I'll sur -

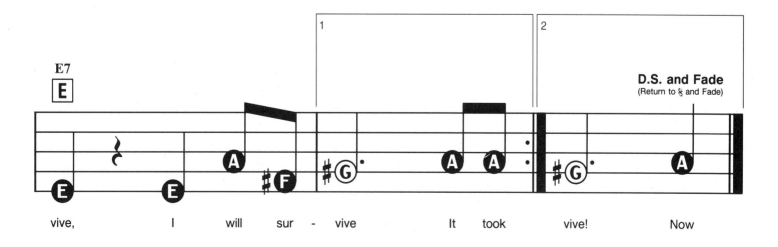

vive, I will sur - vive It took vive! Now

Jive Talkin'

Registration 4
Rhythm: Rock or Disco

Words and Music by Barry Gibb,
Robin Gibb and Maurice Gibb

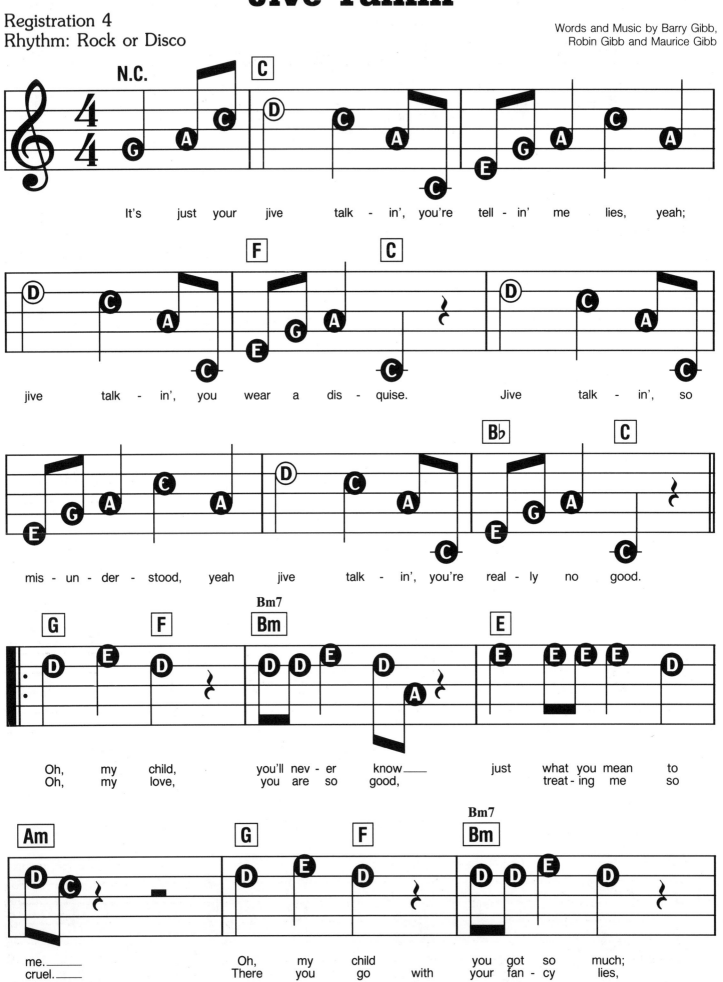

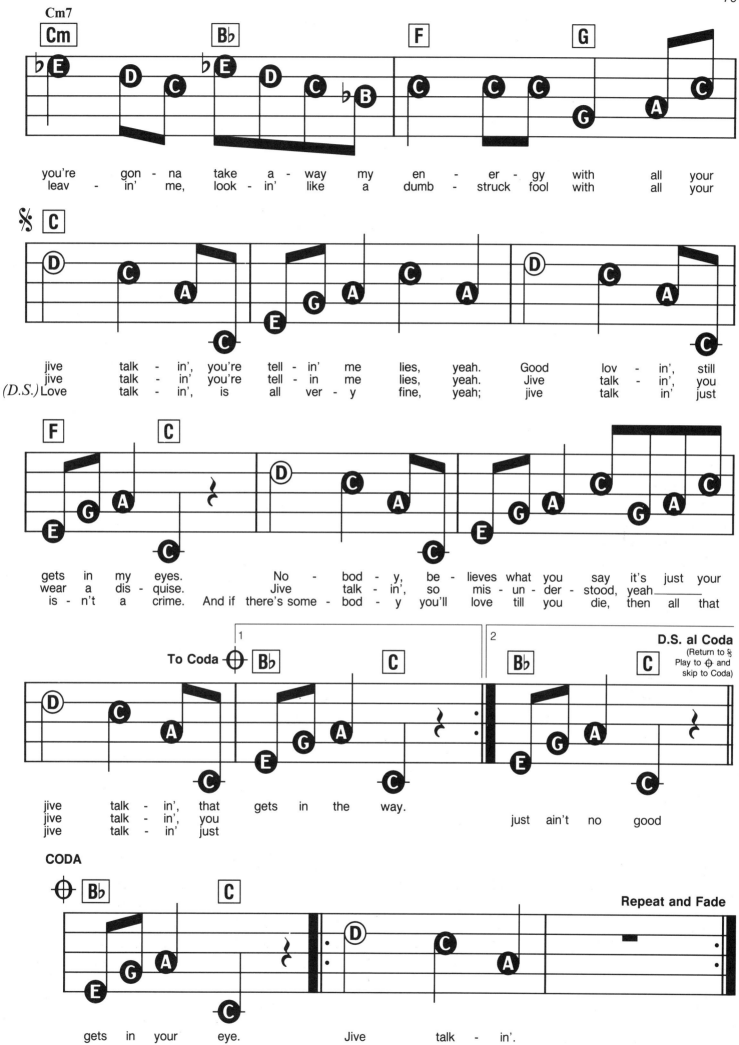

Joy To The World

Registration 2
Rhythm: Rock

Words and Music by
Hoyt Axton

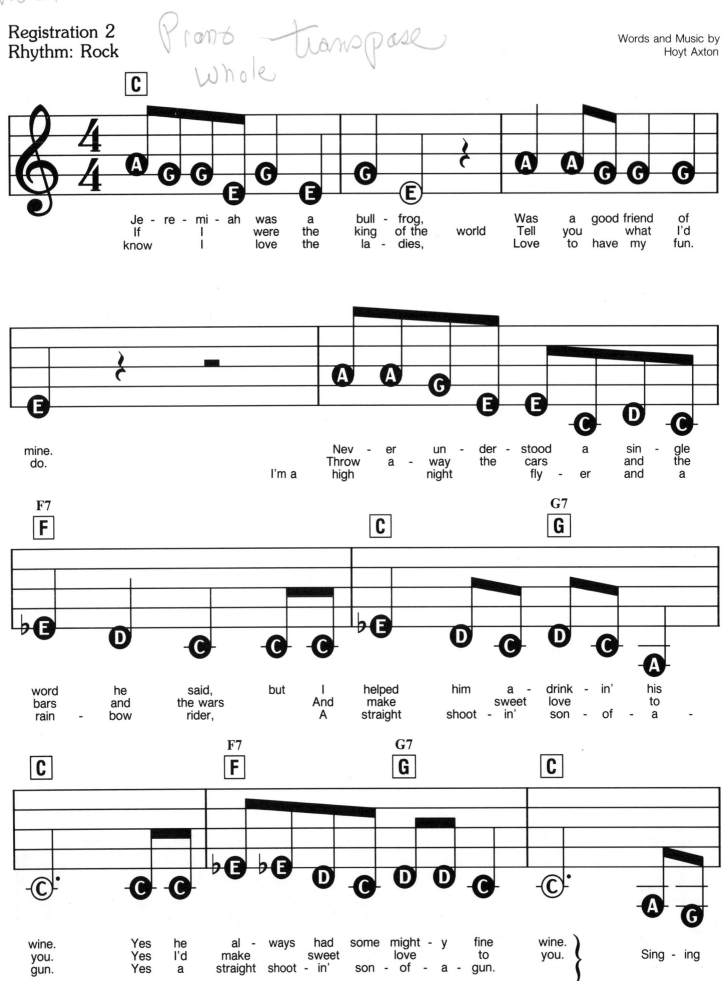

81

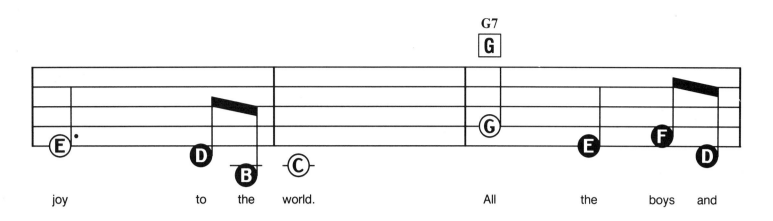

joy   to the world.   All   the   boys and

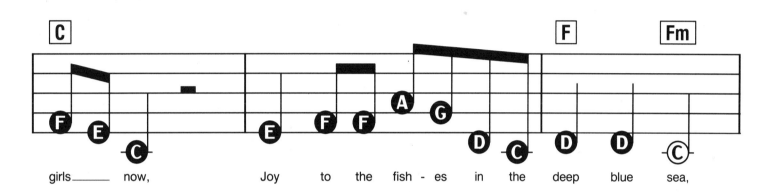

girls _____ now,   Joy   to the fish - es in the deep blue sea,

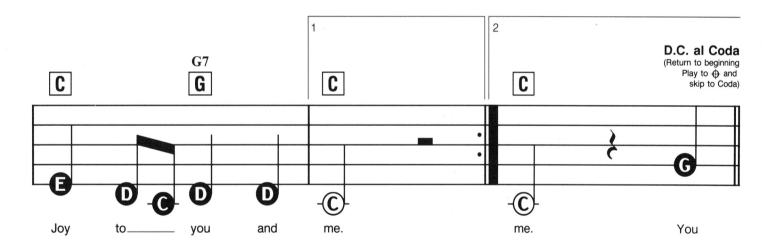

Joy to _____ you and me.   me.   You

CODA

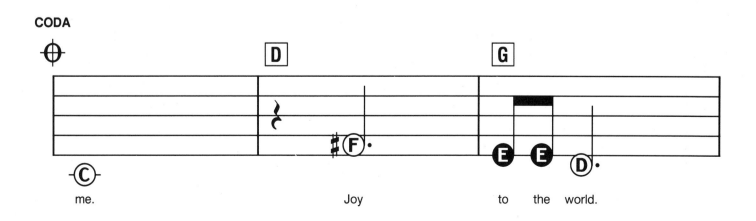

me.   Joy   to the world.

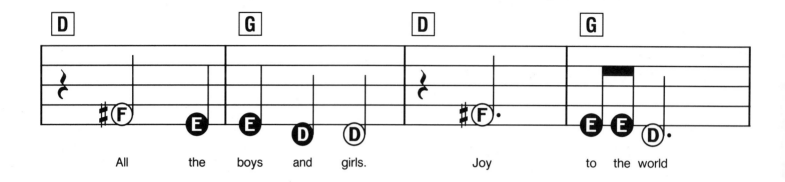

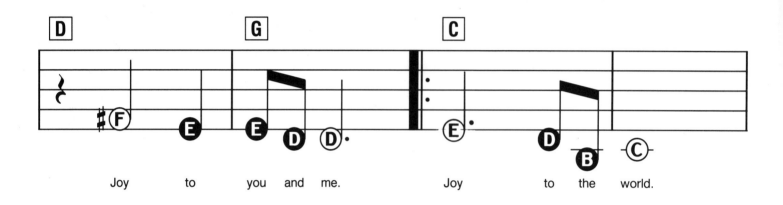

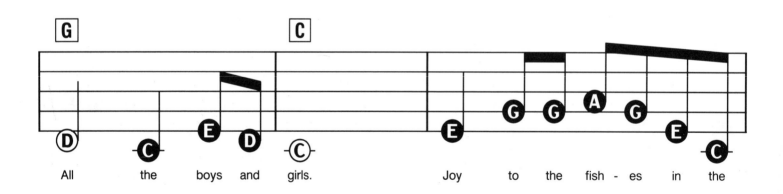

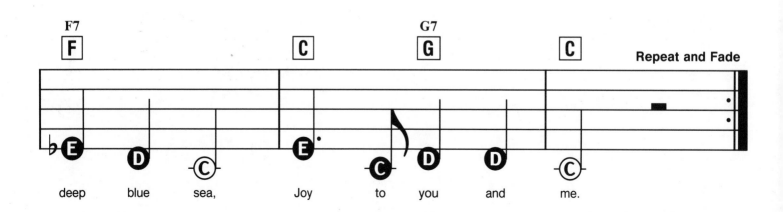

The Long And Winding Road

Registration 4
Rhythm: Rock and Slow Rock

Words and Music by
John Lennon and Paul McCartney

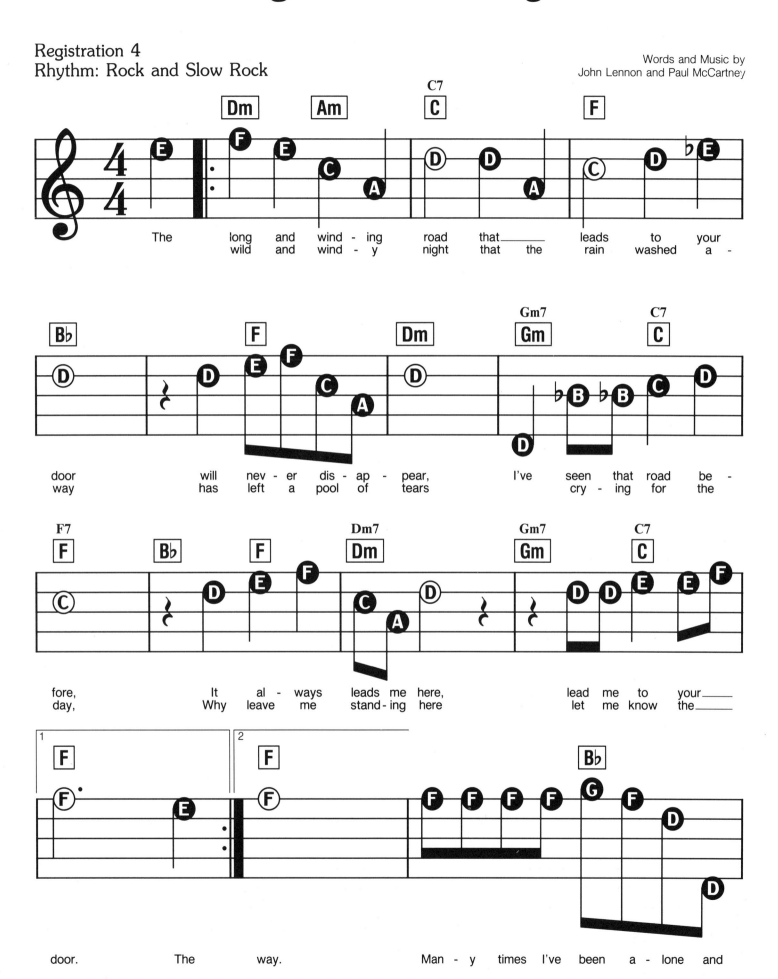

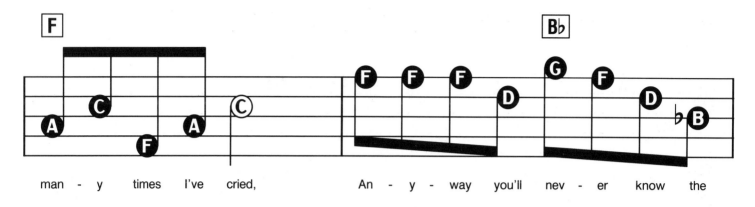

man - y times I've cried, An - y - way you'll nev - er know the

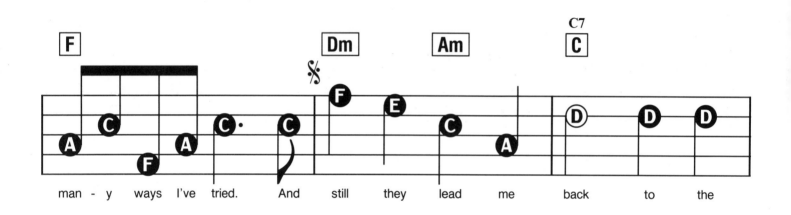

man - y ways I've tried. And still they lead me back to the

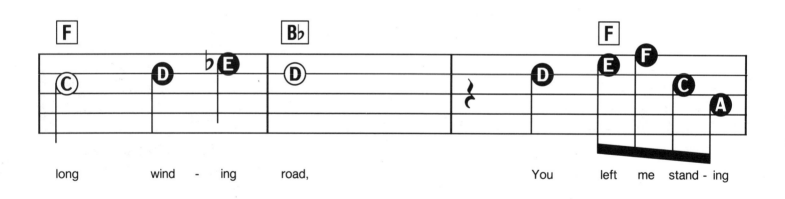

long wind - ing road, You left me stand - ing

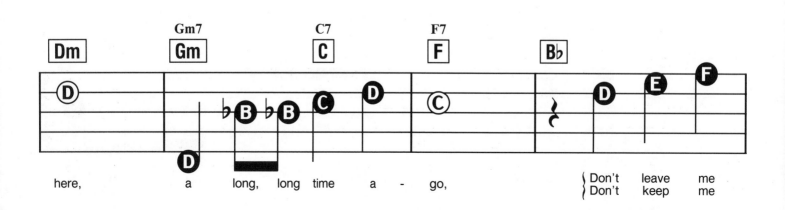

here, a long, long time a - go, { Don't leave me / Don't keep me

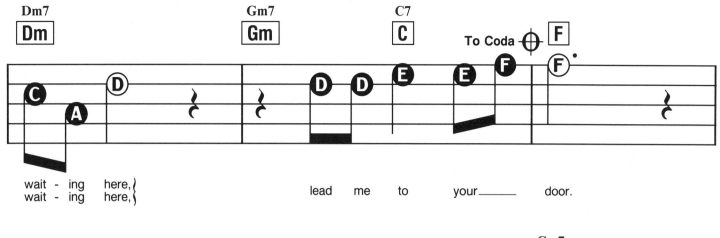

wait - ing here,
wait - ing here,
lead me to your____ door.

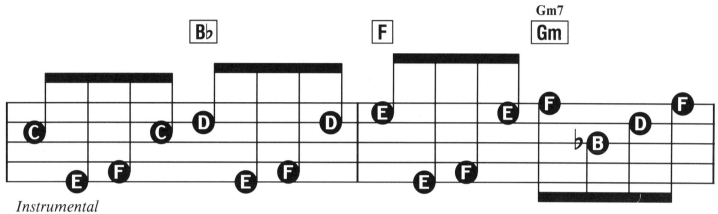

Instrumental

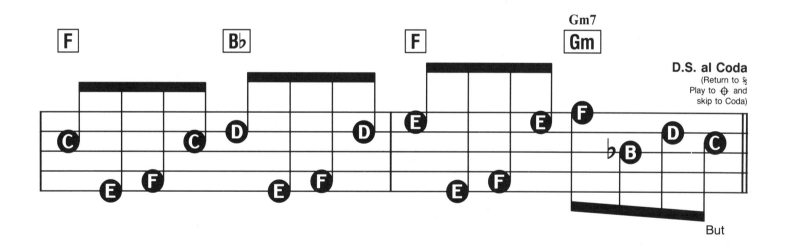

But

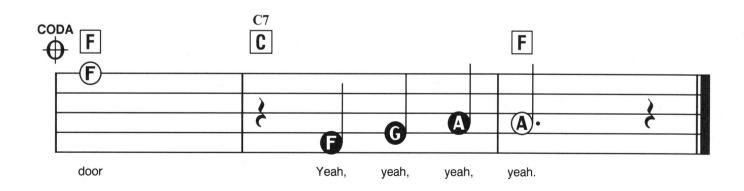

door
Yeah, yeah, yeah, yeah.

Just The Way You Are

Registration 4
Rhythm: Rock or Jazz Rock

Words and Music by Billy Joel

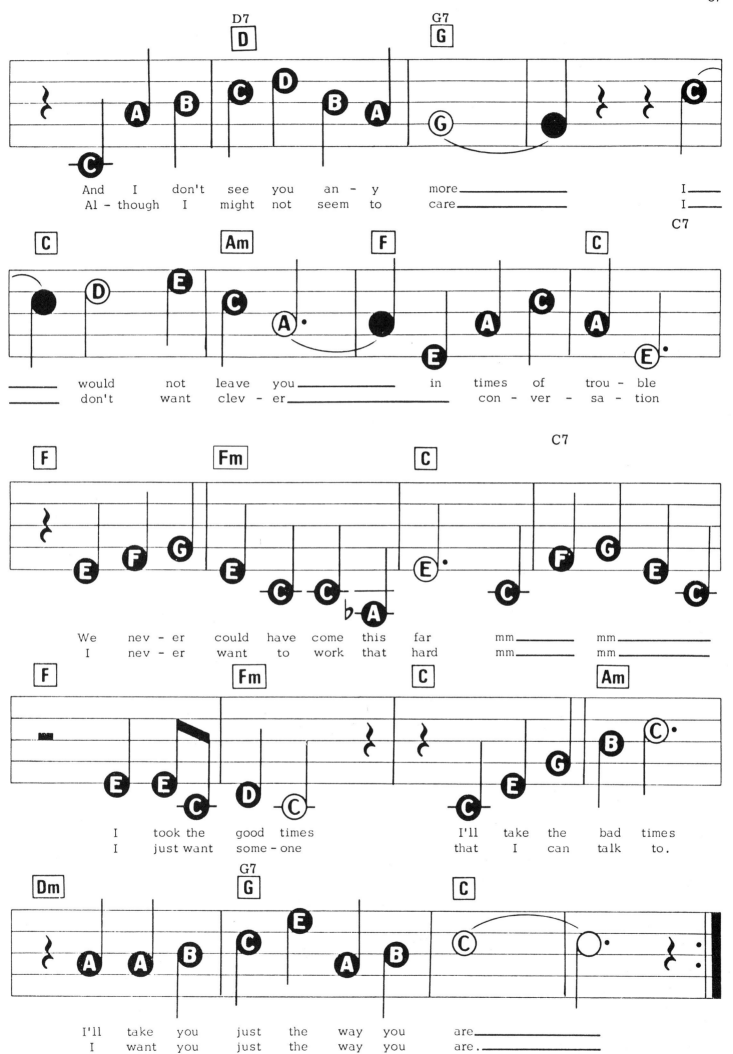

88

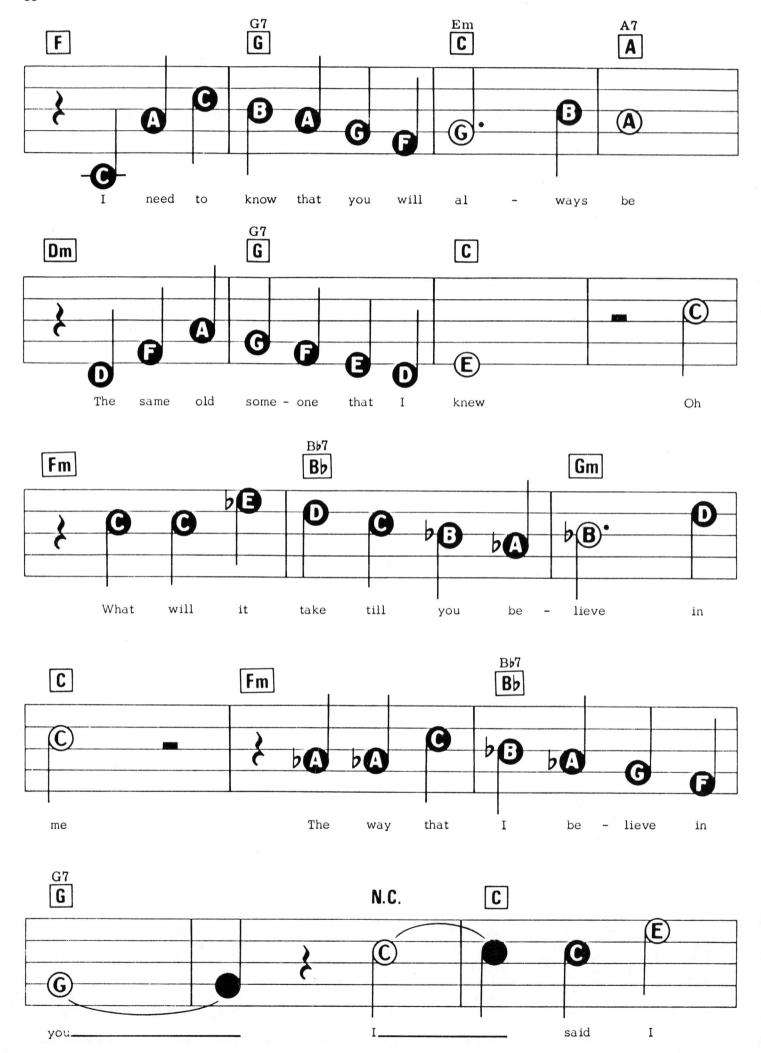

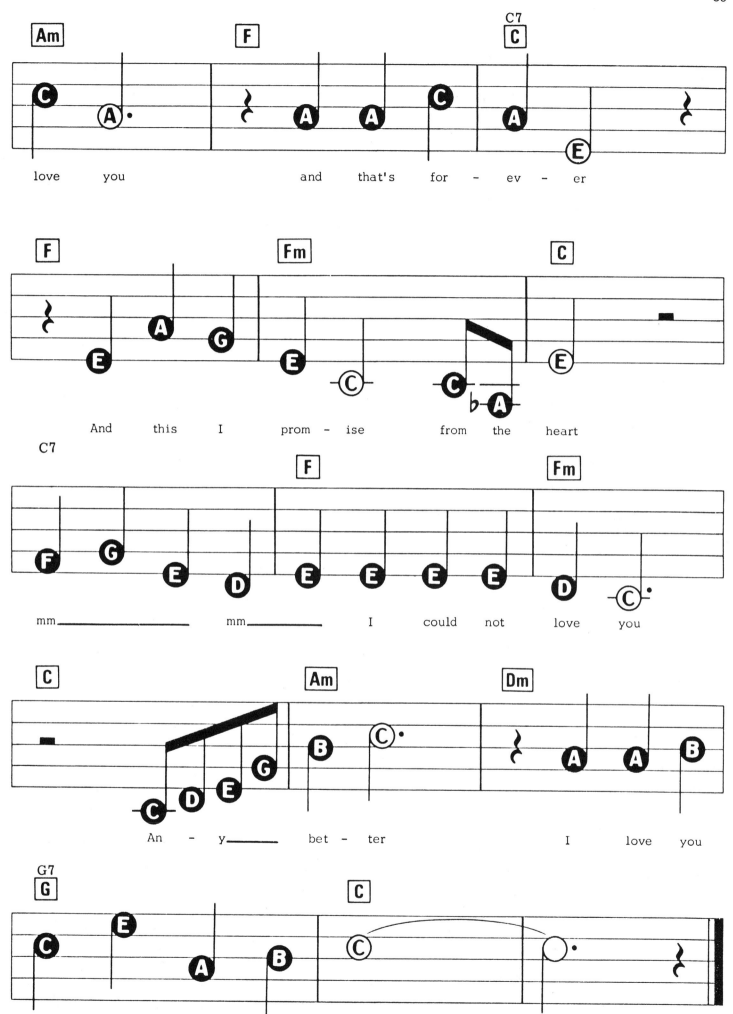

Knock Three Times

Registration 4
Rhythm: Rock

Words and Music by
Irwin Levine and L. Russell Brown

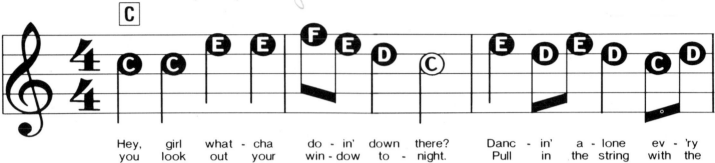

Hey, girl what - cha do - in' down there? Danc - in' a - lone ev - 'ry
you look out your win - dow to - night. Pull in the string with the

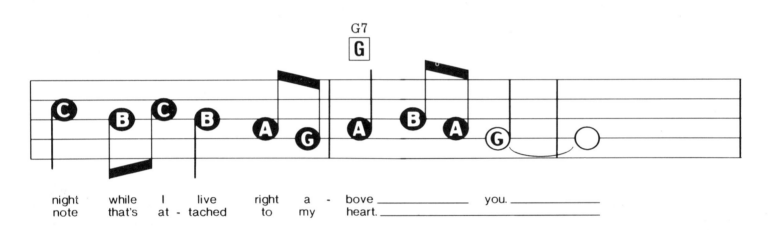

night while I live right a - bove _____ you. _____
note that's at - tached to my heart. _____

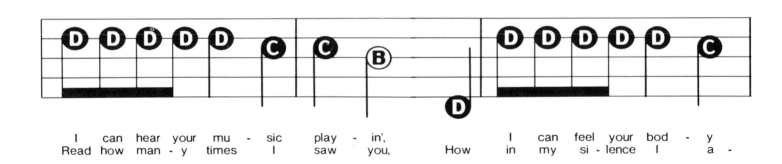

I can hear your mu - sic play - in', I can feel your bod - y
Read how man - y times I saw you, How in my si - lence I a -

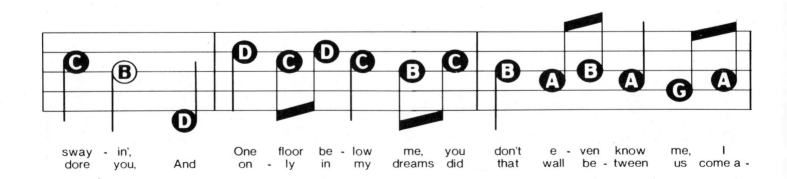

sway - in', One floor be - low me, you don't e - ven know me, I
dore you, And on - ly in my dreams did that wall be - tween us come a -

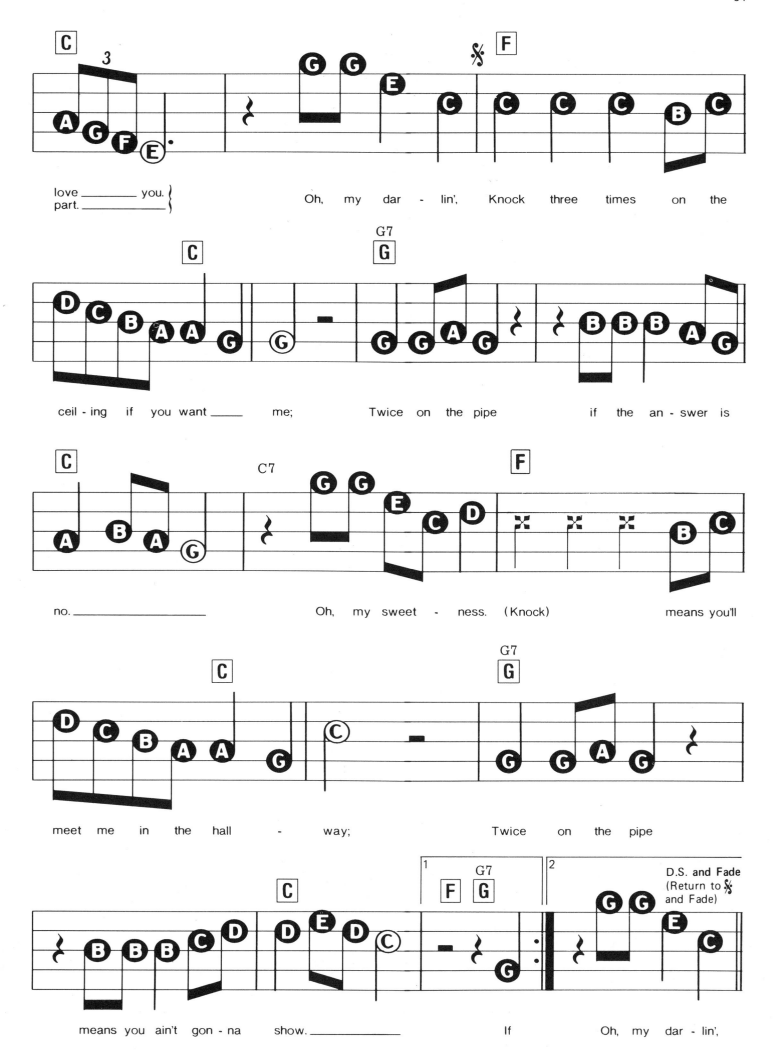

91

Laughter In The Rain

Registration 4
Rhythm: Rock

Words and Music by
Neil Sedaka and Phil Cody

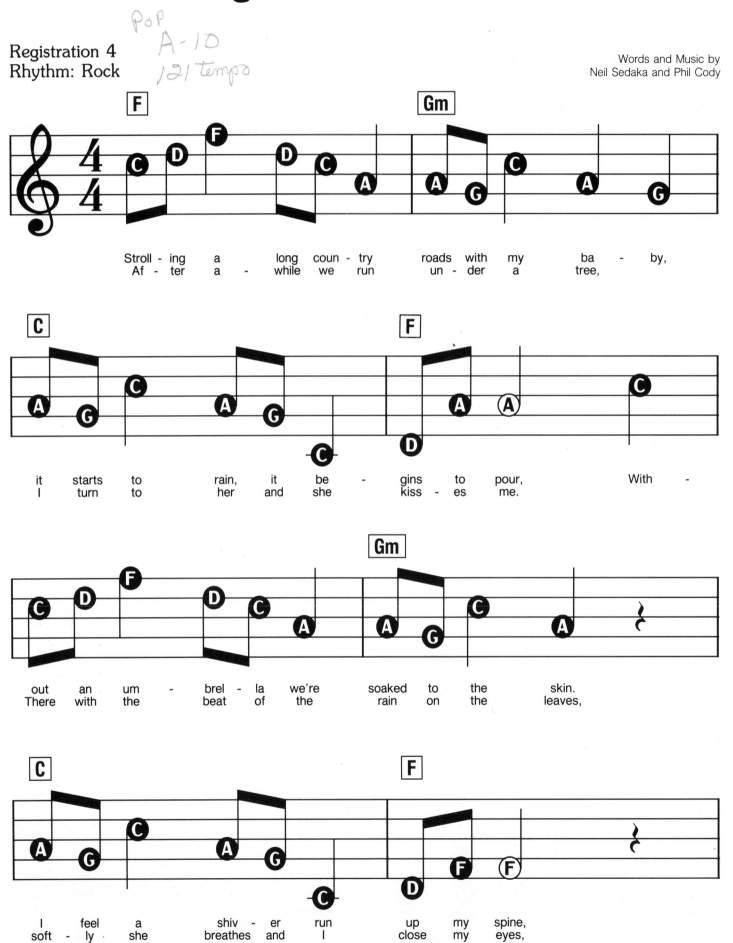

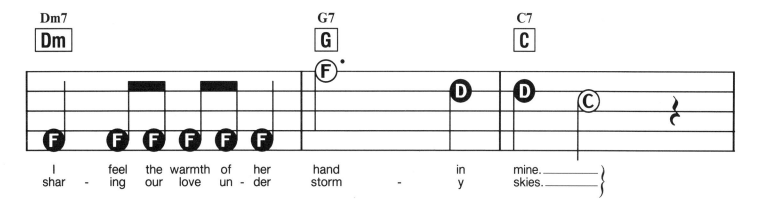

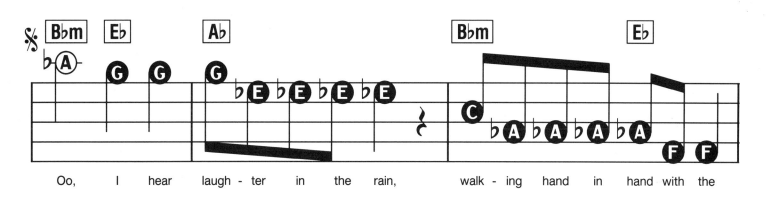

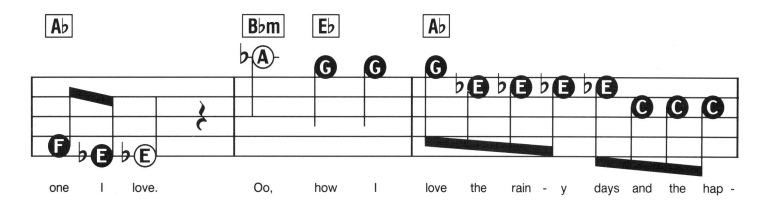

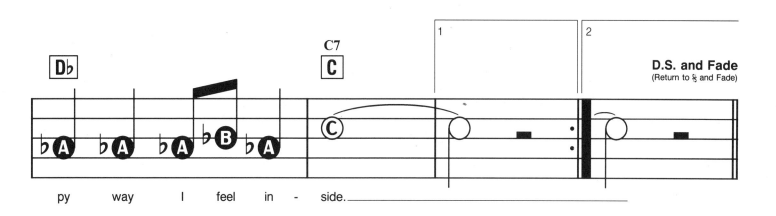

Let it Be

Registration 3
Rhythm: Rock

Words and Music by
John Lennon and Paul McCartney

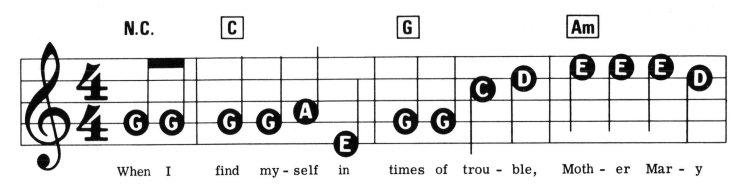

When I find my-self in times of trou - ble, Moth - er Mar - y

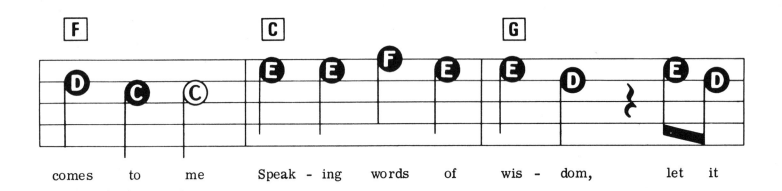

comes to me Speak - ing words of wis - dom, let it

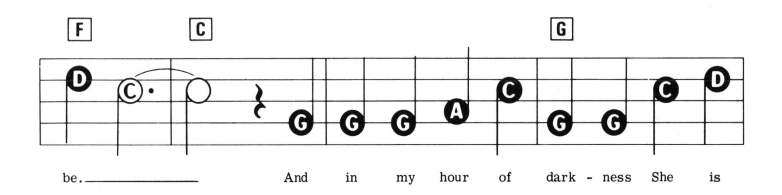

be._____ And in my hour of dark - ness She is

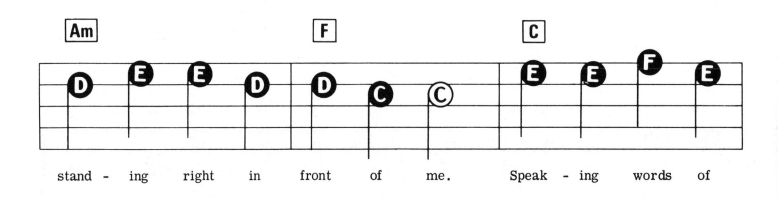

stand - ing right in front of me. Speak - ing words of

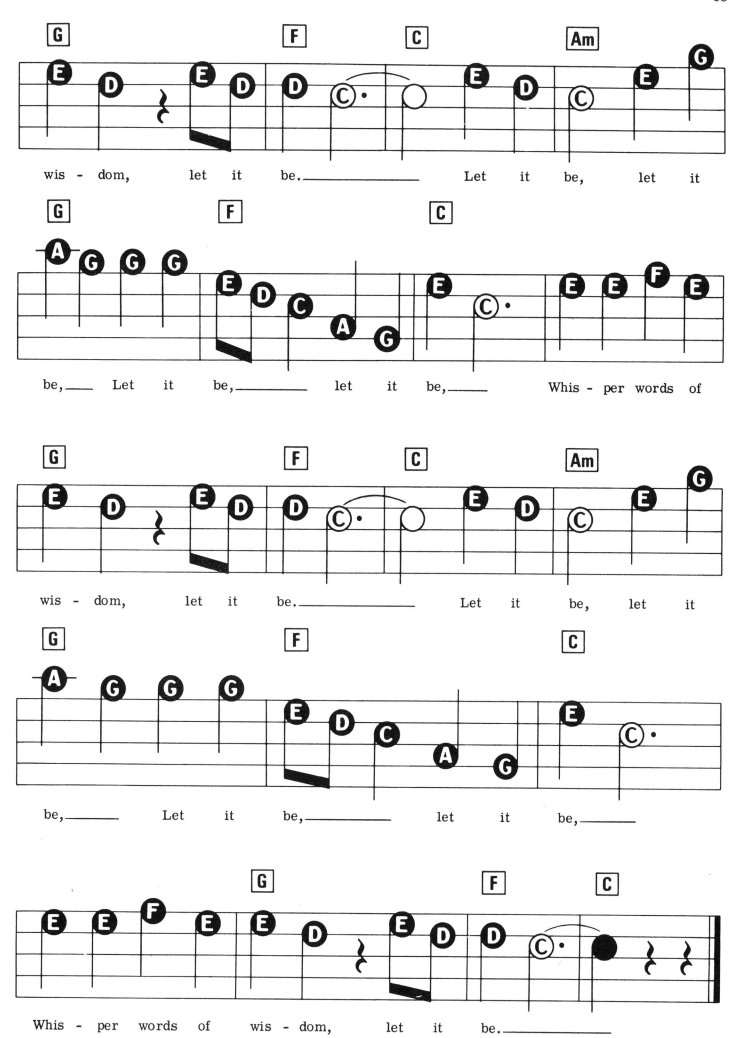

Love Will Keep Us Together

Registration 8
Rhythm: Rock

Words and Music by
Neil Sedaka and Howard Greenfield

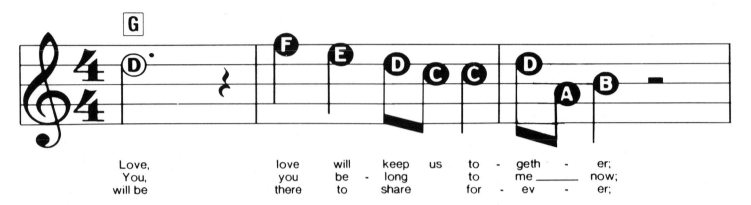

Love,   love   will   keep   us   to - geth - er;
You,   you   be - long   to   me _____ now;
will be   there   to   share   for - ev - er;

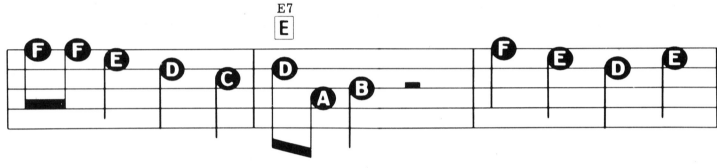

think   of   me,   babe,   when - ev - er   some   sweet - talk - in'
ain't   gon - na   set   you   free _____ now.   When   those   guys   start
love   will   keep   us   to - geth - er.   Said it   be - fore   and I'll

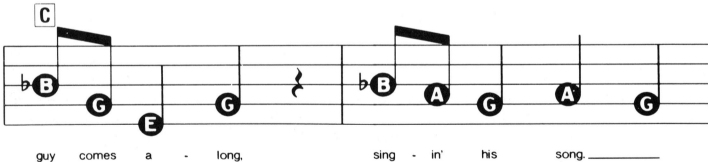

guy   comes   a - long,   sing - in'   his   song. _____
hang - in'   a - round,   talk - in'   me   down, _____
say   it   a - gain, while   oth - ers   pre - tend, _____

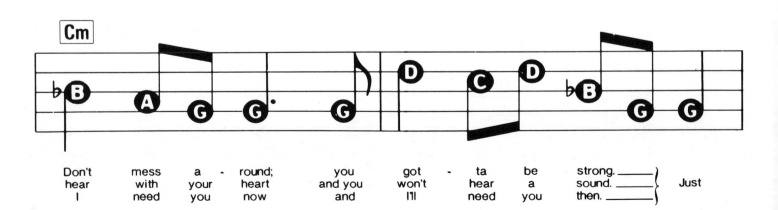

Don't   mess   a - round;   you   got - ta   be   strong. _____ }
hear   with   your   heart   and you   won't   hear   a   sound. _____ } Just
I   need   you   now   and   I'll   need   you   then. _____ }

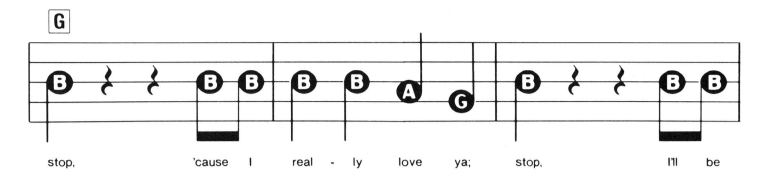

stop, 'cause I real - ly love ya; stop, I'll be

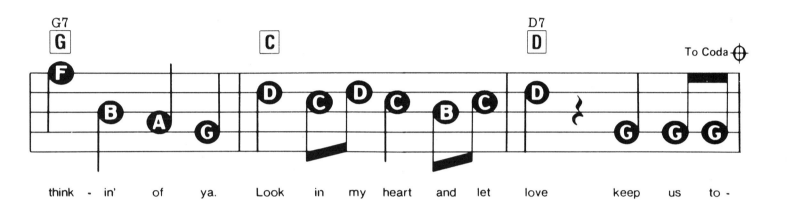

think - in' of ya. Look in my heart and let love keep us to -

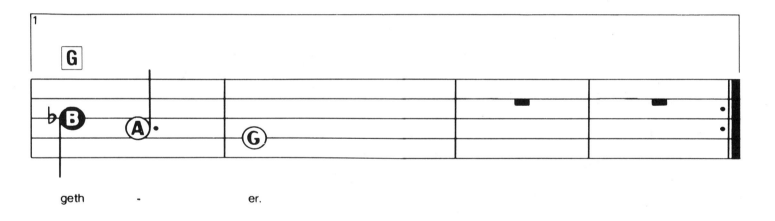

geth - er.

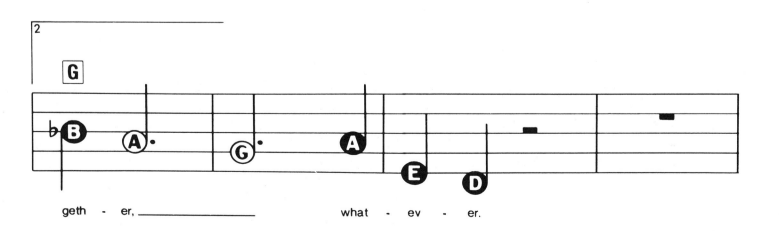

geth - er, _____ what - ev - er.

98

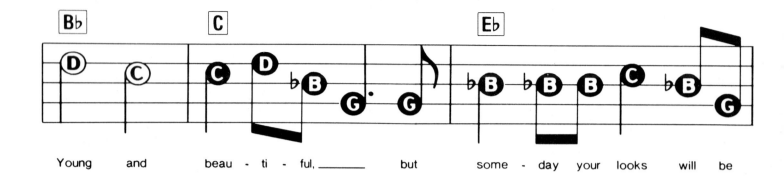

Young and beau - ti - ful, _____ but some - day your looks will be

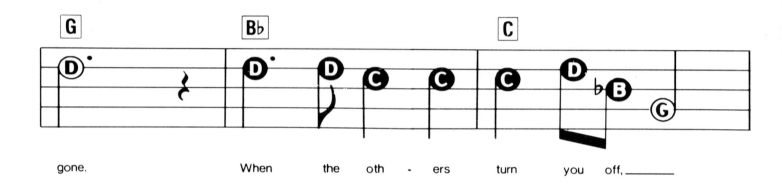

gone. When the oth - ers turn you off, _____

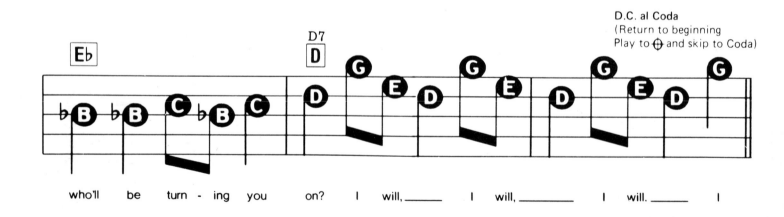

D.C. al Coda
(Return to beginning
Play to ⊕ and skip to Coda)

who'll be turn - ing you on? I will, _____ I will, _____ I will. _____ I

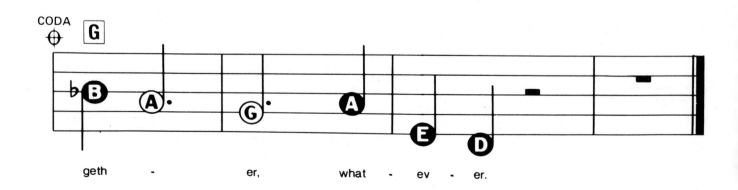

geth - er, what - ev - er.

Mandy

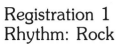

Registration 1
Rhythm: Rock

Words and Music by
Scott English and Richard Kerr

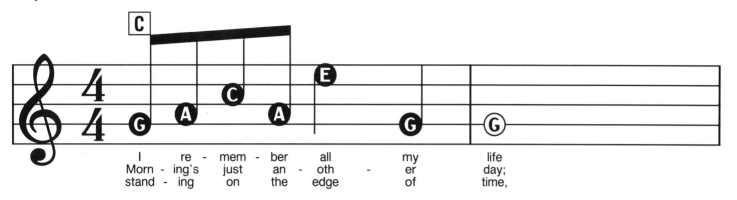

I re - mem - ber all my life
Morn - ing's just an - oth - er day;
stand - ing on the edge of time,

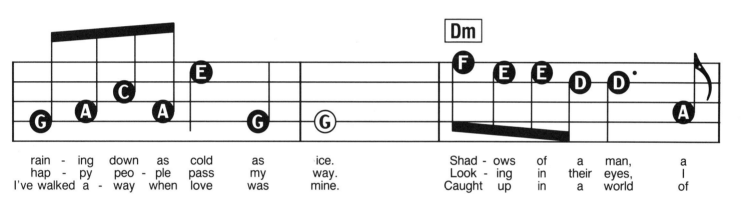

rain - ing down as cold as ice.
hap - py peo - ple pass my way.
I've walked a - way when love was mine.

Shad - ows of a man, a
Look - ing in their eyes, I
Caught up in a world of

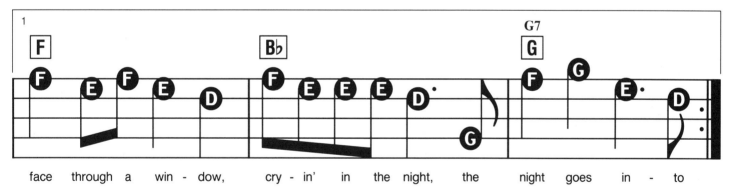

face through a win - dow, cry - in' in the night, the night goes in - to

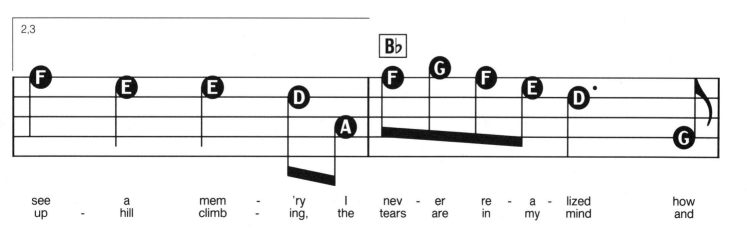

see a mem - 'ry I nev - er re - a - lized how
up - hill climb - ing, the tears are in my mind and

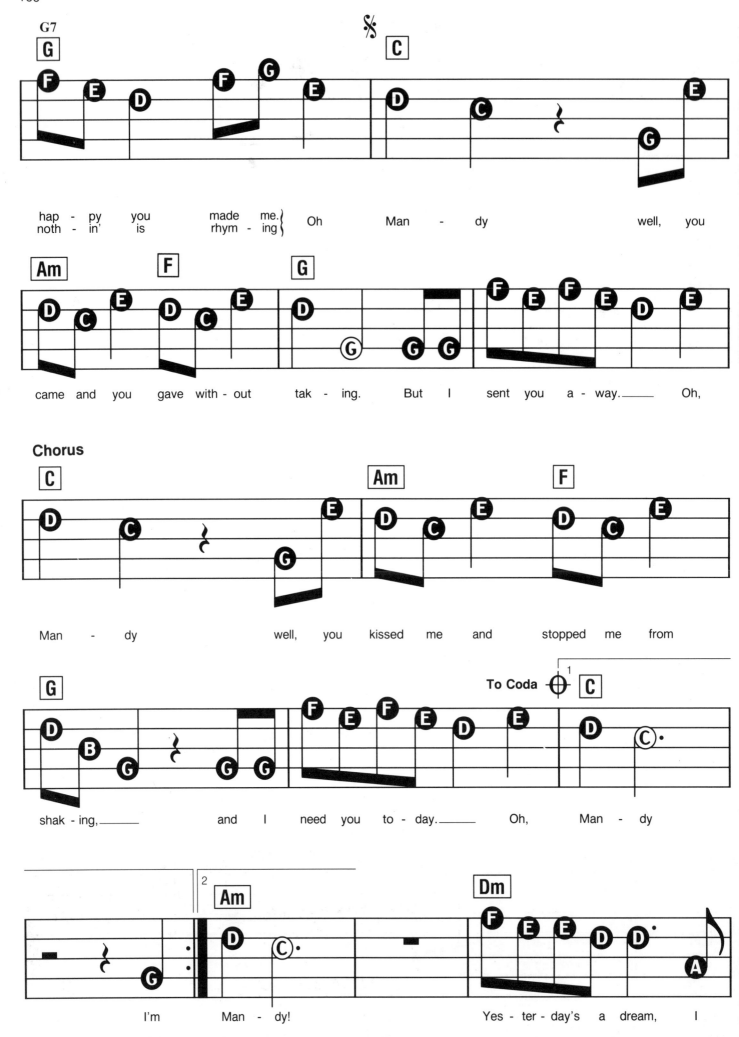

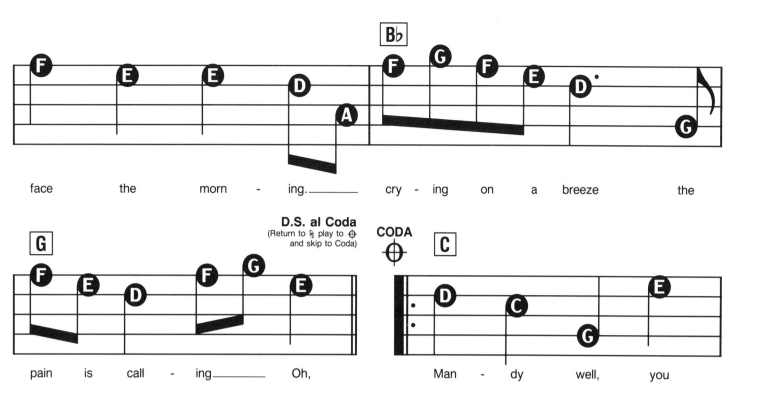

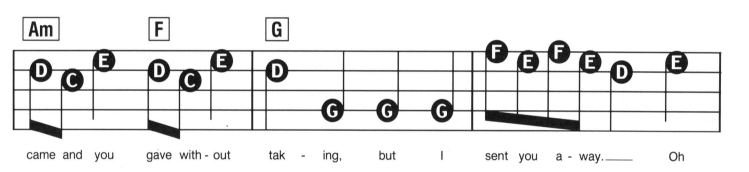

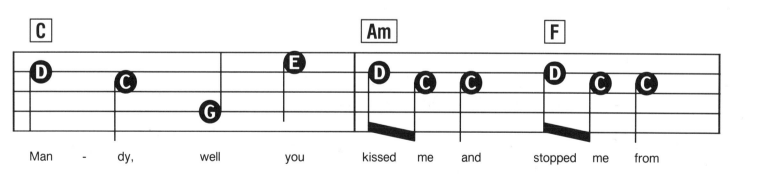

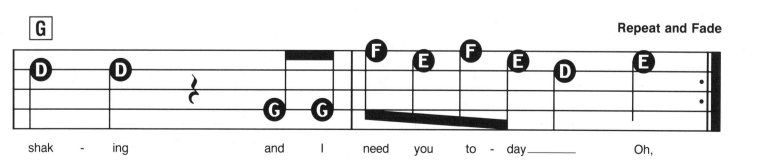

Love's Theme

Registration 3
Rhythm: Rock or Disco

Words and Music by
Barry White

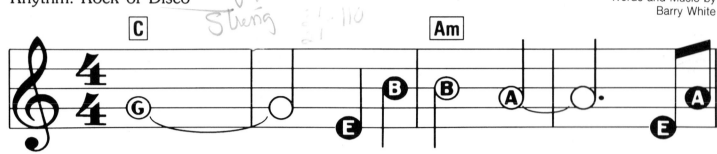

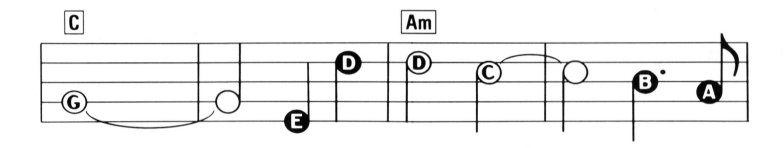

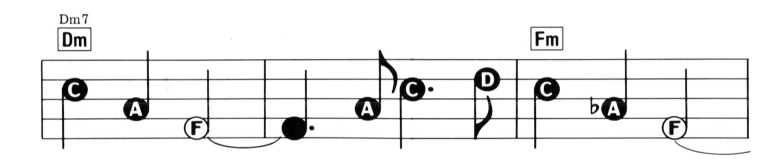

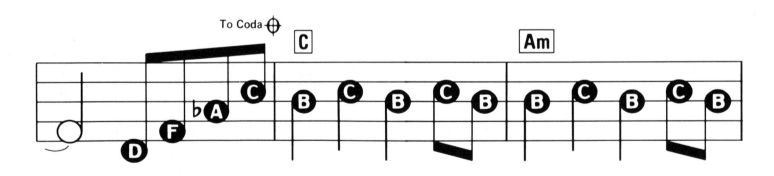

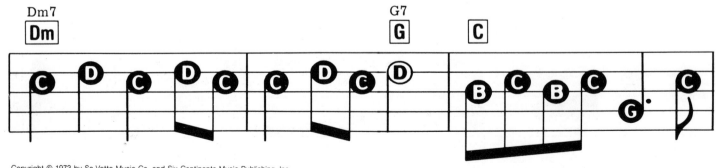

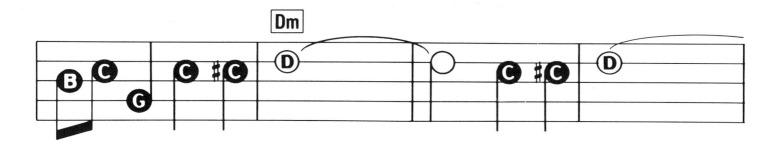

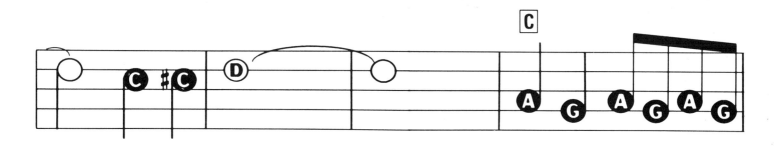

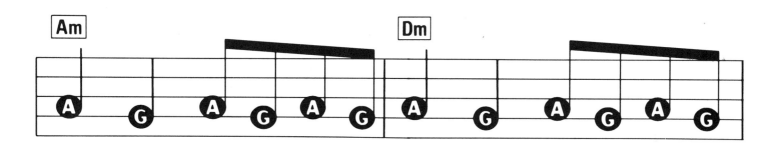

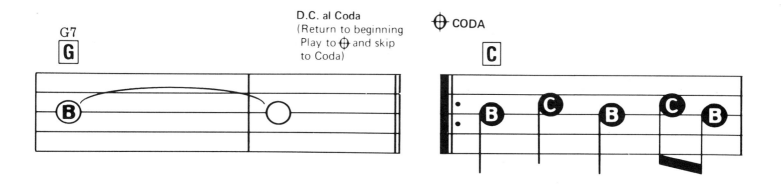

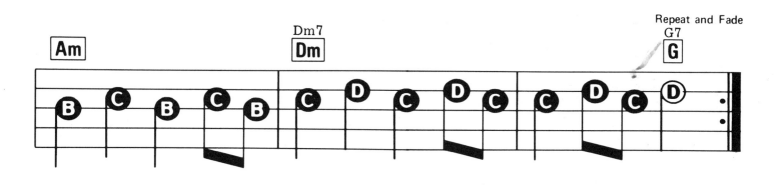

Me And Bobby McGee

Registration 3
Rhythm: Country or Swing

Words and Music by
Kris Kristofferson and Fred Foster

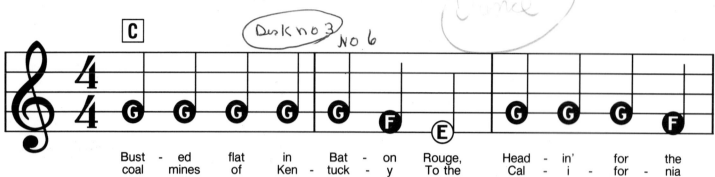

Bust - ed flat in Bat - on Rouge, Head - in' for the
coal mines of Ken - tuck - y To the Cal - i - for - nia

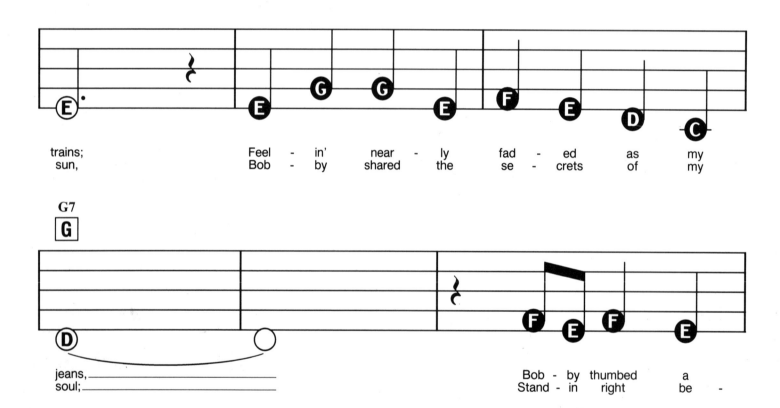

trains; Feel - in' near - ly fad - ed as my
sun, Bob - by shared the se - crets of my

jeans,_____
soul;_____

Bob - by thumbed a
Stand - in right be -

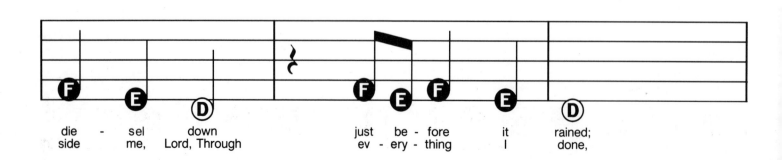

die - sel down just be - fore it rained;
side me, Lord, Through ev - ery - thing I done,

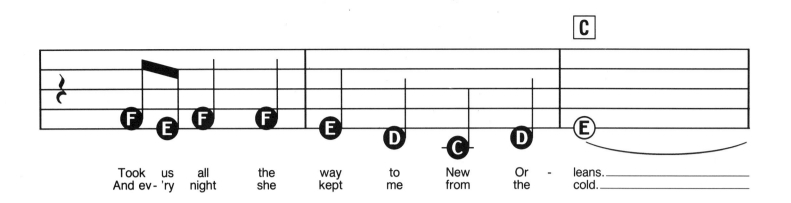

Took us all the way to New Or - leans._____
And ev - 'ry night she kept me from the cold._____

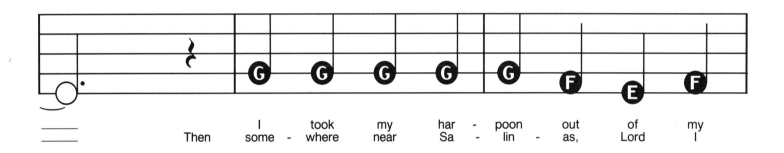

_____ I took my har - poon out of my
_____ Then some - where near Sa - lin - as, Lord I

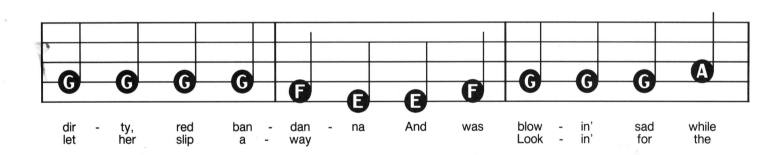

dir - ty, red ban - dan - na And was blow - in' sad while
let her slip a - way Look - in' for the

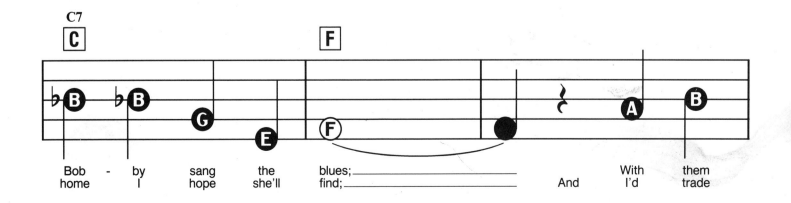

Bob - by sang the blues;_____ And With them
home I hope she'll find;_____ I'd trade

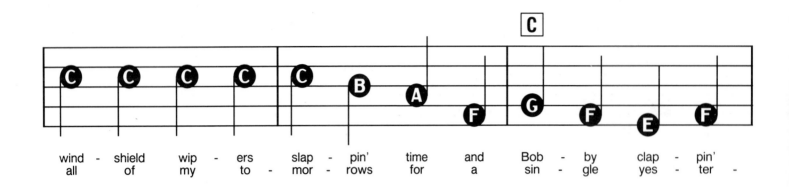

wind - shield wip - ers slap - pin' time and a Bob - by clap - pin'
all of my to - mor - rows for a sin - gle yes - ter -

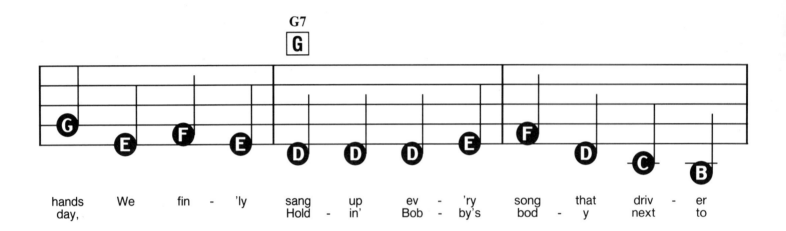

hands We fin - 'ly sang up ev - 'ry song that driv - er
day, Hold - in' Bob - by's bod - y next to

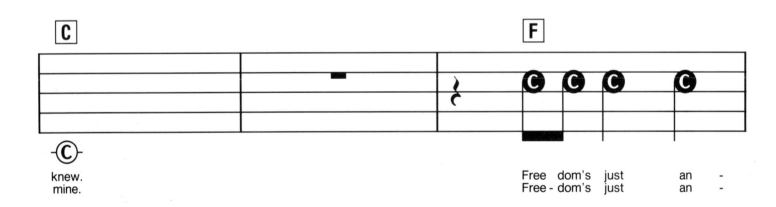

knew.
mine.

Free dom's just an -
Free - dom's just an -

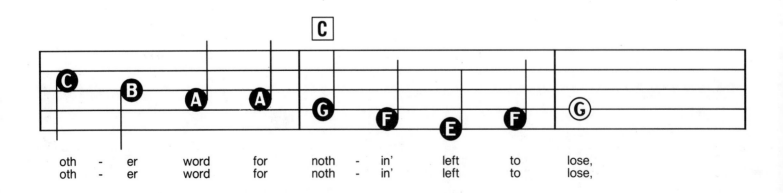

oth - er word for noth - in' left to lose,
oth - er word for noth - in' left to lose,

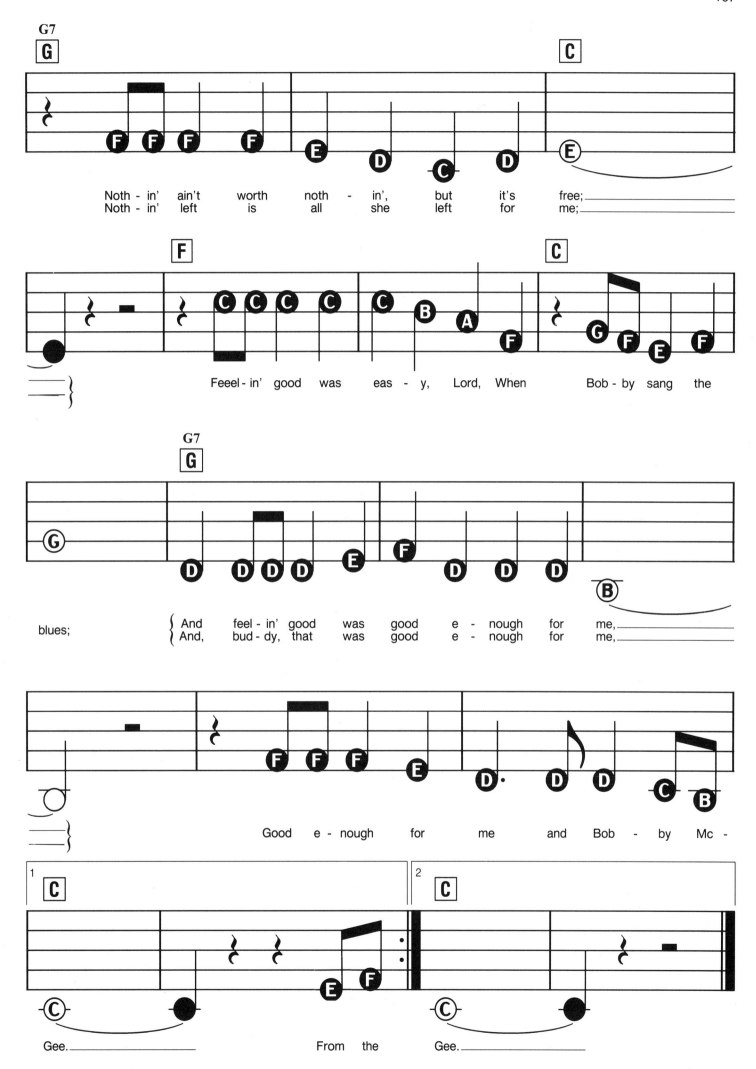

Midnight Train To Georgia

Registration 4
Rhythm: Rock

Words and Music by
Jim Weatherly

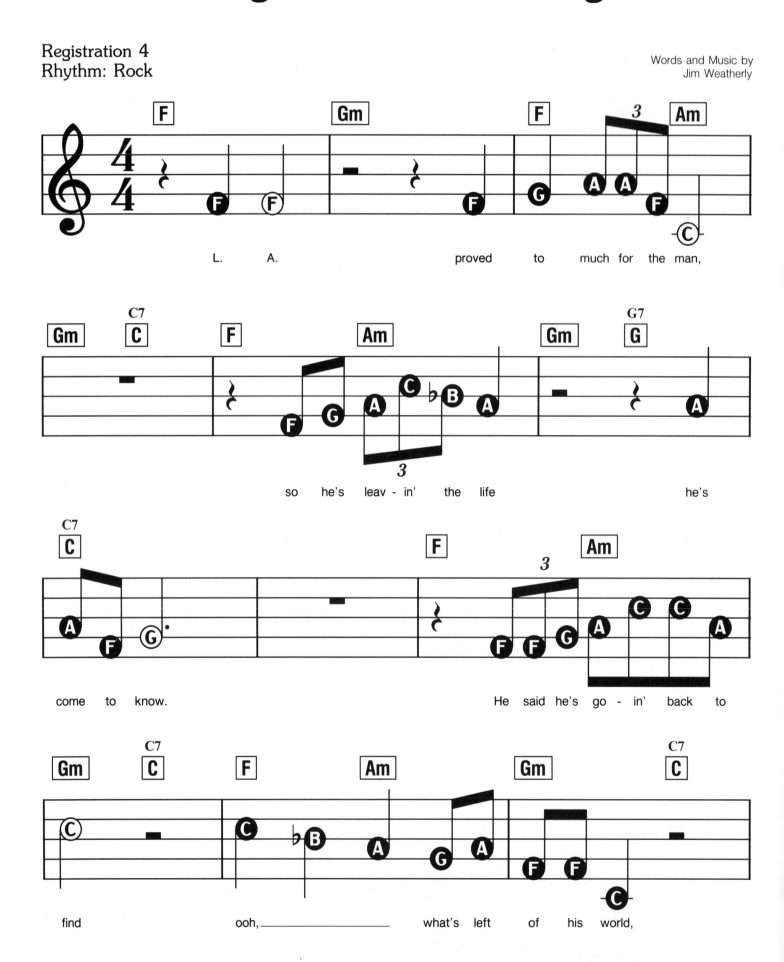

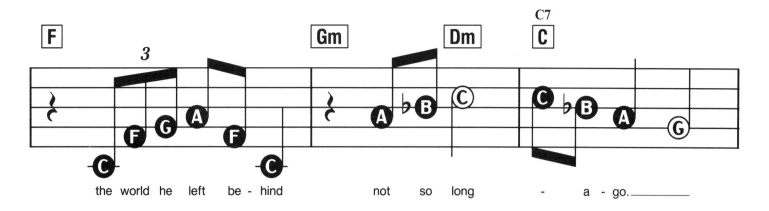

the world he left be-hind   not so long - a go.

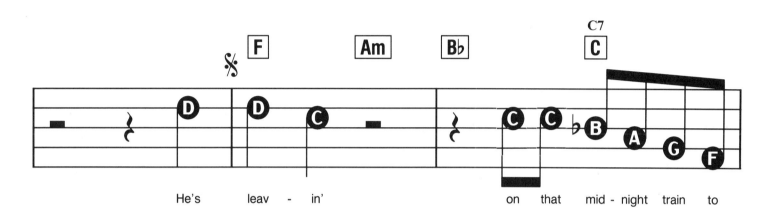

He's leav-in'   on that mid-night train to

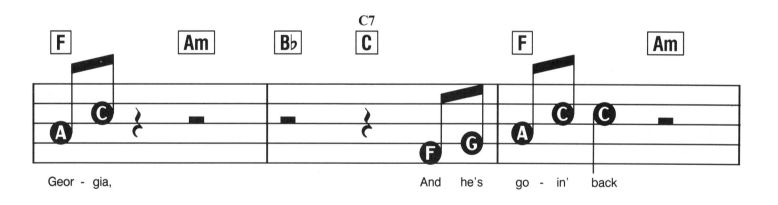

Geor-gia,   And he's go-in' back

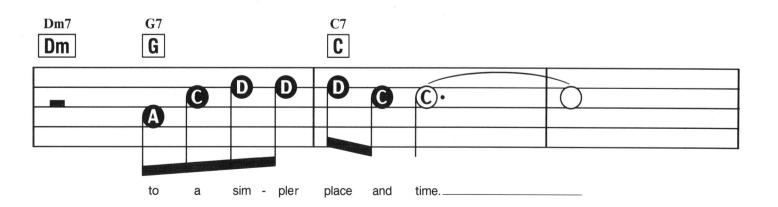

to a sim-pler place and time.

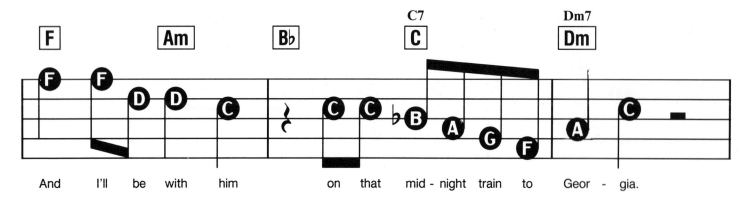

And I'll be with him on that mid - night train to Geor - gia.

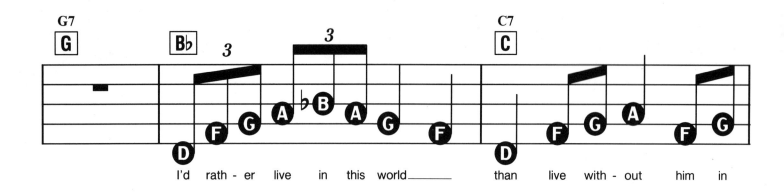

I'd rath - er live in this world_____ than live with - out him in

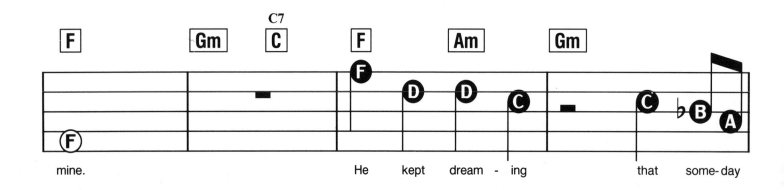

mine. He kept dream - ing that some-day

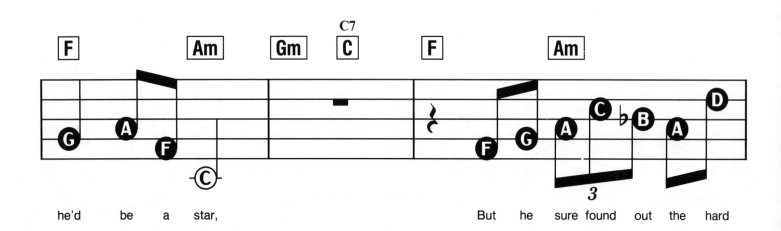

he'd be a star, But he sure found out the hard

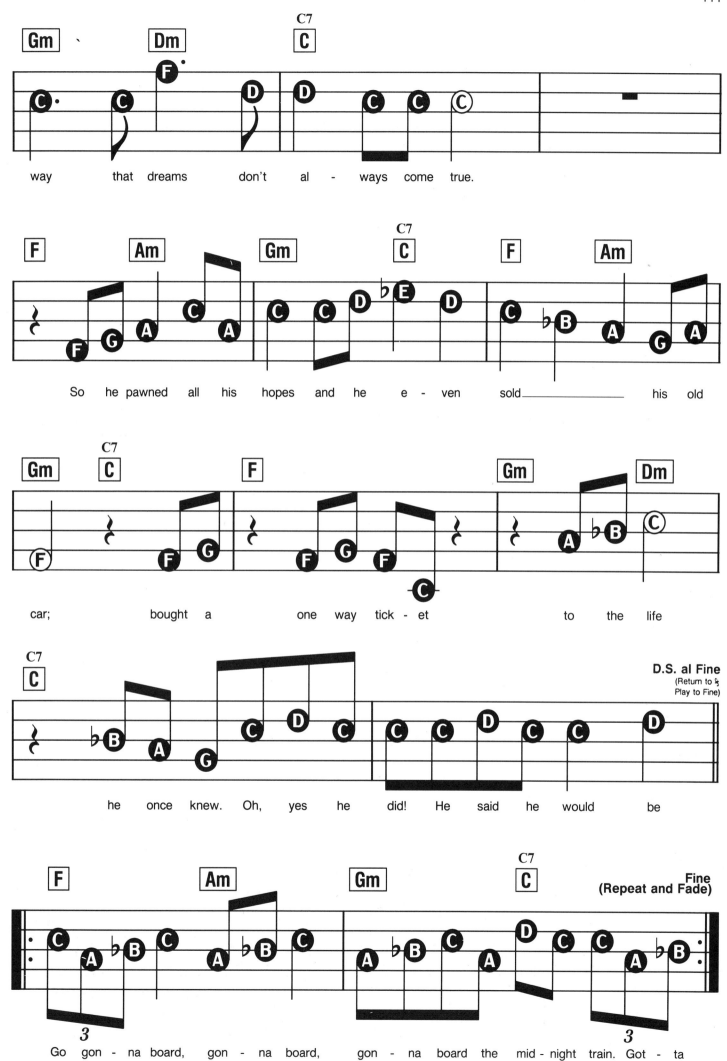

My Life

Registration 2
Rhythm: Rock

Words and Music by
Billy Joel

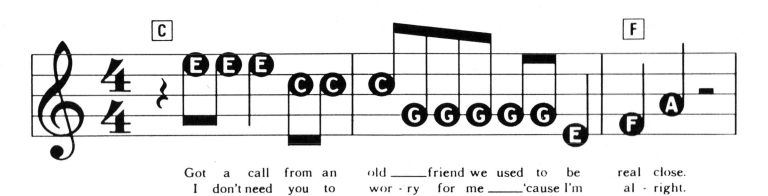

Got a call from an old ____ friend we used to be real close.
I don't need you to wor-ry for me ____ 'cause I'm al-right.

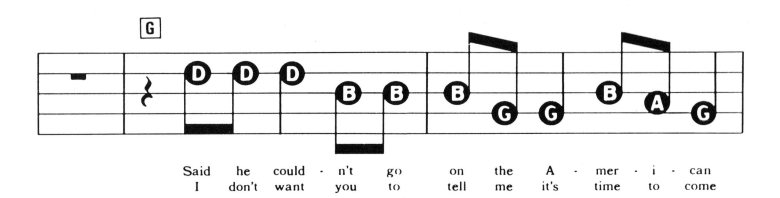

Said he could-n't go on the A-mer-i-can
I don't want you to tell me it's time to come

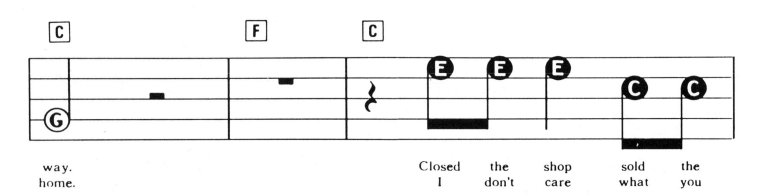

way.
home.

Closed the shop sold the
I don't care what you

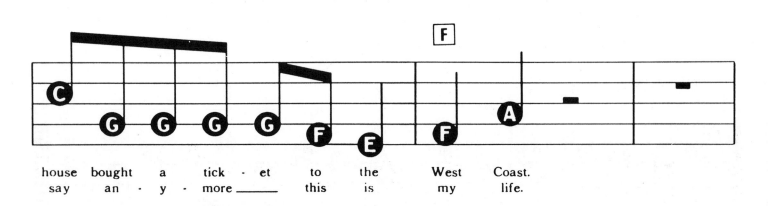

house bought a tick-et to the West Coast.
say an-y-more ____ this is my life.

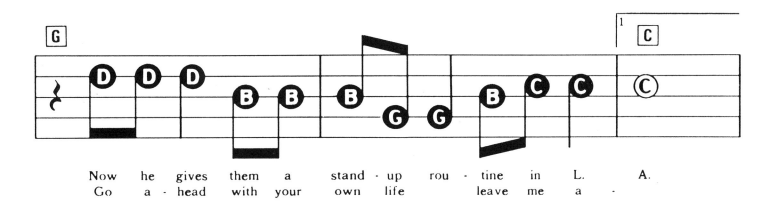

Now he gives them a stand - up rou - tine in L. A.
Go a - head with your own life leave me a -

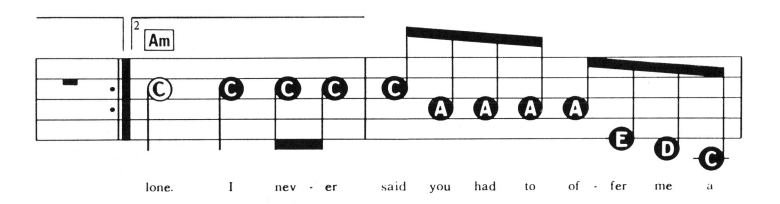

lone. I nev - er said you had to of - fer me a

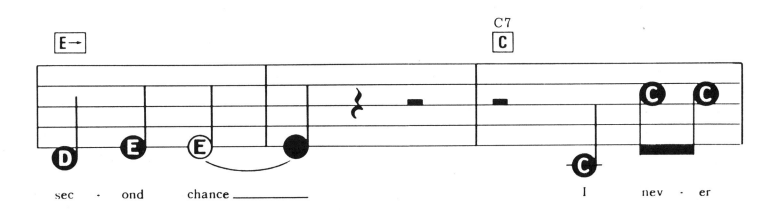

sec - ond chance _____ I nev - er

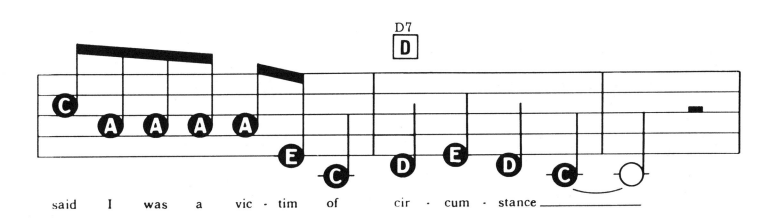

said I was a vic - tim of cir - cum - stance _____

114

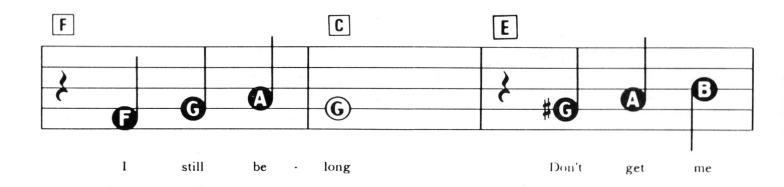

I still be - long   Don't get me

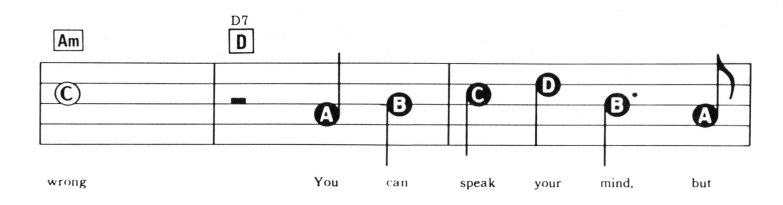

wrong   You can speak your mind, but

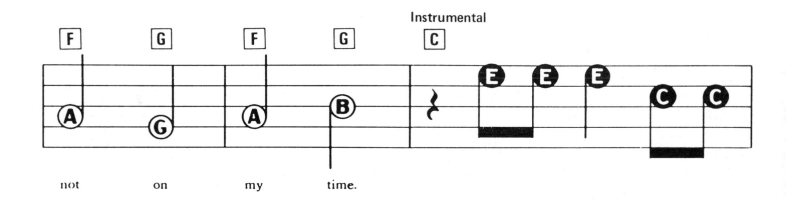

not   on   my   time.

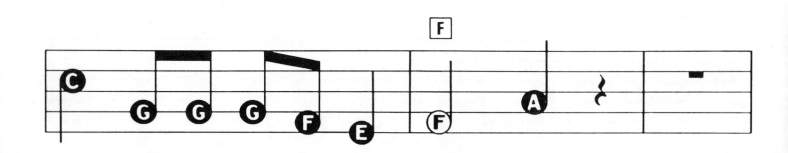

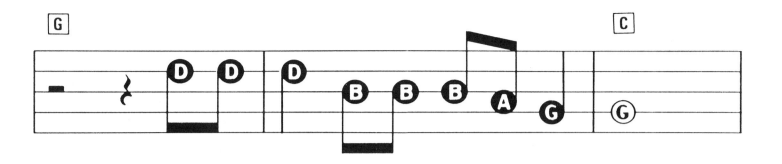
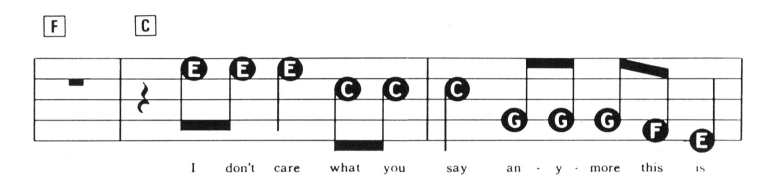

I don't care what you say an-y-more this is

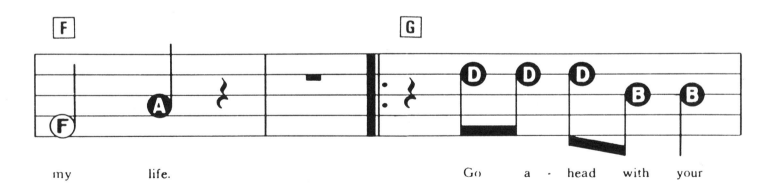

my life. Go a-head with your

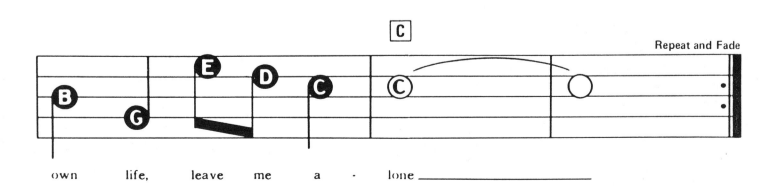

own life, leave me a-lone

Repeat and Fade

My Love

Registration 10
Rhythm: Ballad

Words and Music by
McCartney

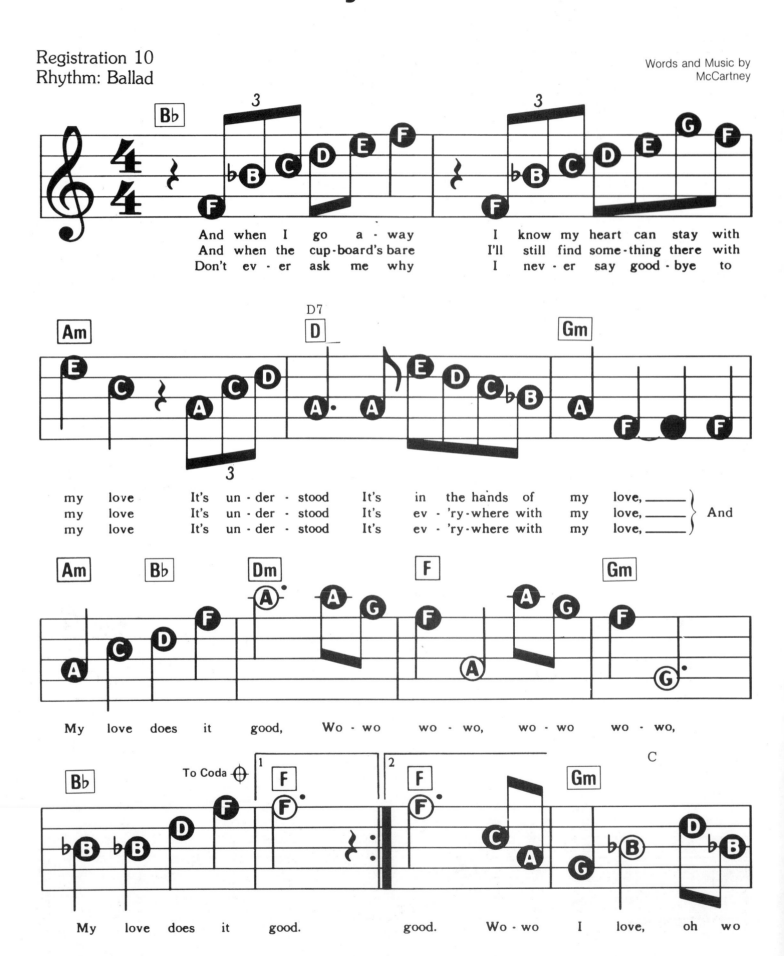

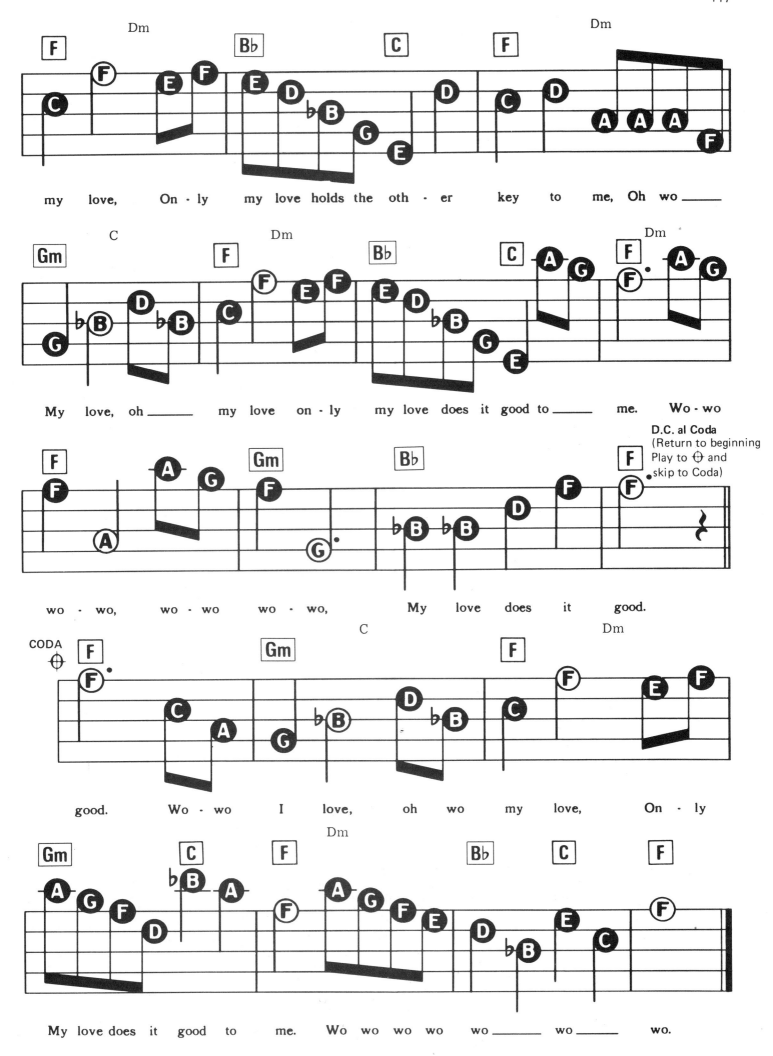

EGB

Nights In White Satin

Words and Music by
Justin Hayward

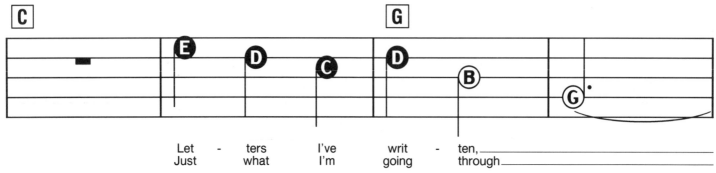

Nights in white sat - in,_____
Gaz - ing at peo - ple,_____

Nev - er reach - ing the end,_____
Some - ing hand in hand,_____

Let - ters I've writ - ten,_____
Just what I'm going through_____

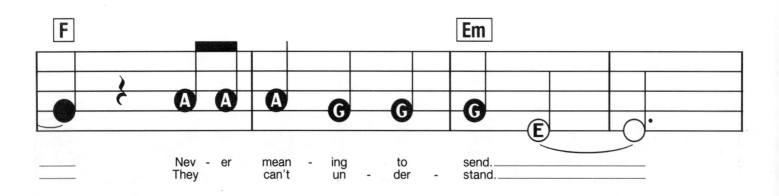

Nev - er mean - ing to send._____
They can't un - der - stand._____

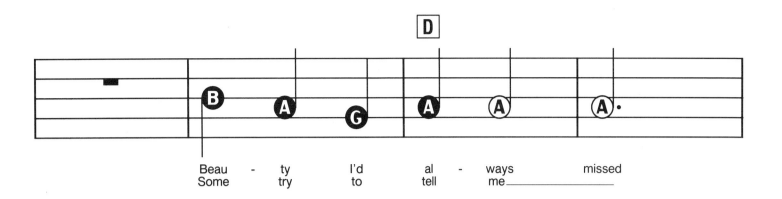

Beau - ty I'd al - ways missed
Some try to tell me____

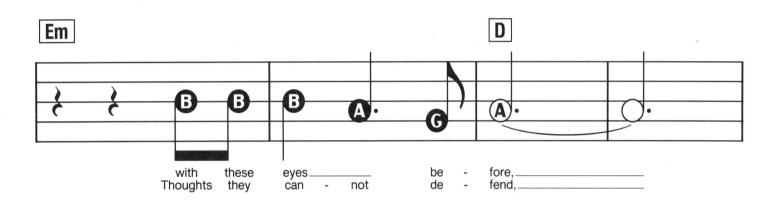

with these eyes____ be - fore,____
Thoughts they can - not de - fend,____

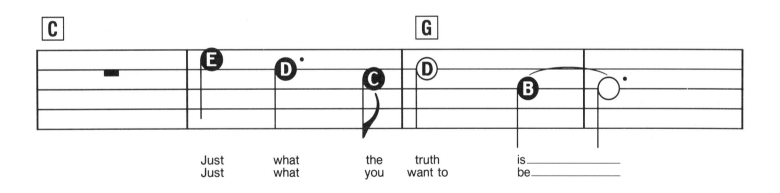

Just what the truth is____
Just what you want to be____

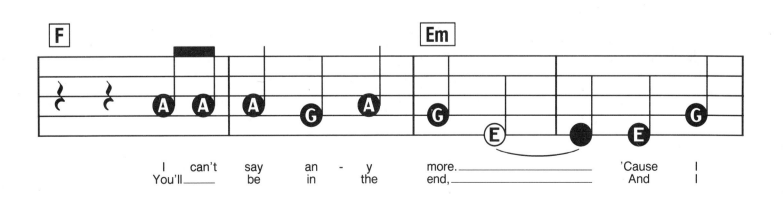

I can't say an - y more.____ 'Cause I
You'll____ be in the end,____ And I

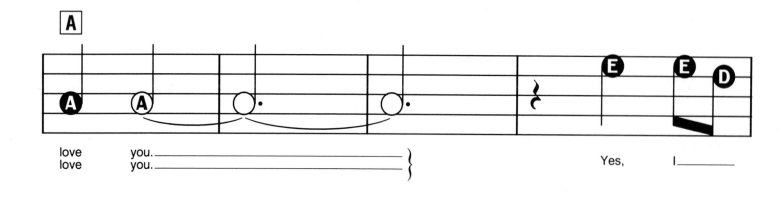

love   you.
love   you.   Yes,   I

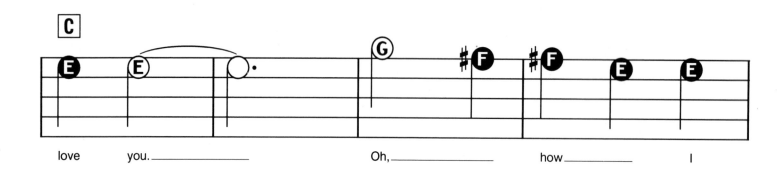

love   you.   Oh,   how   I

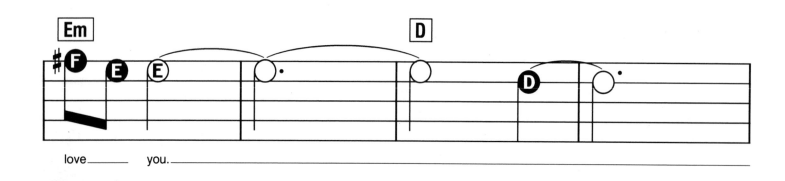

love   you.

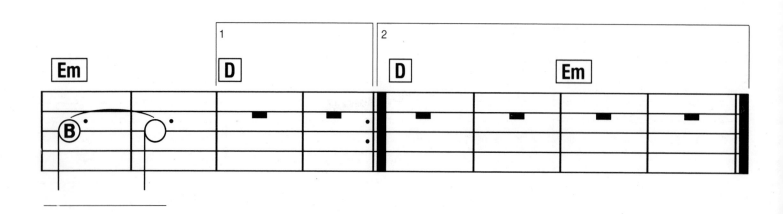

Piano Man

Registration 4
Rhythm: Waltz

Words and Music by
Billy Joel

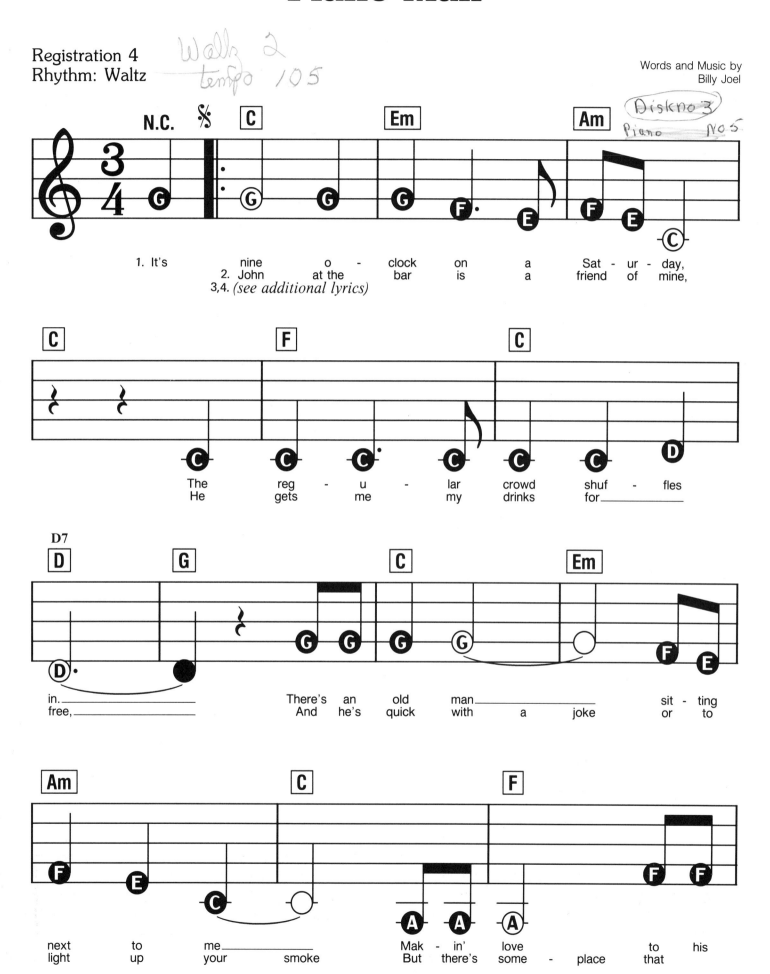

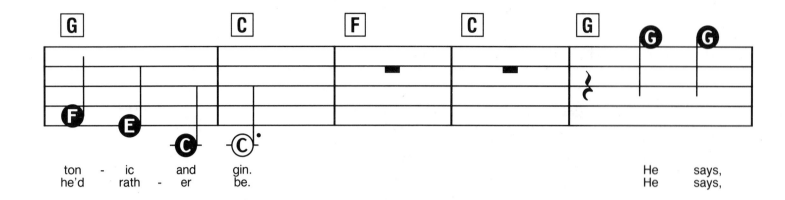

ton - ic and gin.
he'd rath - er be. He says,
He says,

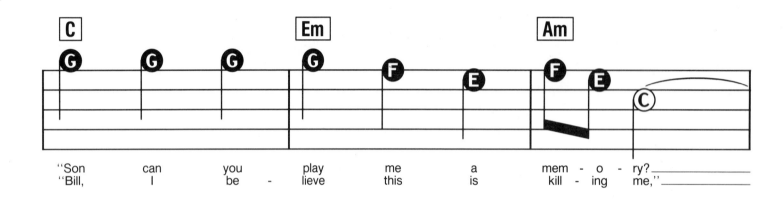

"Son can you play me a mem - o - ry?
"Bill, I be - lieve this is kill - ing me,"

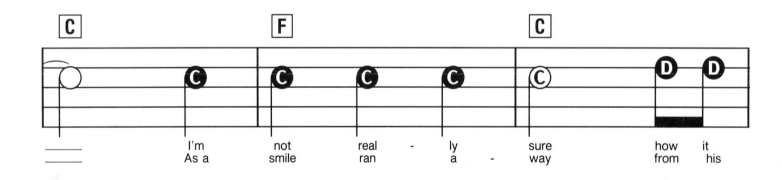

I'm not real - ly sure how it
As a smile ran a - way from his

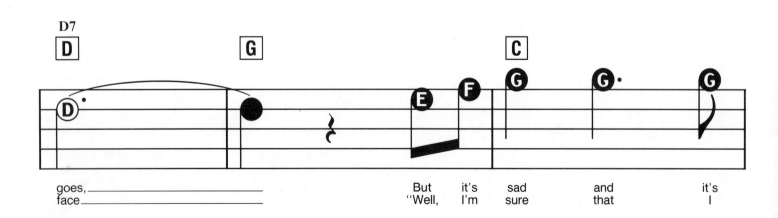

goes,
face
But it's sad and it's
"Well, I'm sure that I

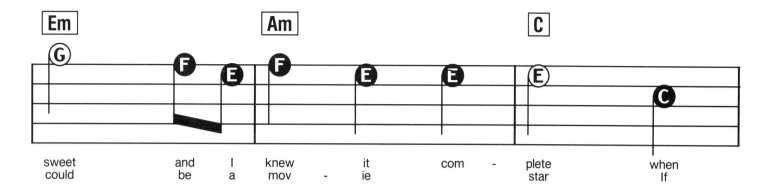

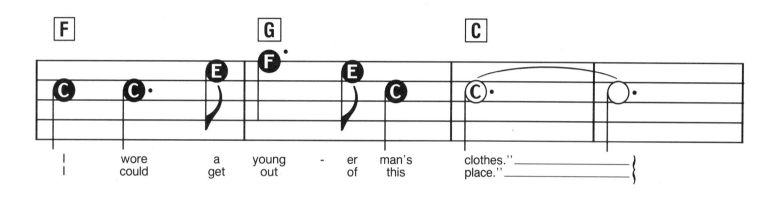

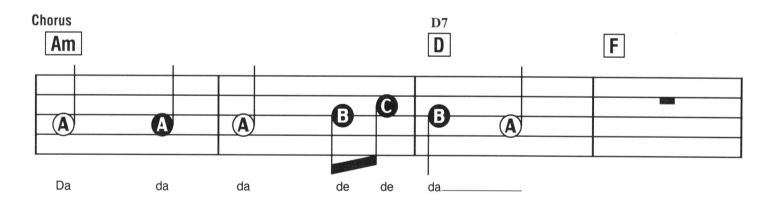

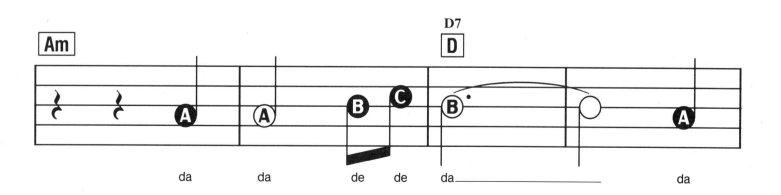

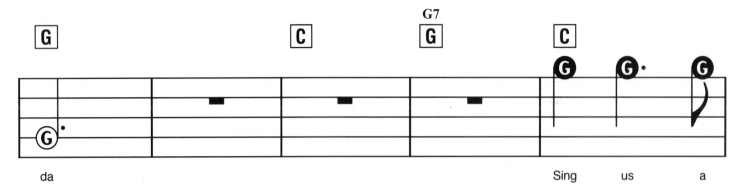

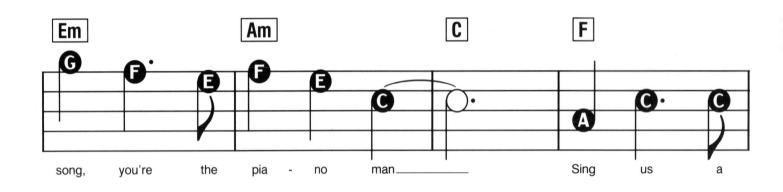

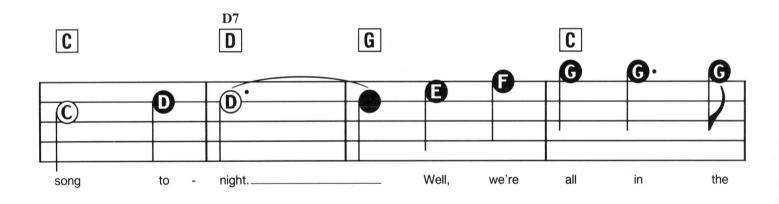

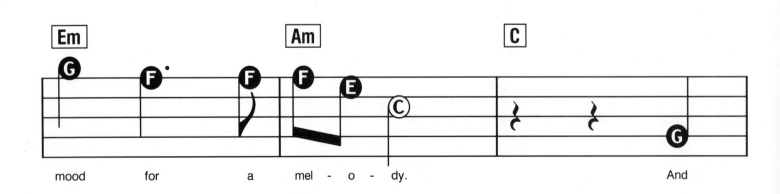

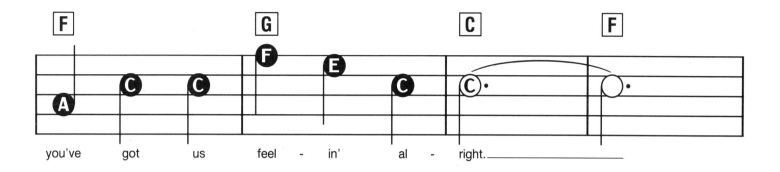

you've got us feel - in' al - right._____

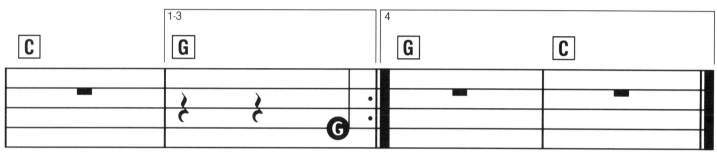

2. Now
3. Now

Additional Lyrics

3. Now Paul is a real estate novelist,
Who never had time for a wife,
And he's talkin' with Davey who's still in the Navy
And probably will be for life.
And the waitress is practicing politics,
As the businessmen slowly get stoned
Yes, they're sharing a drink they call loneliness
But it's better than drinkin' alone.

CHORUS

4. It's a pretty good crowd for a Saturday,
And the manager gives me a smile
'Cause he knows that it's me they've been comin' to see
To forget about life for a while.
And the piano sounds like a carnival
And the microphone smells like a beer
And they sit at the bar and put bread in my jar
And say "Man, what are you doin' here?"

CHORUS

Peg

Registration 7
Rhythm: Rock or 8 Beat

Words and Music by
Walter Becker and Donald Fagen

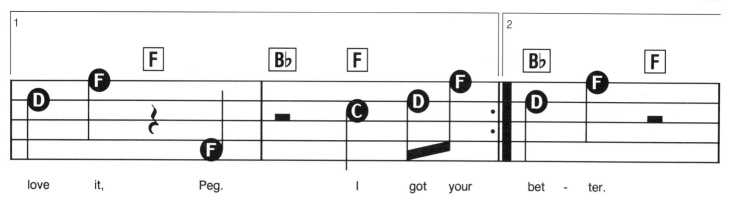

love it, Peg. I got your bet - ter.

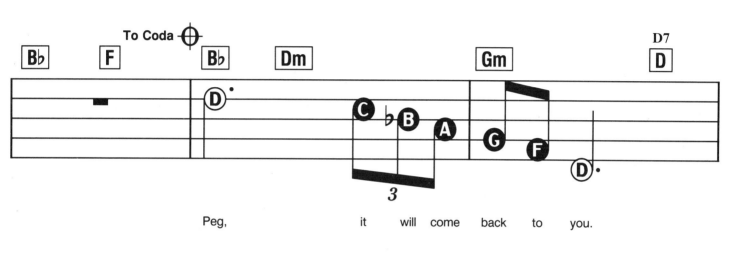

Peg, it will come back to you.

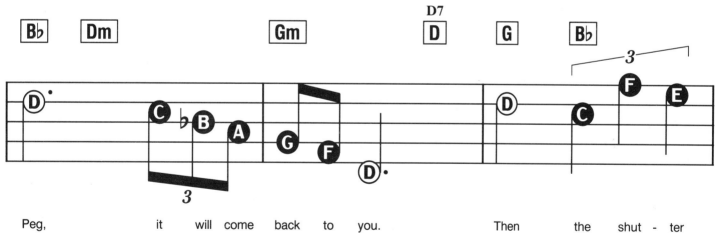

Peg, it will come back to you. Then the shut - ter

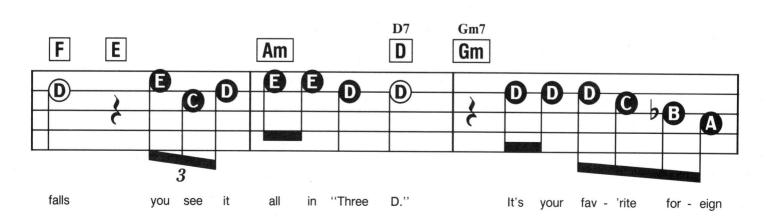

falls you see it all in "Three D." It's your fav - 'rite for - eign

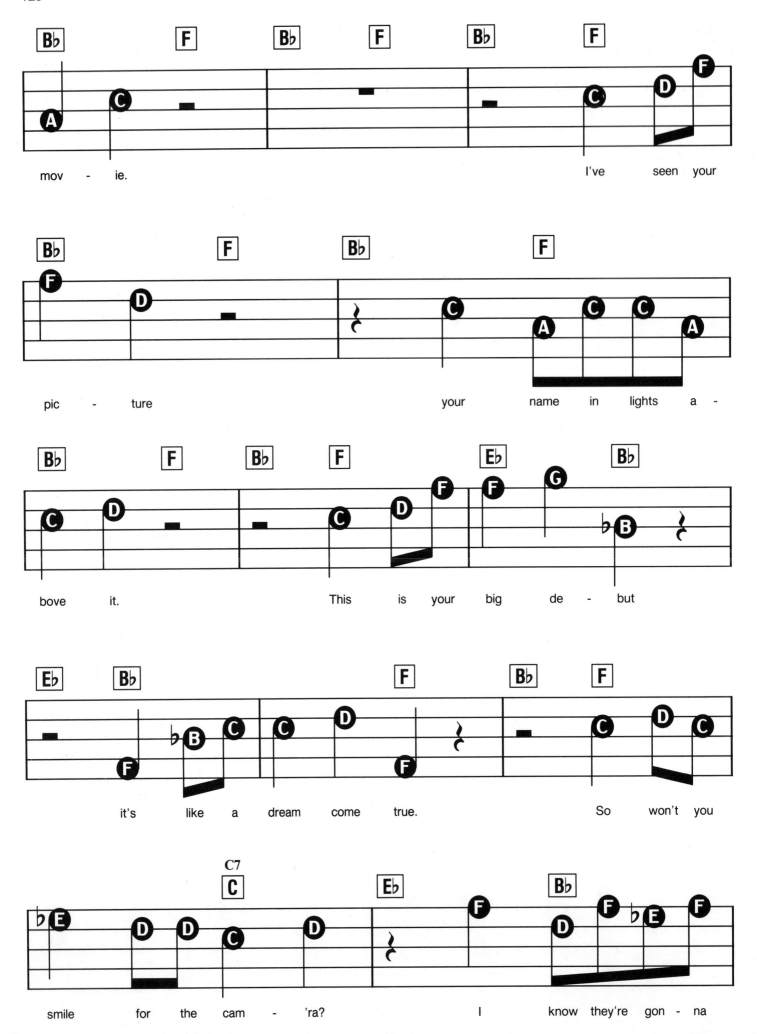

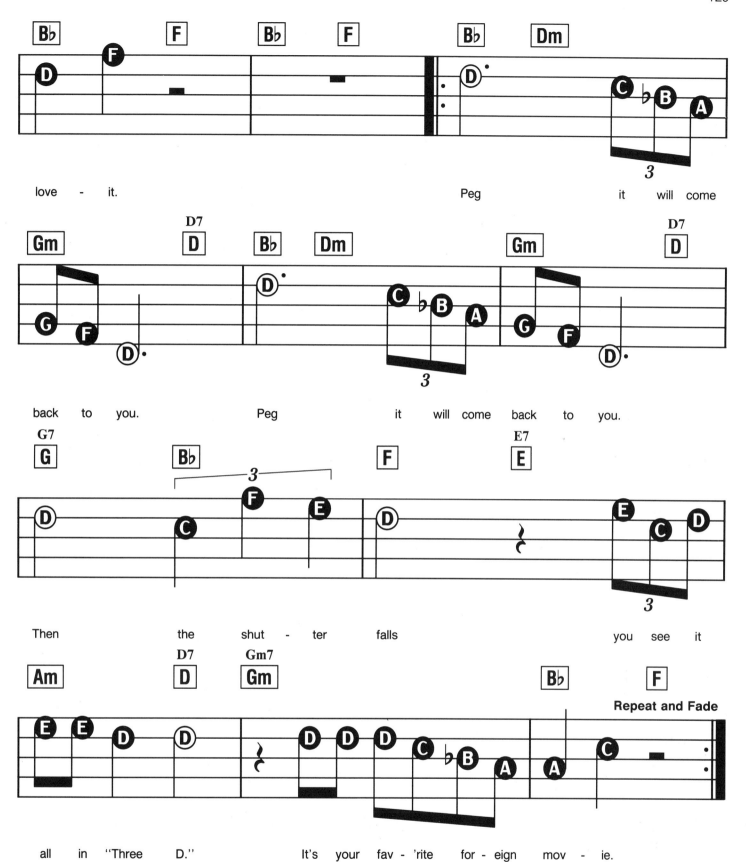

love - it.   Peg   it   will come

back   to   you.   Peg   it will come back to you.

Then   the   shut - ter falls   you see it

all in "Three D."   It's your fav - 'rite for - eign mov - ie.

Additional Lyrics

2. I got your pin shot
I keep it with your letter
Done up in a blueprint blue,
It sure looks good on you.
So won't you smile for the camera,
I know I'll love you better.

Reunited

Registration 4
Rhythm: Rock

Words and Music by
Dino Fekaris and Freddie Perren

132

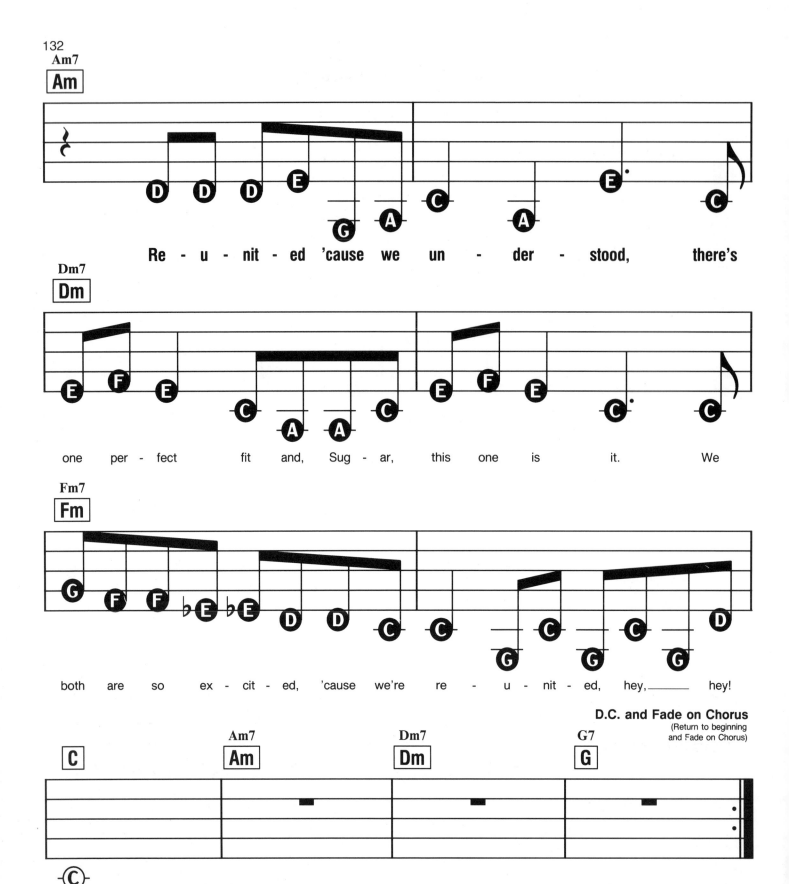

D.C. and Fade on Chorus
(Return to beginning
and Fade on Chorus)

Additional Lyrics

3. Lover, lover this is solid love,
and you're exactly what I'm dreaming of.
All through the day and all through the night,
I'll give you all the love I have with all my might,
hey, hey!

Lyric for Fade Ending:

Ooo, listen baby, I won't ever make you cry, I won't let one day go by
without holding you, without kissing you, without loving you.
Ooo, you're my everything, only you know how to free
all the love there is in me.
I wanna let you know, I won't let you go.
I wanna let you know, I won't let you go.
Ooo, feels so good!

Sara Smile

Registration 3
Rhythm: Rock

Words and Music by
Daryl Hall and John Oates

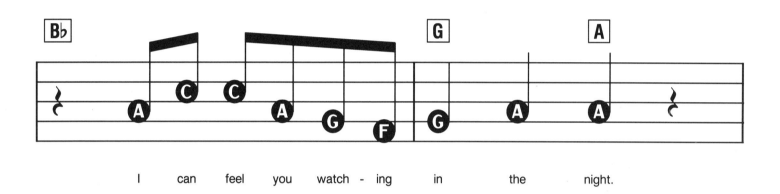

Ba - by hair_____ with a wom - an's eyes_____

I can feel you watch - ing in the night.

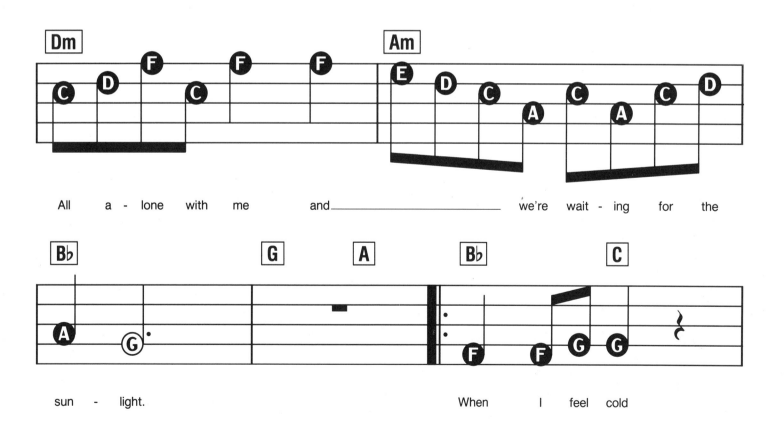

All a - lone with me and_____ we're wait - ing for the

sun - light.

When I feel cold

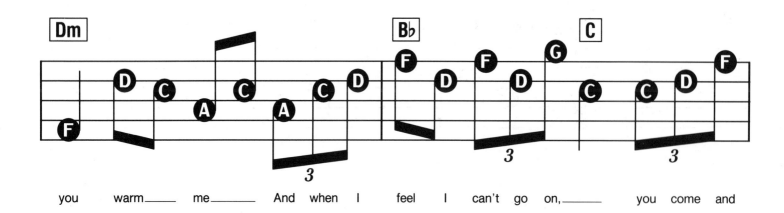

you warm____ me____ And when I feel I can't go on,____ you come and

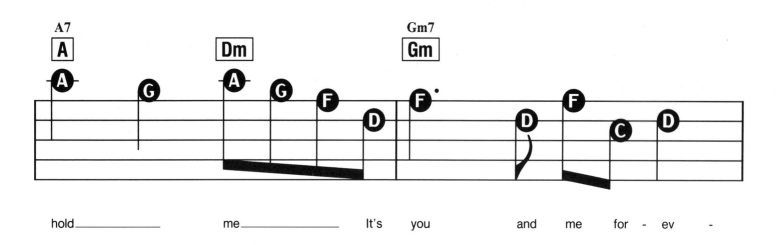

hold_____ me_____ It's you and me for - ev -

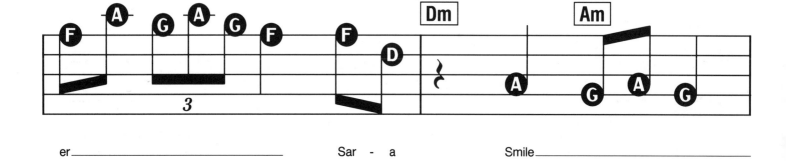

er_____ Sar - a Smile_____

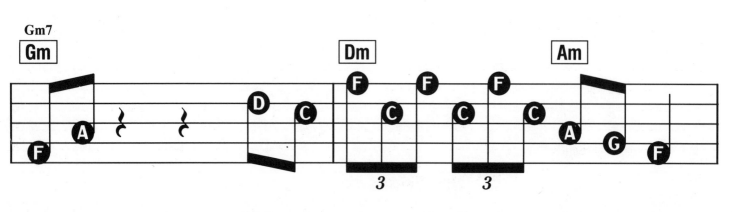

_____ Won't you smile a while for me____ Sar - a____

135

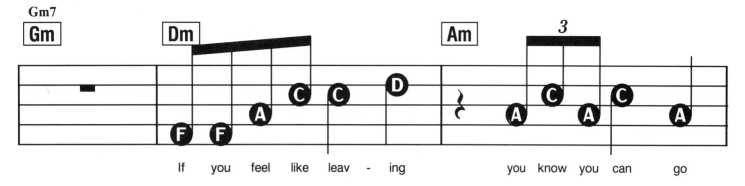

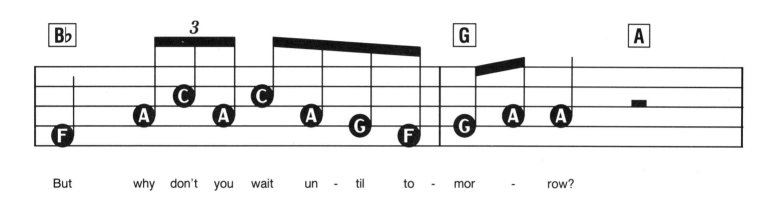

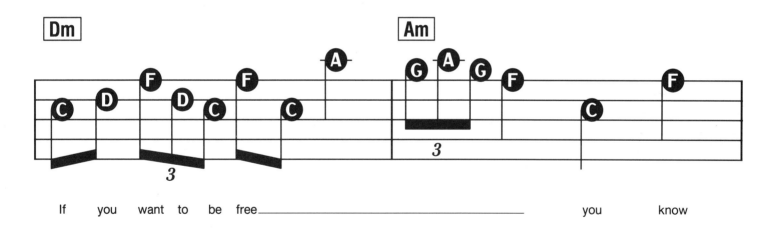

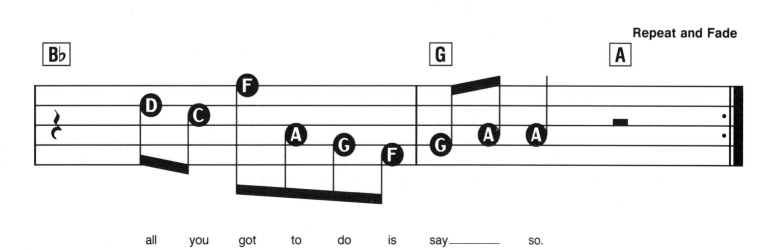

Seasons In The Sun

Ballade 3
Tempo 95

Registration 4
Rhythm: March or Polka

English Lyric by Rod McKuen
Music by Jacques Brel

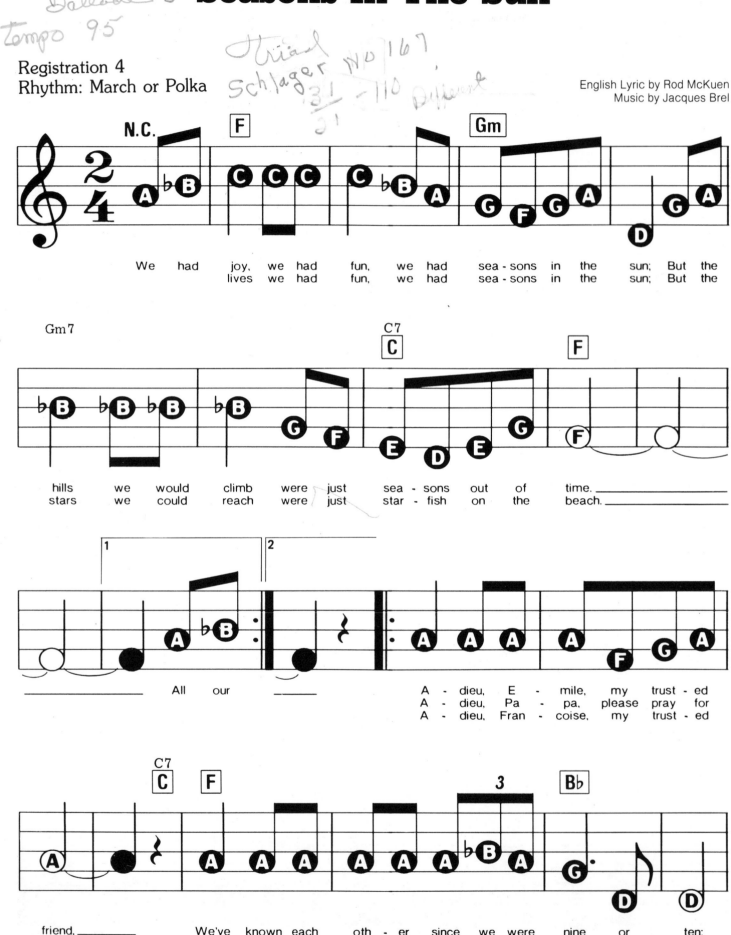

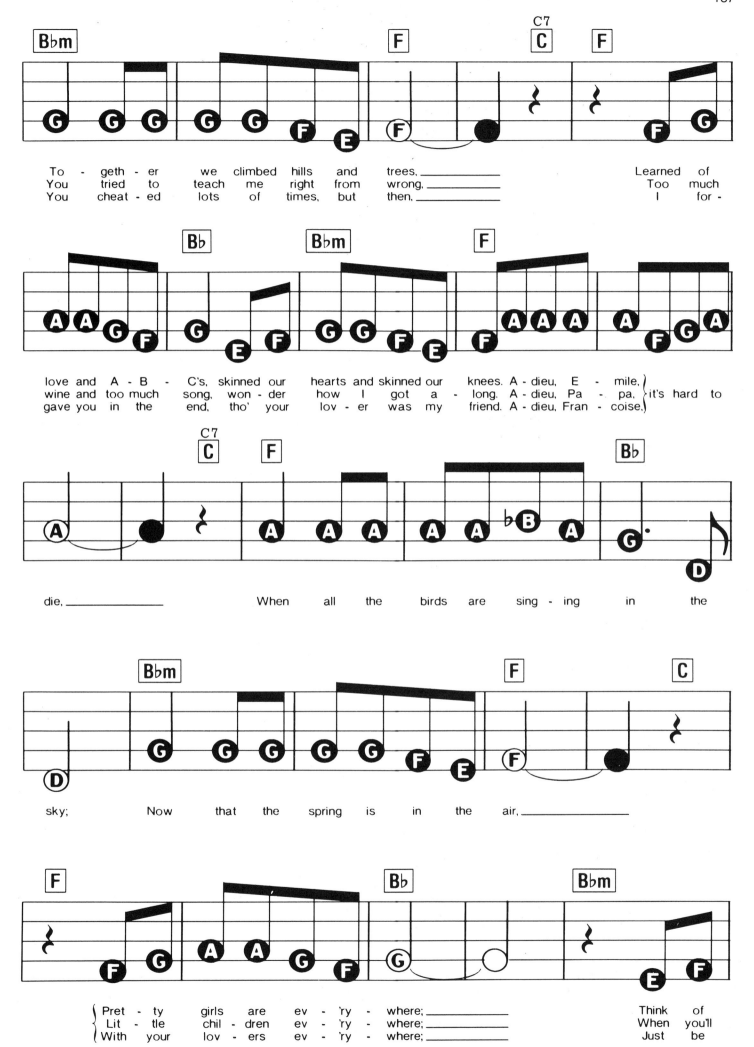

137

Lyrics:

To - geth - er we climbed hills and trees, _____ Learned of
You tried to teach me right from wrong, _____ Too much
You cheat - ed lots of times, but then, _____ I for -

love and A - B - C's, skinned our hearts and skinned our knees. A - dieu, E - mile,
wine and too much song, won - der how I got a - long. A - dieu, Pa - pa, } it's hard to
gave you in the end, tho' your lov - er was my friend. A - dieu, Fran - coise,

die, _____ When all the birds are sing - ing in the

sky; Now that the spring is in the air, _____

Pret - ty girls are ev - 'ry - where; _____ Think of
Lit - tle chil - dren ev - 'ry - where; _____ When you'll
With your lov - ers ev - 'ry - where; _____ Just be

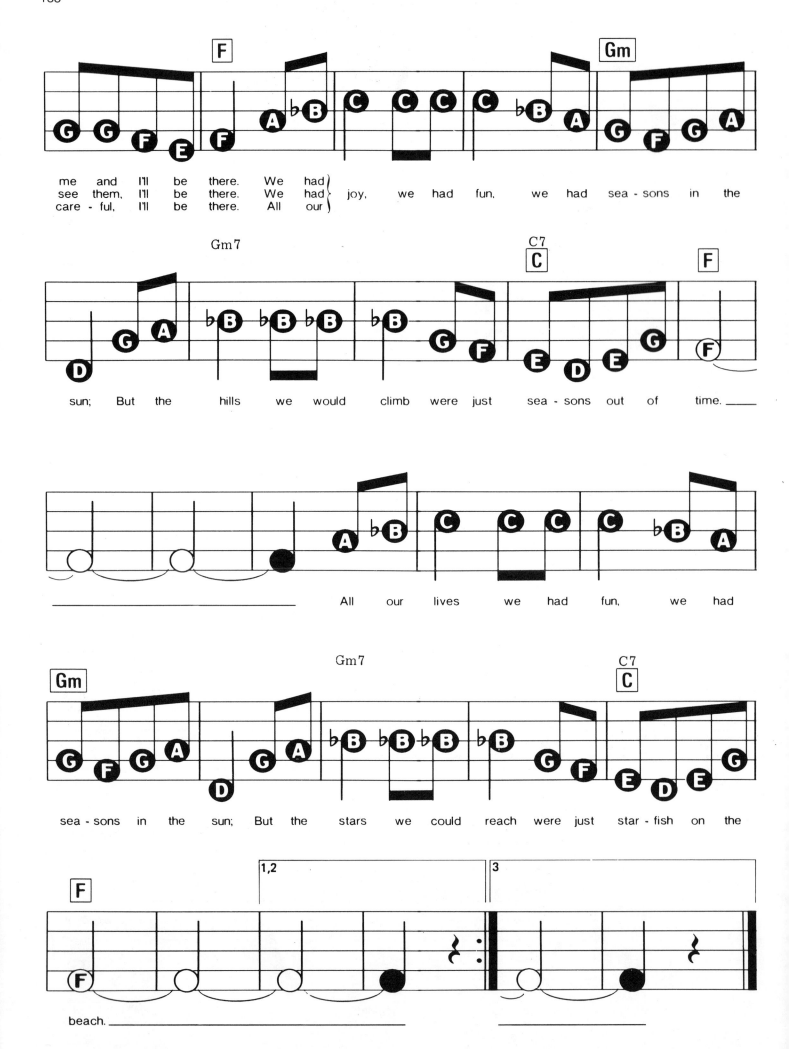

me and I'll be there. We had
see them, I'll be there. We had joy, we had fun, we had sea - sons in the
care - ful, I'll be there. All our

sun; But the hills we would climb were just sea - sons out of time. _____

_____ All our lives we had fun, we had

sea - sons in the sun; But the stars we could reach were just star - fish on the

beach. _____

Send In The Clowns
(From the Musical "A LITTLE NIGHT MUSIC")

Registration 1
Rhythm: Slow rock or Ballad

Music and Lyrics by
Stephen Sondheim

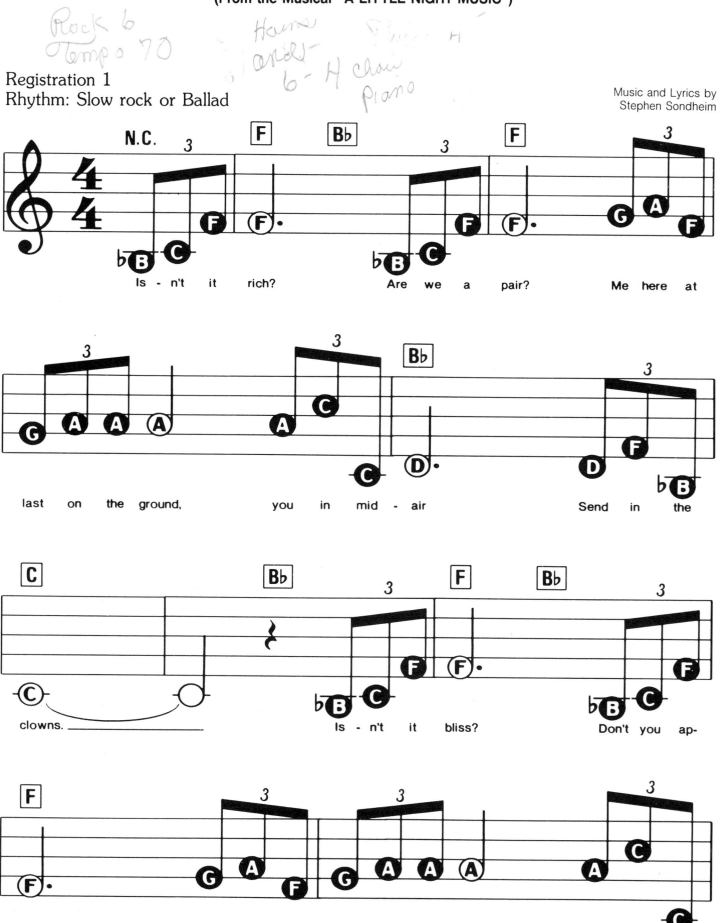

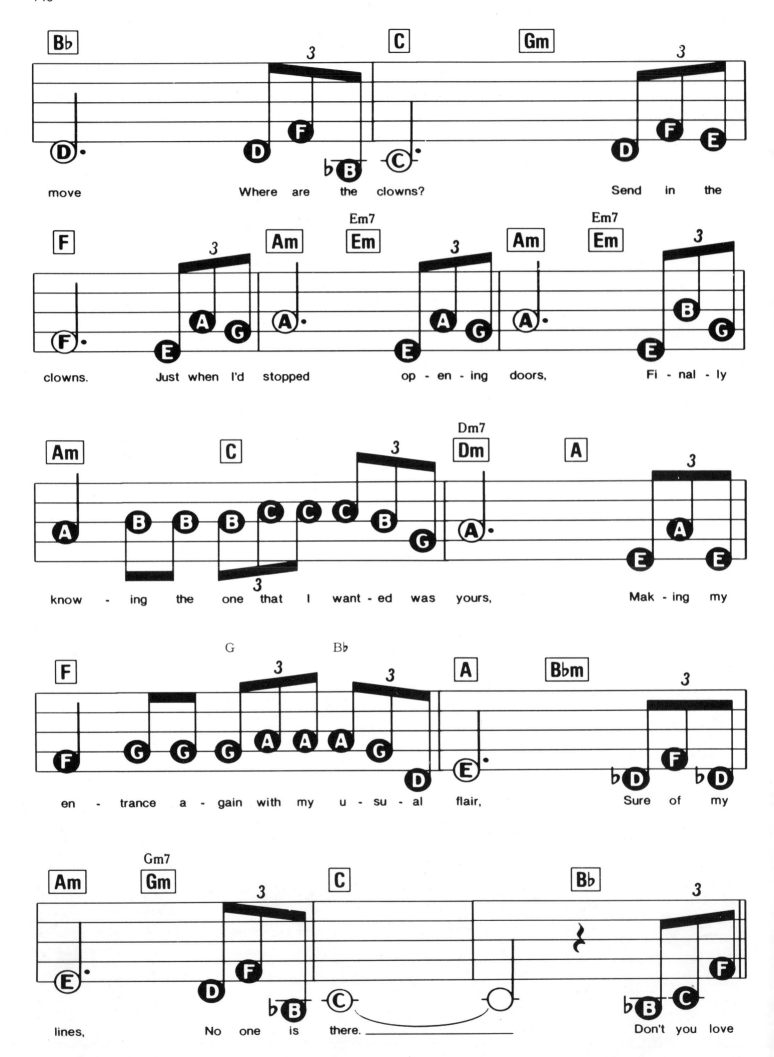

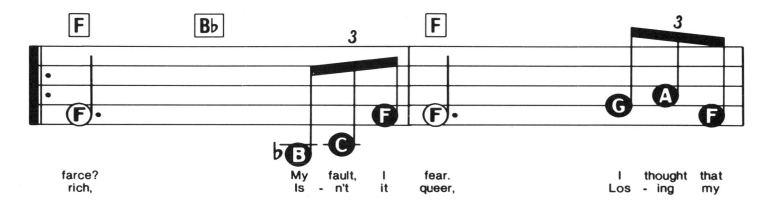

farce?
rich,
My fault, I fear. Is - n't it queer, I thought that Los - ing my

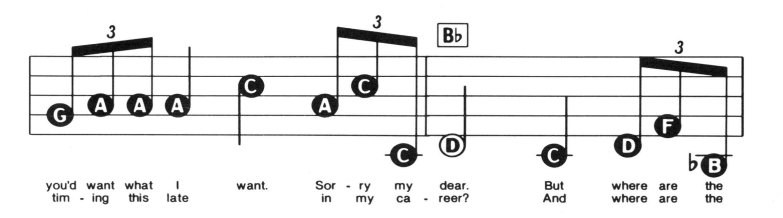

you'd want what I want. Sor - ry my dear. But where are the
tim - ing this late in my ca - reer? And where are the

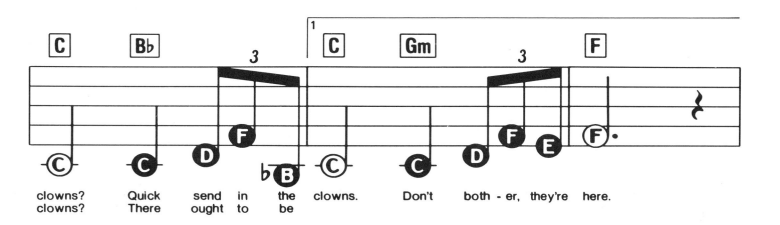

clowns? Quick send in the clowns. Don't both - er, they're here.
clowns? There ought to be

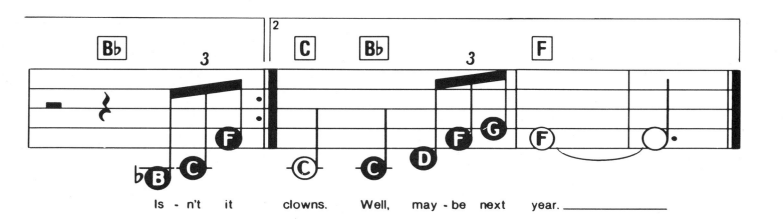

Is - n't it clowns. Well, may - be next year._____

Silly Love Songs

Registration 7
Rhythm: Rock

Words and Music by
McCartney

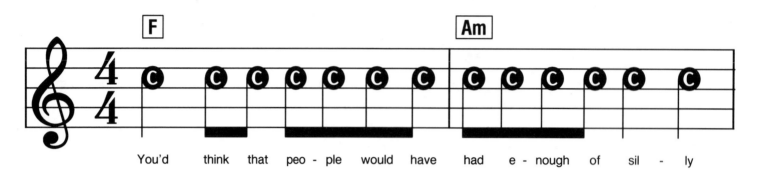

You'd think that peo - ple would have had e - nough of sil - ly

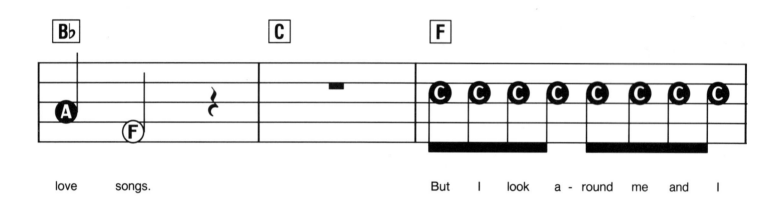

love songs. But I look a - round me and I

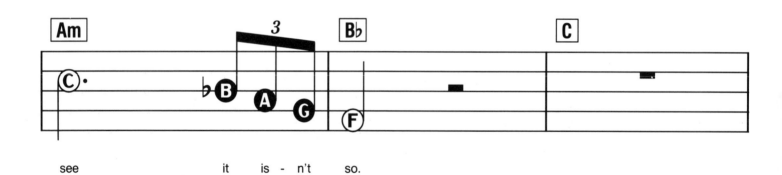

see it is - n't so.

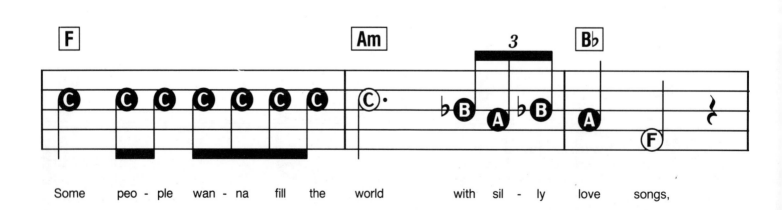

Some peo - ple wan - na fill the world with sil - ly love songs,

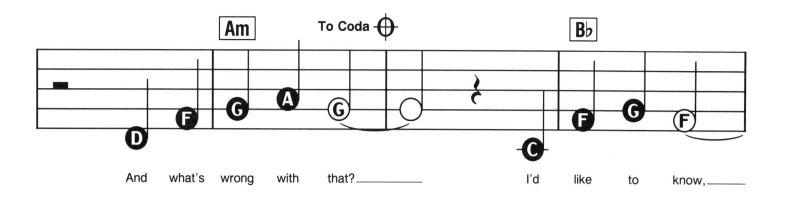

And what's wrong with that?_____ I'd like to know,_____

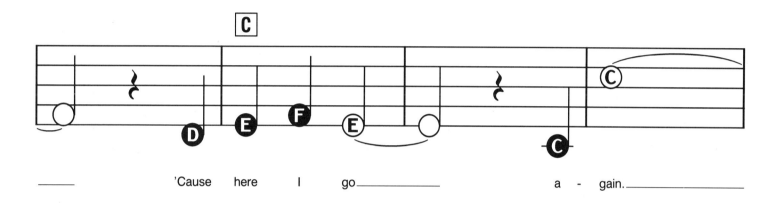

_____ 'Cause here I go_____ a - gain._____

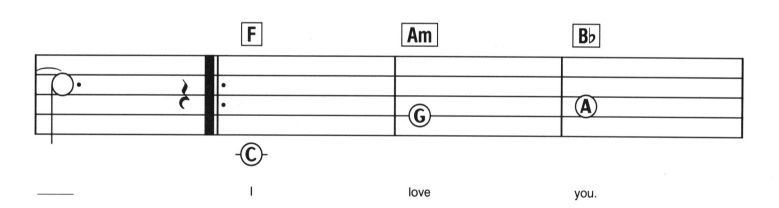

_____ I love you.

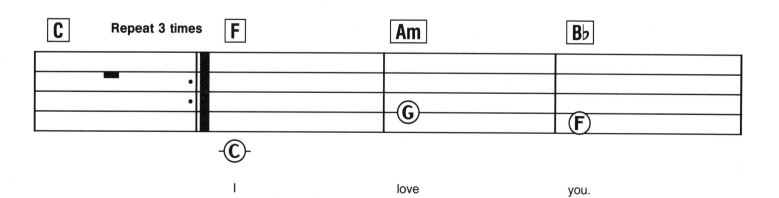

I love you.

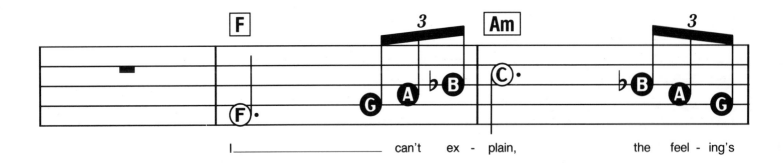

I_____ can't ex - plain,   the feel - ing's

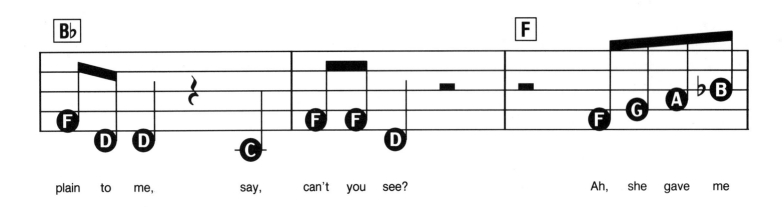

plain to me,   say,   can't you see?   Ah, she gave me

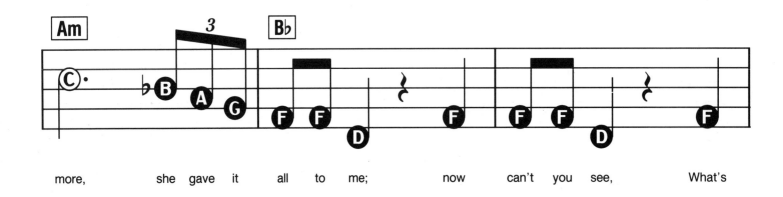

more,   she gave it all to me;   now   can't you see,   What's

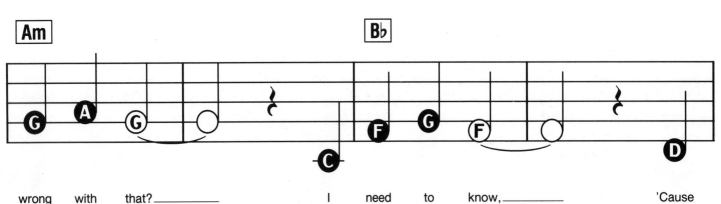

wrong with that?_____   I need to know,_____   'Cause

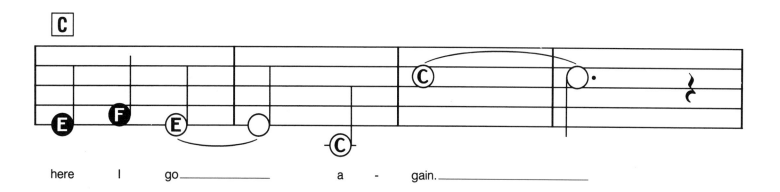

here I go_____ a - gain._____

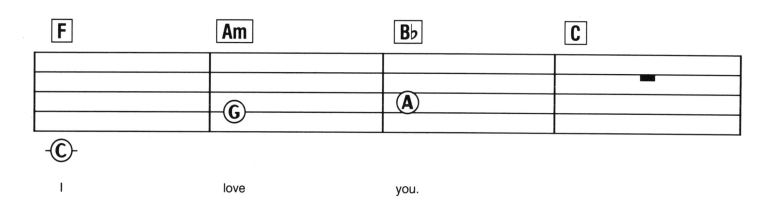

I   love   you.

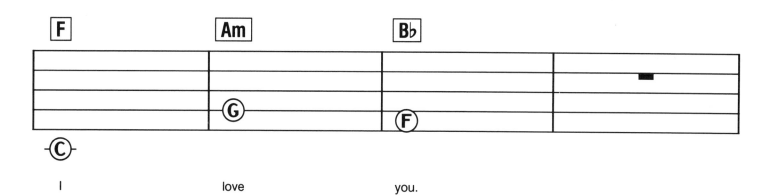

I   love   you.

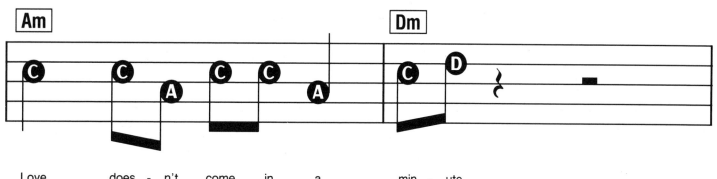

Love   does - n't   come   in   a   min - ute,

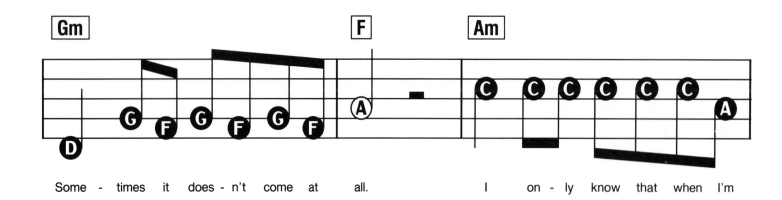

Some - times it does - n't come at all. I on - ly know that when I'm

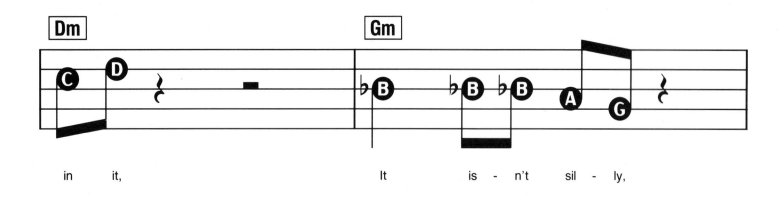

in it, It is - n't sil - ly,

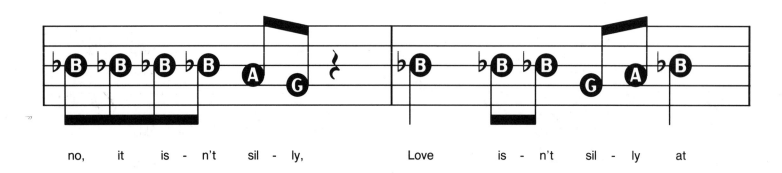

no, it is - n't sil - ly, Love is - n't sil - ly at

D.C. al Coda
(Return to beginning
Play to ⊕ and
skip to Coda)

CODA

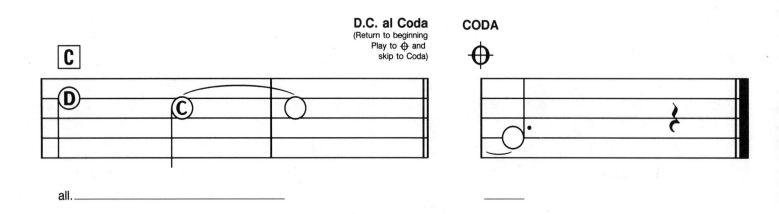

all.

Stayin' Alive

Registration 7
Rhythm: Disco or Rock

Words and Music by Barry Gibb,
Robin Gibb and Maurice Gibb

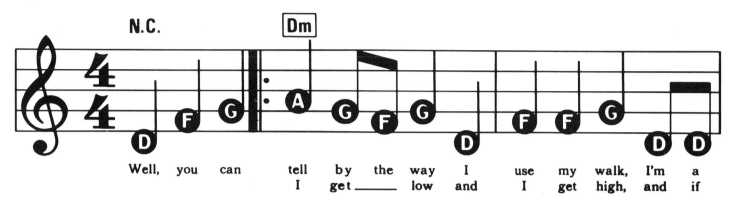

Well, you can   tell   by the   way   I   use my walk, I'm a
I get _____ low   and   I   get high, and if

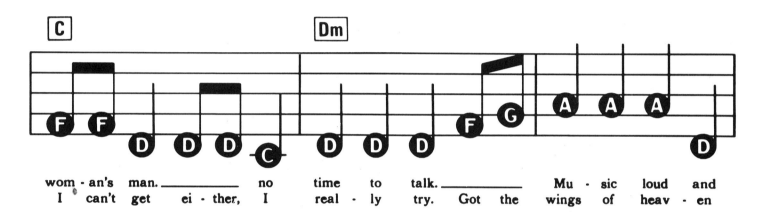

wom - an's man. _____ no   time to   talk. _____ Mu - sic loud and
I   can't get ei - ther, I   real - ly try. Got the wings of heav - en

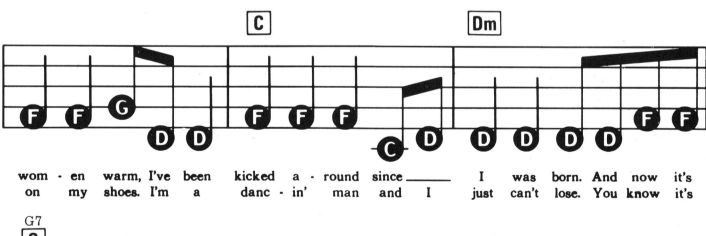

wom - en warm, I've been kicked a - round since _____ I   was born. And now it's
on   my shoes. I'm a   danc - in' man and I   just can't lose. You know it's

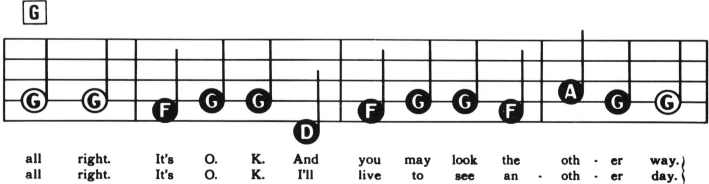

all   right.   It's O. K.   And you may look the oth - er way.}
all   right.   It's O. K.   I'll live to see an - oth - er day.}

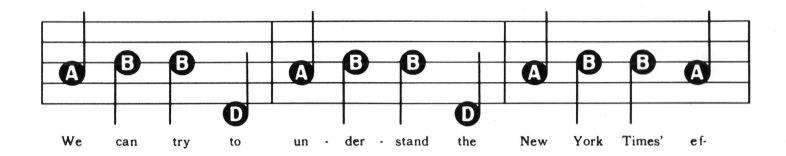

We can try to un - der - stand the New York Times' ef-

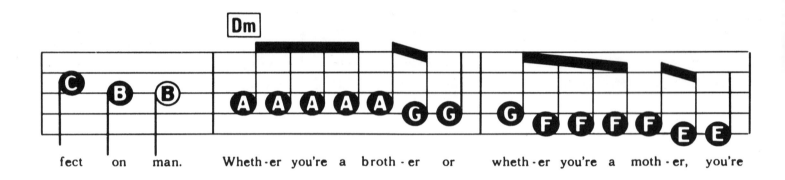

fect on man. Wheth-er you're a broth-er or wheth-er you're a moth-er, you're

stay-in' a - live, stay-in' a - live. Feel the cit-y break-in' and

ev - 'ry-bod - y shak-in', and we're stay-in' a - live, stay-in' a - live.

Ah,   ha,   ha,   ha,   stay - in' a - live,   stay - in' a - live.

Ah,   ha,   ha,   ha,   stay - in' a - live. _____

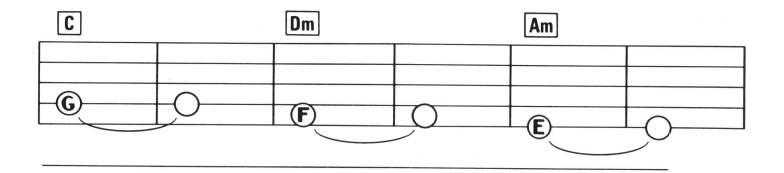

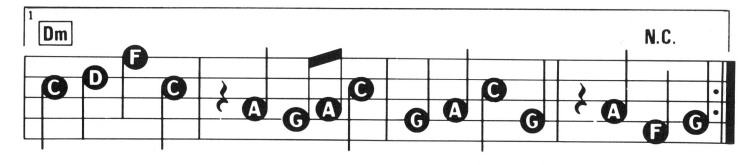

Well now

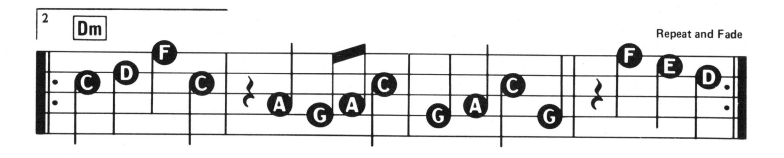

Sometimes When We Touch

Registration 8
Rhythm: Rock or Slow Rock

Words by Dan Hill
Music by Barry Mann

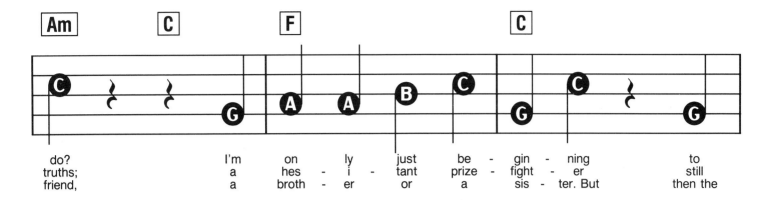
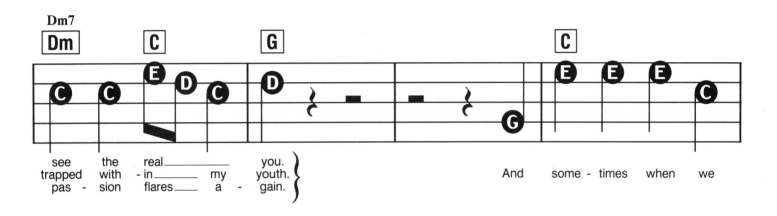
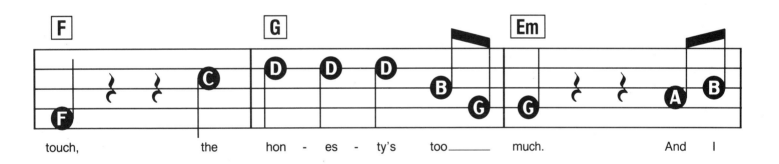
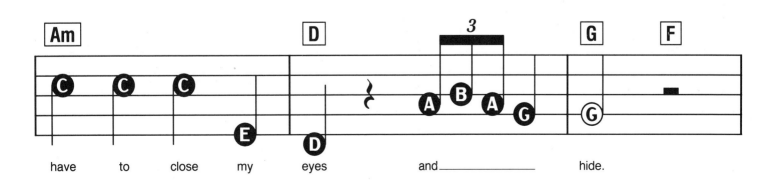

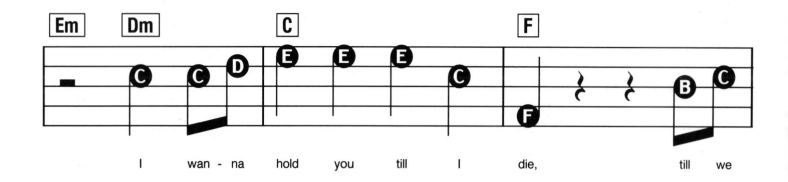

I wan - na hold you till I die, till we

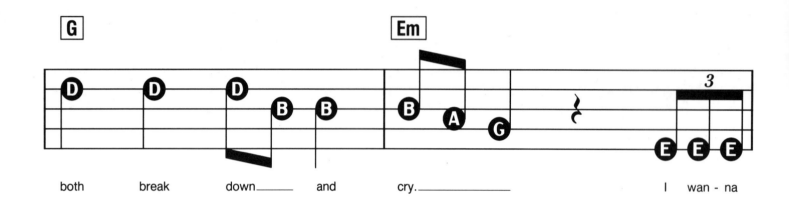

both break down and cry. I wan - na

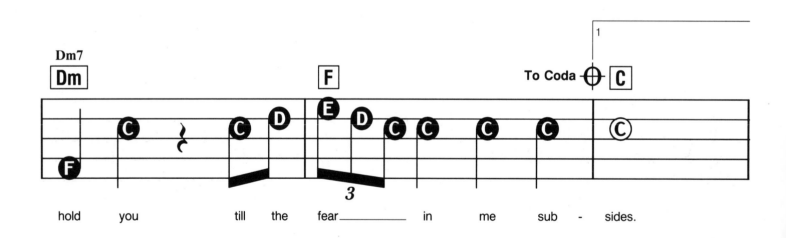

hold you till the fear in me sub - sides.

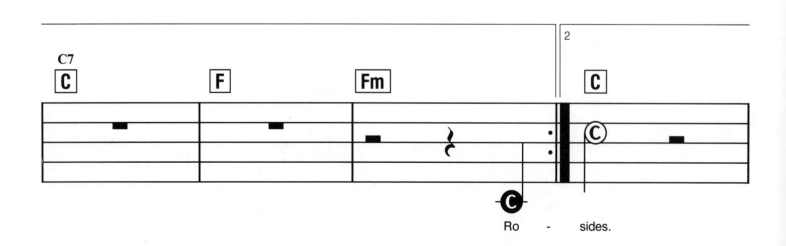

Ro - sides.

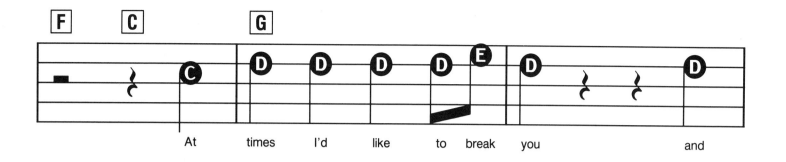

At times I'd like to break you and

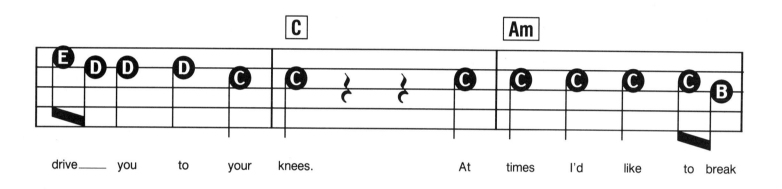

drive you to your knees. At times I'd like to break

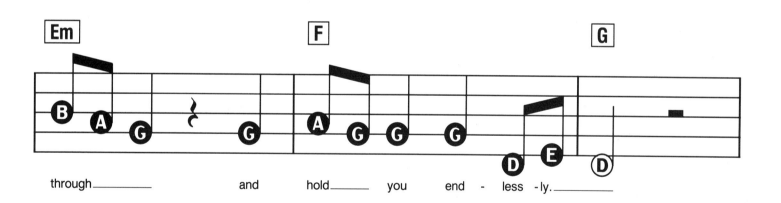

through and hold you end - less - ly.

CODA

D.S. al Coda
(Return to 𝄋
Play to ⊕ and
skip to Coda)

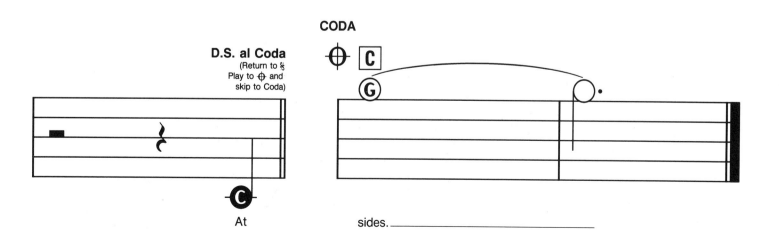

At   sides.

Song Sung Blue

Registration 2
Rhythm: Fox Trot or Ballad

Words and Music by
Neil Diamond

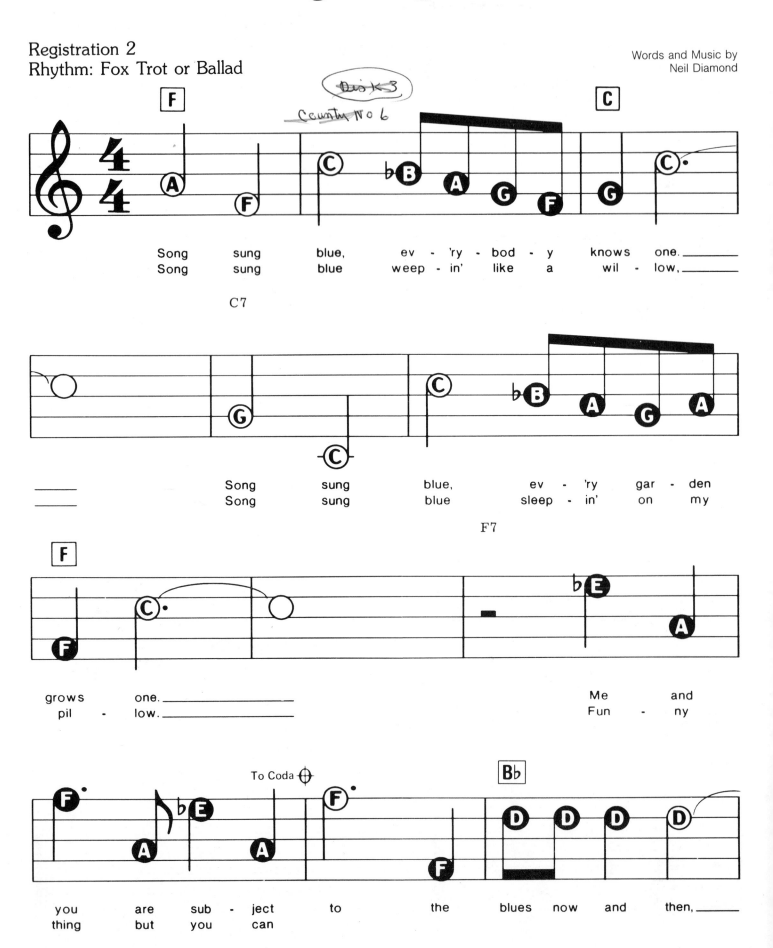

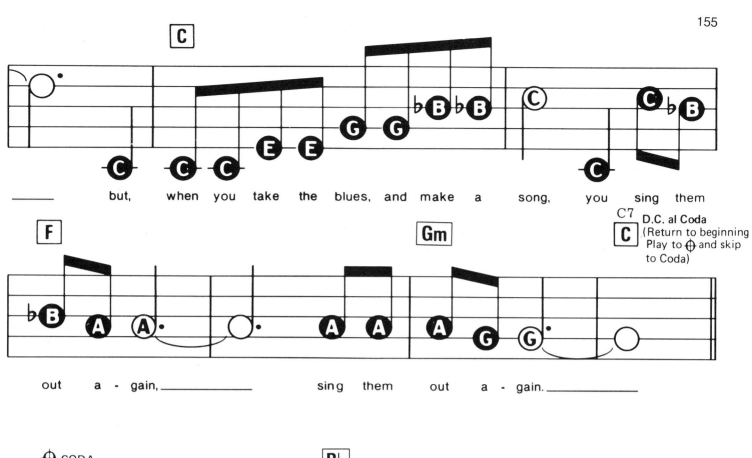

but, when you take the blues, and make a song, you sing them

out a - gain, _____ sing them out a - gain. _____

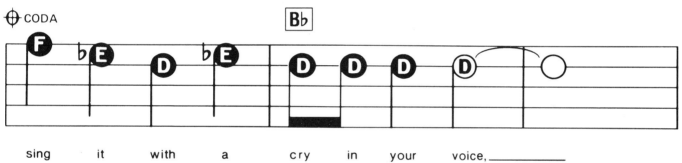

C7 D.C. al Coda
(Return to beginning
Play to ⊕ and skip
to Coda)

⊕ CODA

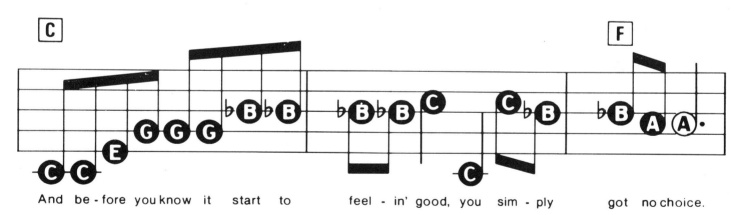

sing it with a cry in your voice, _____

And be - fore you know it start to feel - in' good, you sim - ply got no choice.

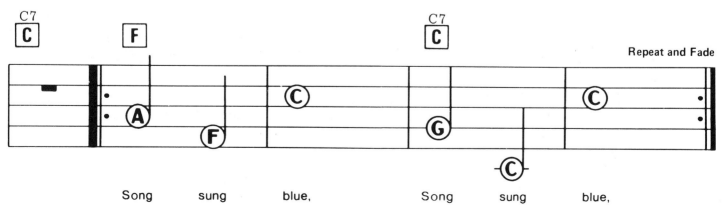

Repeat and Fade

Song sung blue, Song sung blue,

Summer Breeze

Registration 7
Rhythm: Moderate Rock Ballad

Words and Music by
James Seals and Dash Crofts

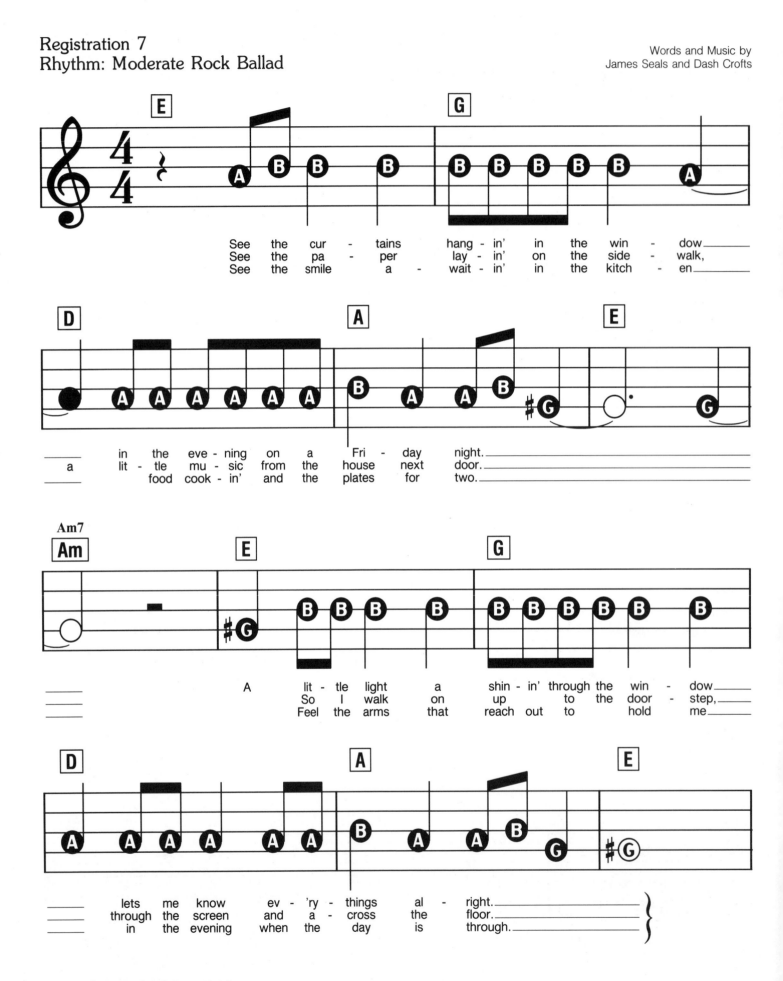

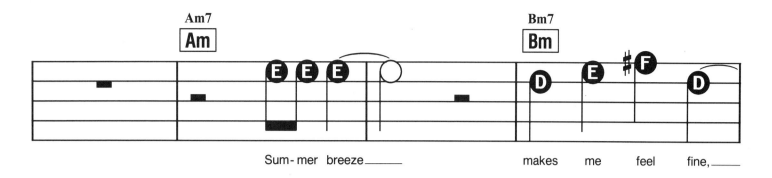

Sum-mer breeze _____ makes me feel fine, _____

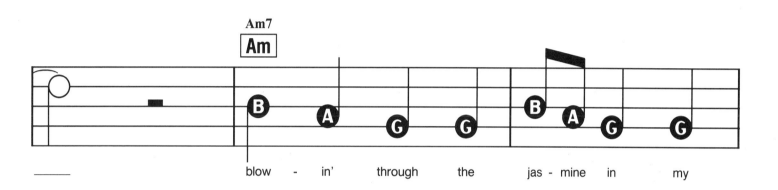

_____ blow - in' through the jas - mine in my

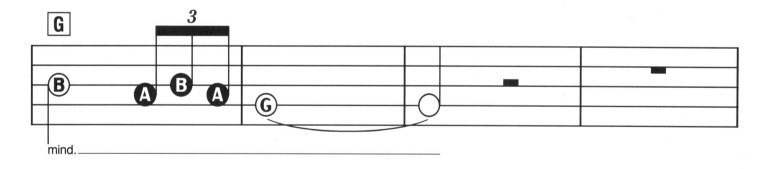

mind. _____

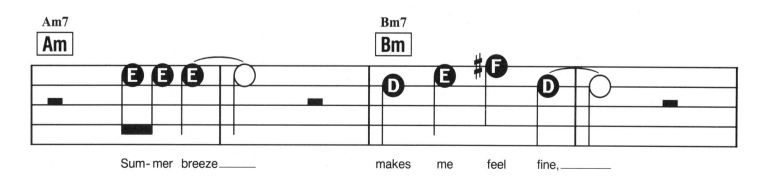

Sum-mer breeze _____ makes me feel fine, _____

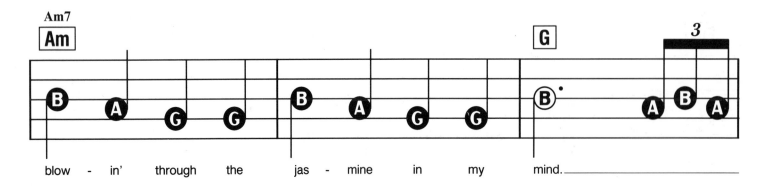

blow - in' through the jas - mine in my mind.

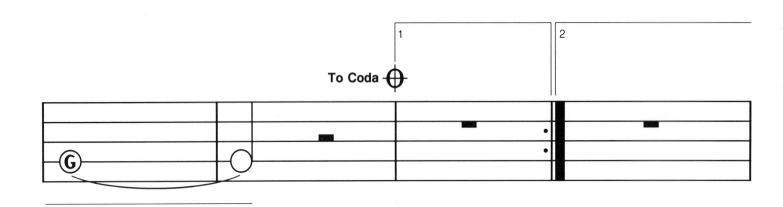

To Coda

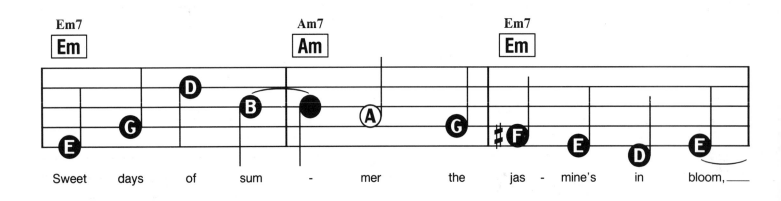

Sweet days of sum - mer the jas - mine's in bloom,

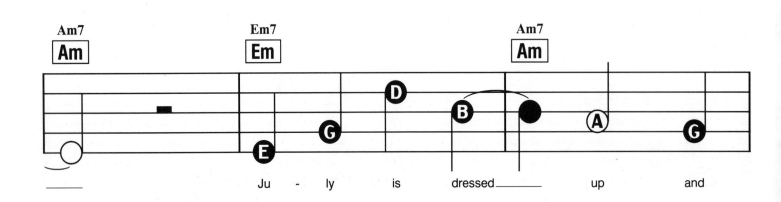

Ju - ly is dressed up and

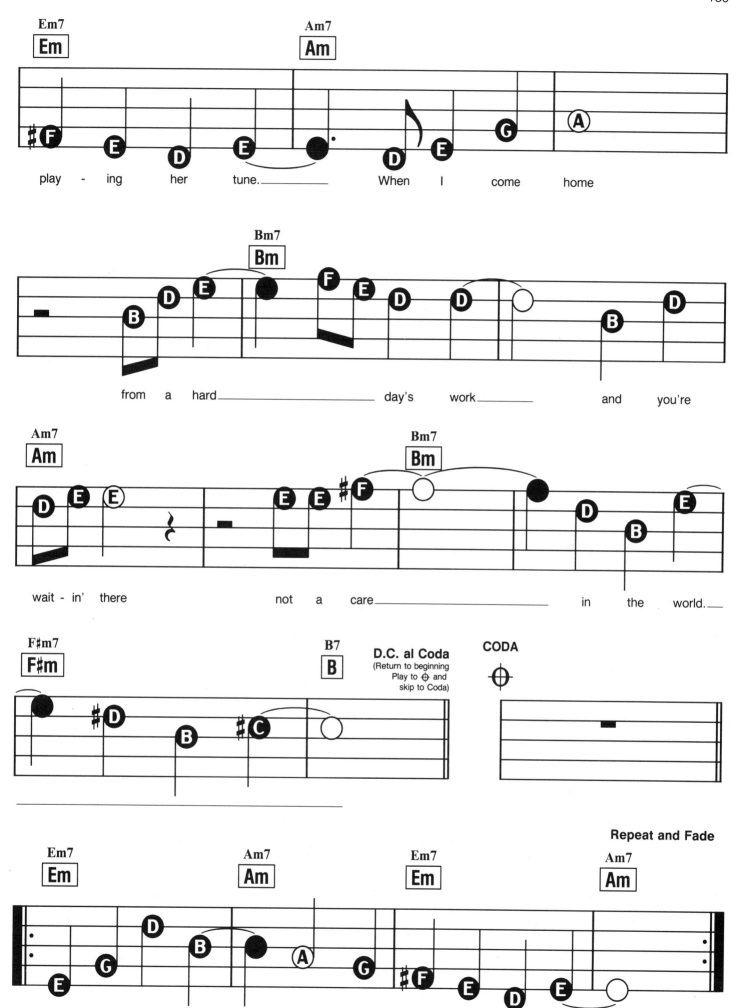

Registration 1
Rhythm: Swing or Jazz

Tomorrow
(From "ANNIE")

Lyric by Martin Charnin
Music by Charles Strouse

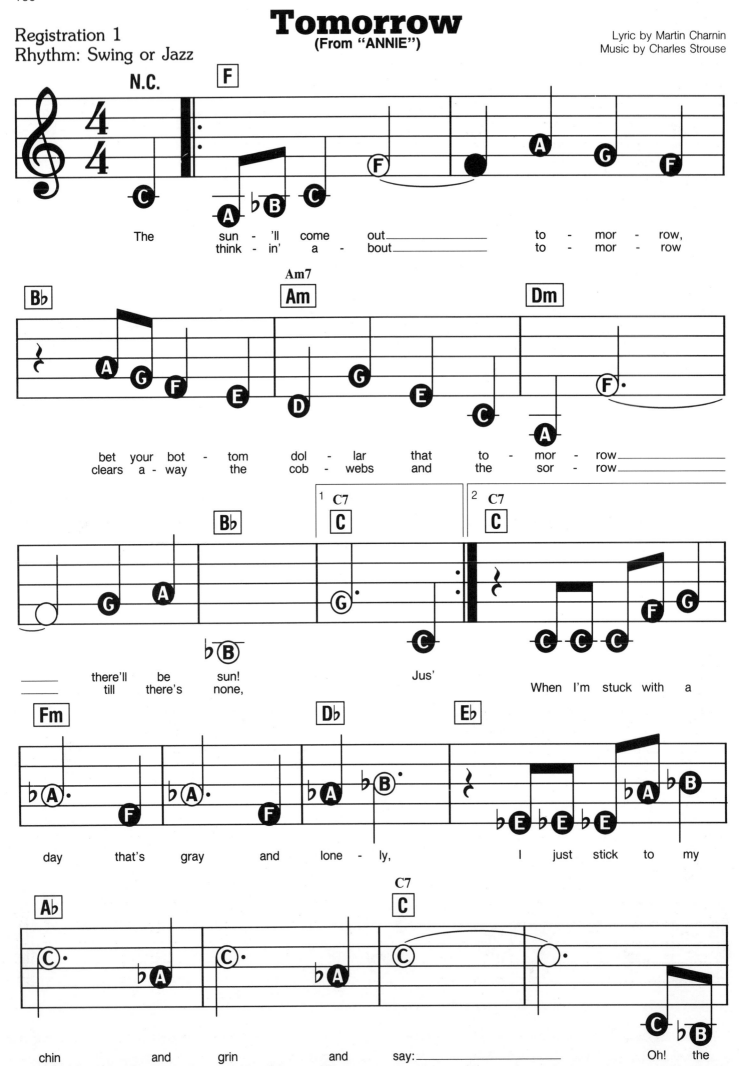

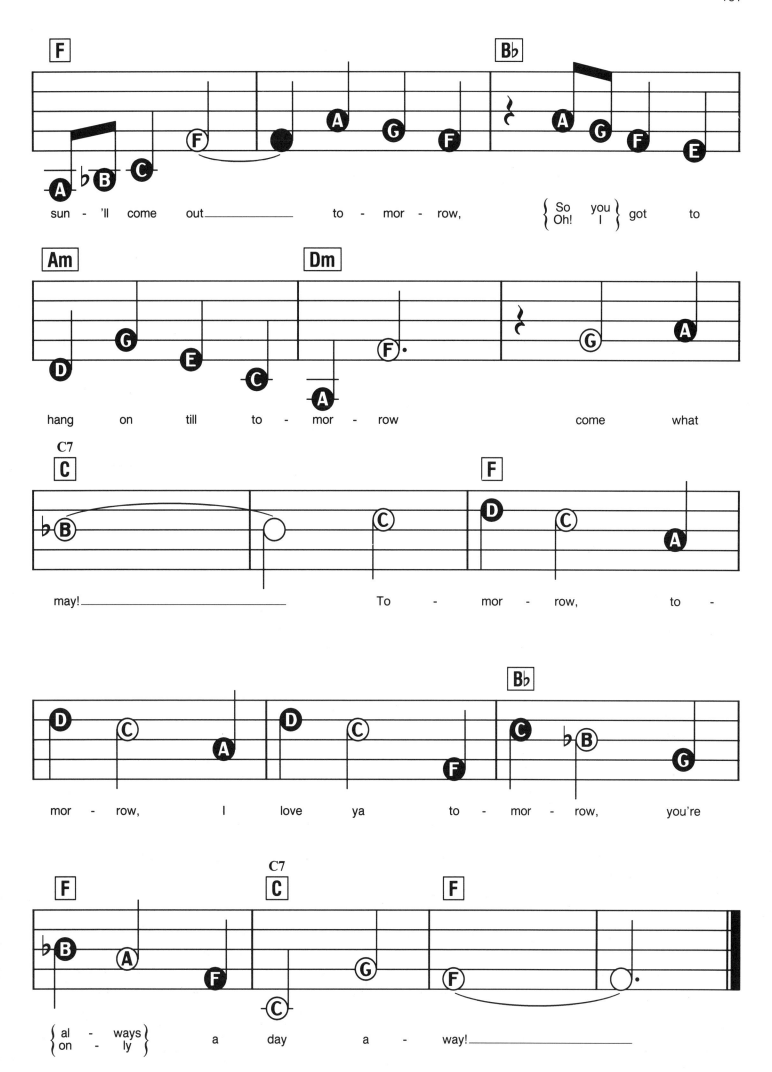

What I Did For Love

(From "A CHORUS LINE")

Registration 3
Rhythm: Ballad

Music by Marvin Hamlisch
Lyric by Edward Kleban

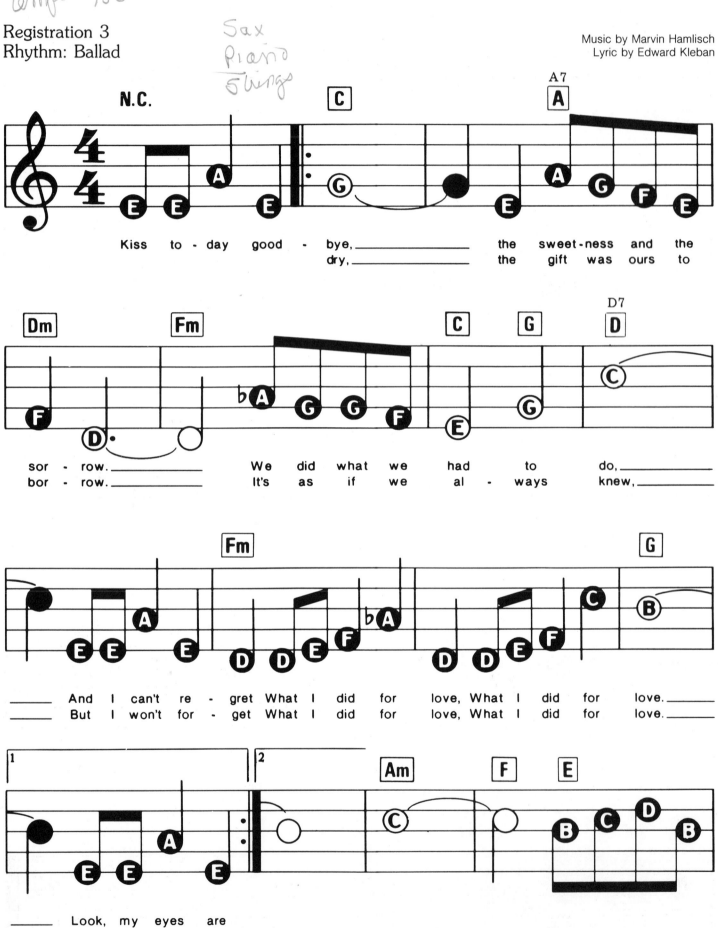

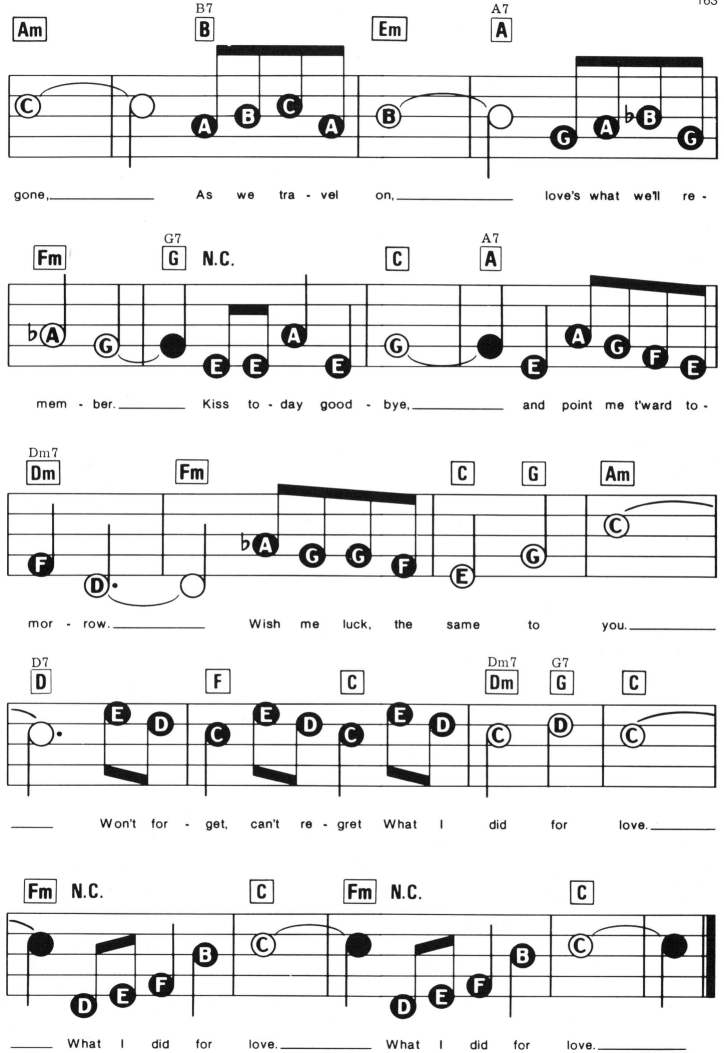

You Don't Bring Me Flowers

Words by Neil Diamond,
Marilyn Bergman, Alan Bergman
Music by Neil Diamond

Registration 4
Rhythm: Ballad or Fox Trot

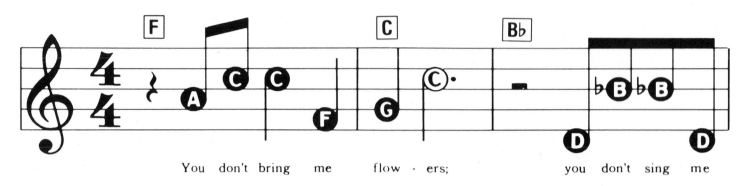

You don't bring me flow - ers; you don't sing me

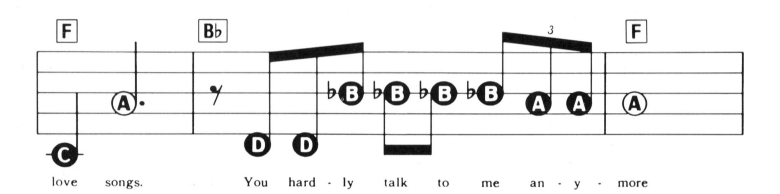

love songs. You hard - ly talk to me an - y - more

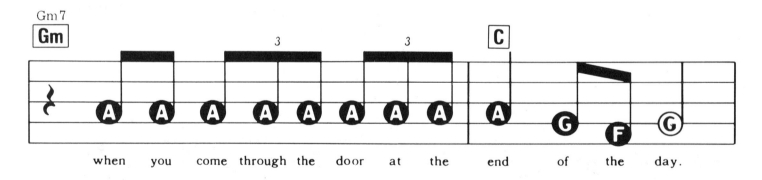

when you come through the door at the end of the day.

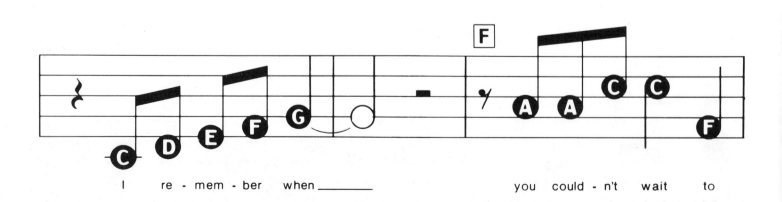

I re - mem - ber when you could - n't wait to

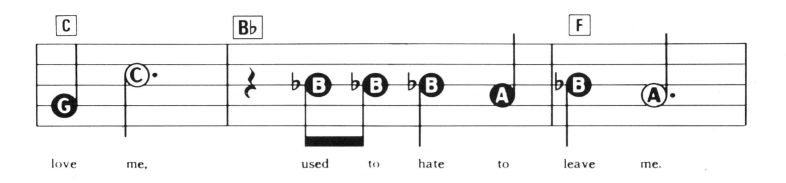

love me, used to hate to leave me.

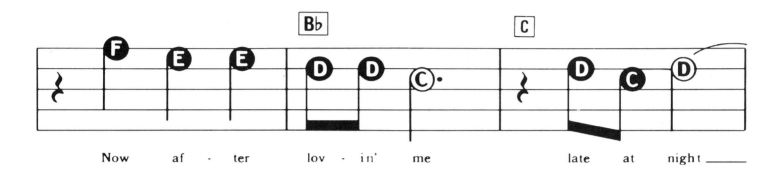

Now af - ter lov - in' me late at night ____

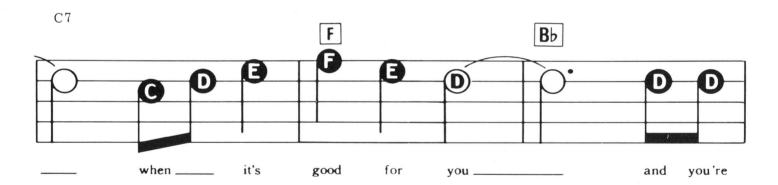

C7

____ when ____ it's good for you _____ and you're

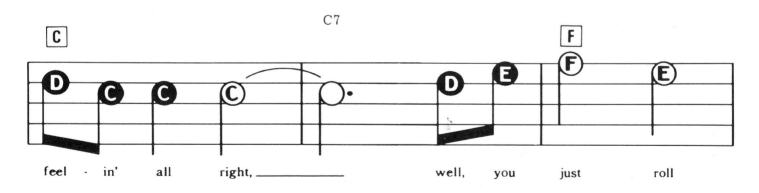

C7

feel - in' all right, _____ well, you just roll

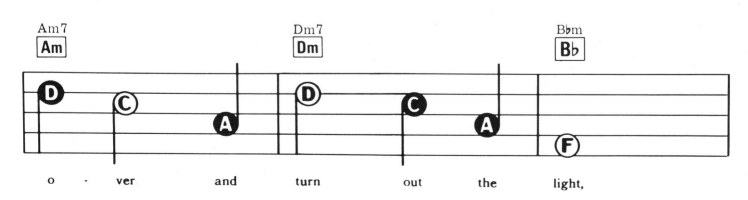

Am7

Dm7

Bbm

o - ver and turn out the light,

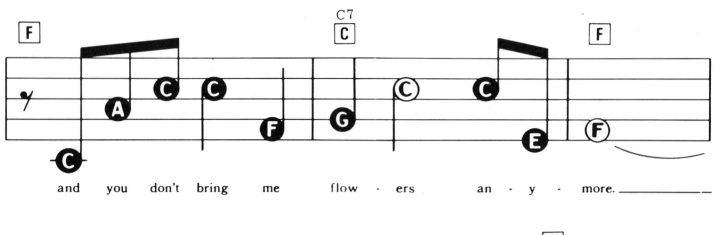

and you don't bring me flow - ers an - y - more. _____

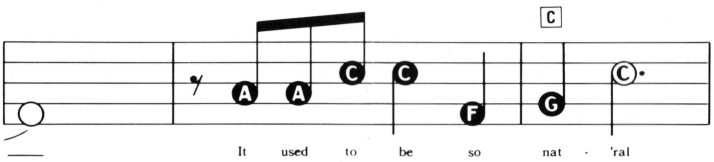

_____ It used to be so nat - 'ral

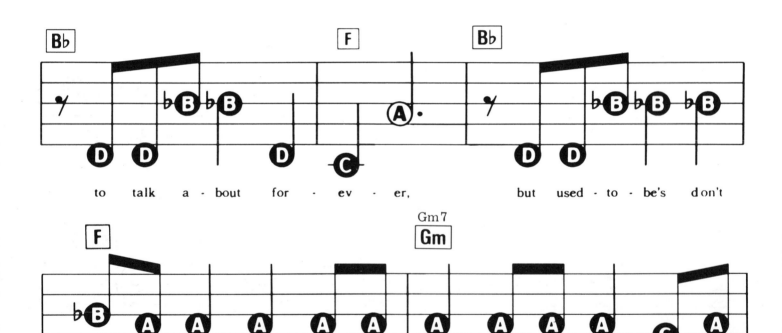

to talk a - bout for - ev - er, but used - to - be's don't

count an - y - more. They just lay on the floor till we

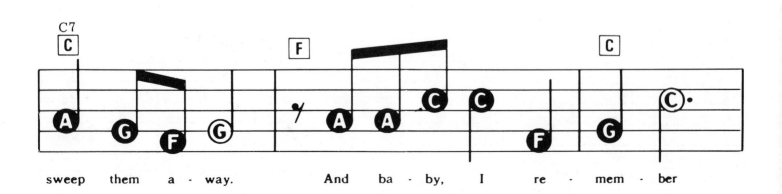

sweep them a - way. And ba - by, I re - mem - ber

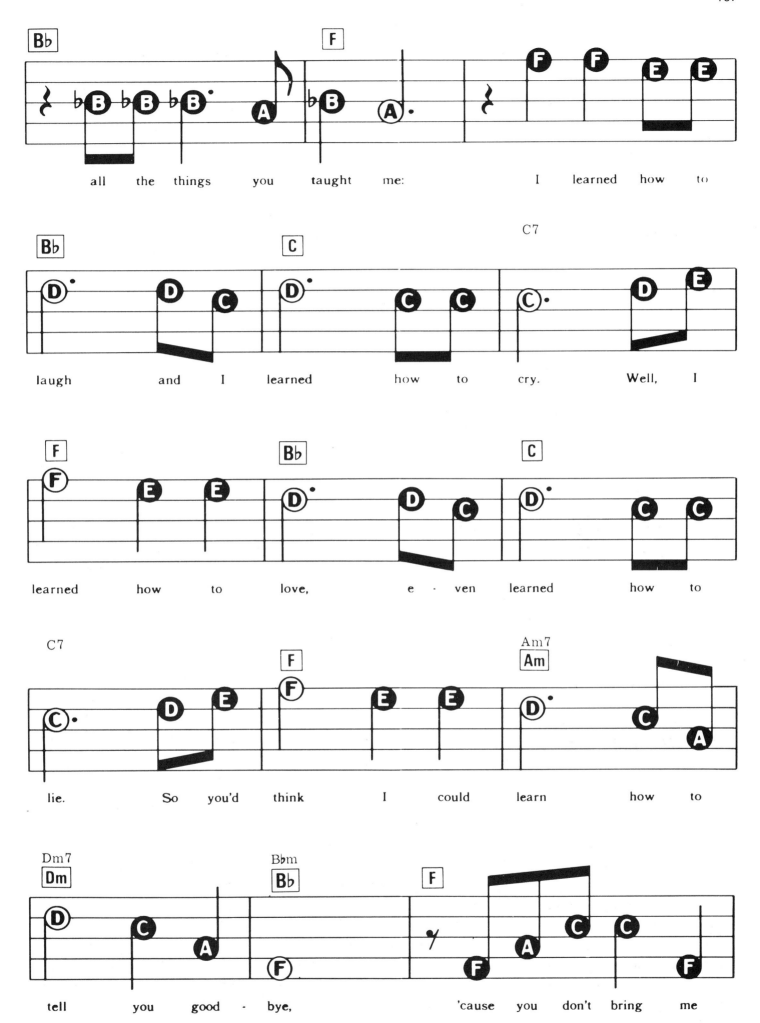

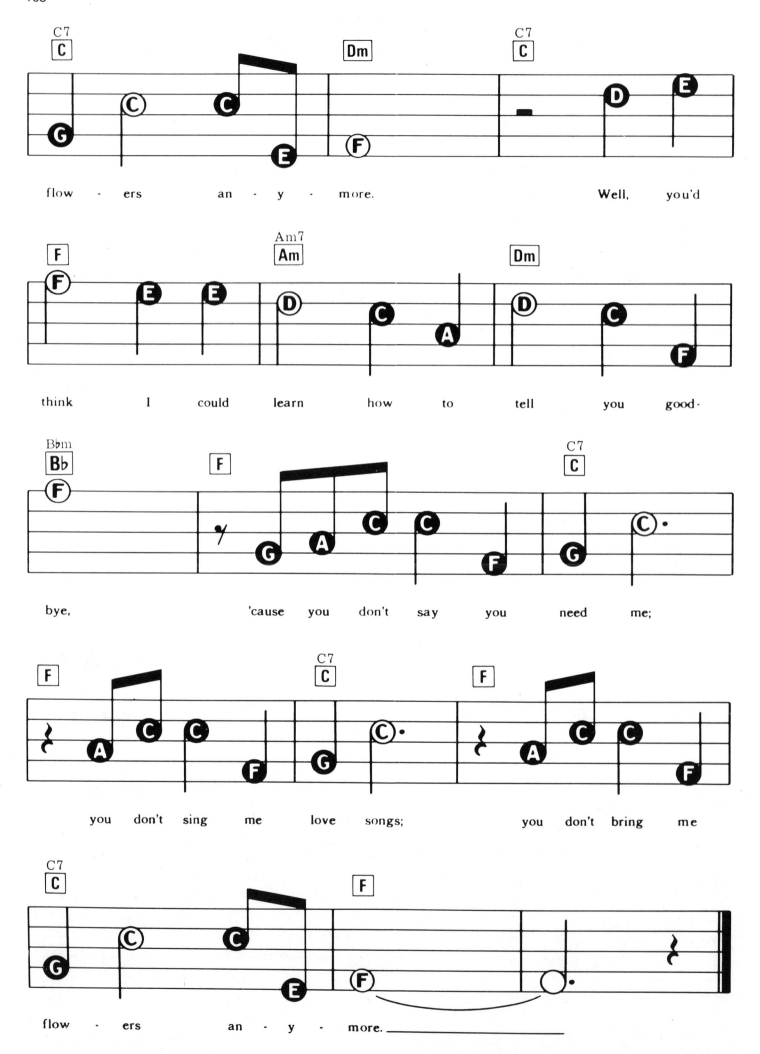

You Needed Me

Registration 2
Rhythm: Country

Words and Music by Randy Goodrum

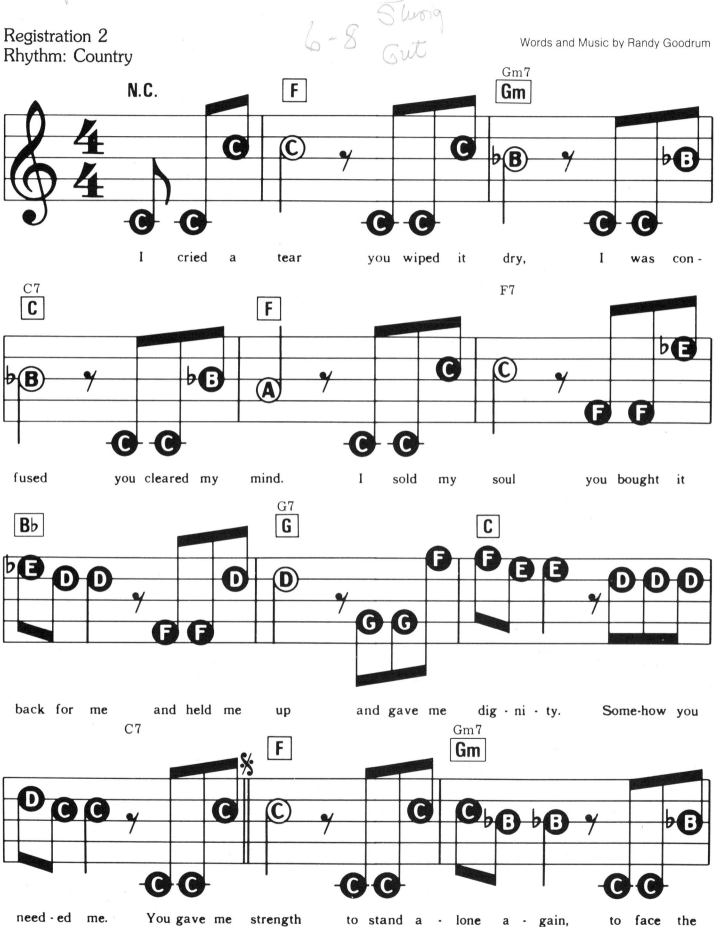

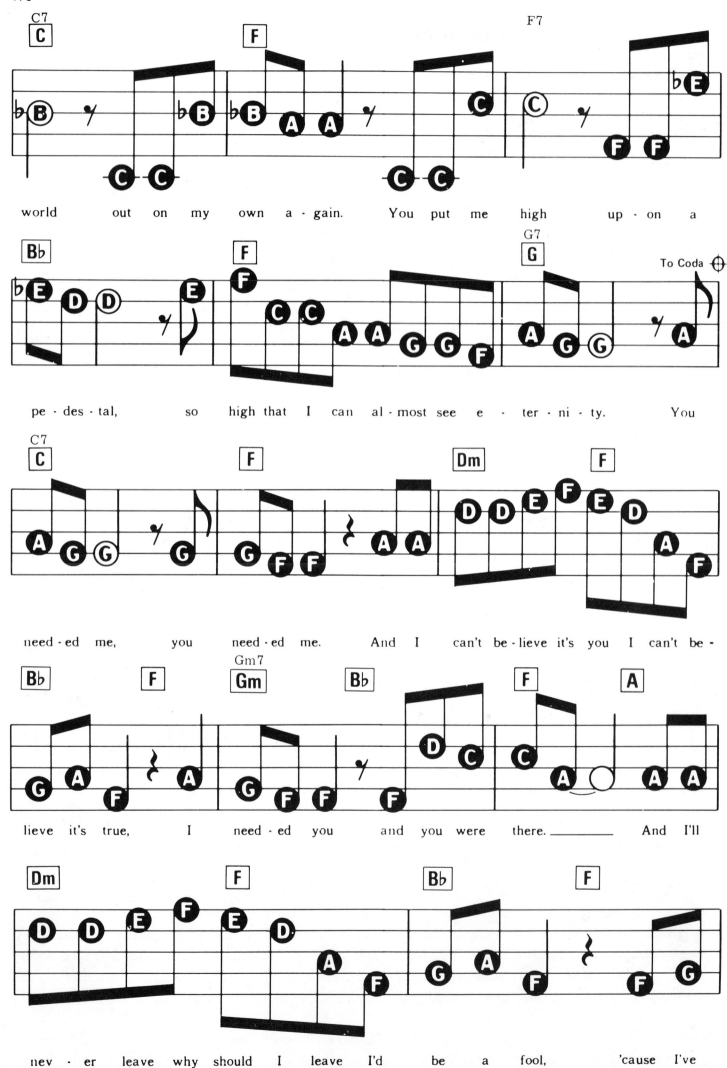

world out on my own a-gain. You put me high up-on a

pe-des-tal, so high that I can al-most see e-ter-ni-ty. You

need-ed me, you need-ed me. And I can't be-lieve it's you I can't be-

lieve it's true, I need-ed you and you were there._____ And I'll

nev-er leave why should I leave I'd be a fool, 'cause I've

171

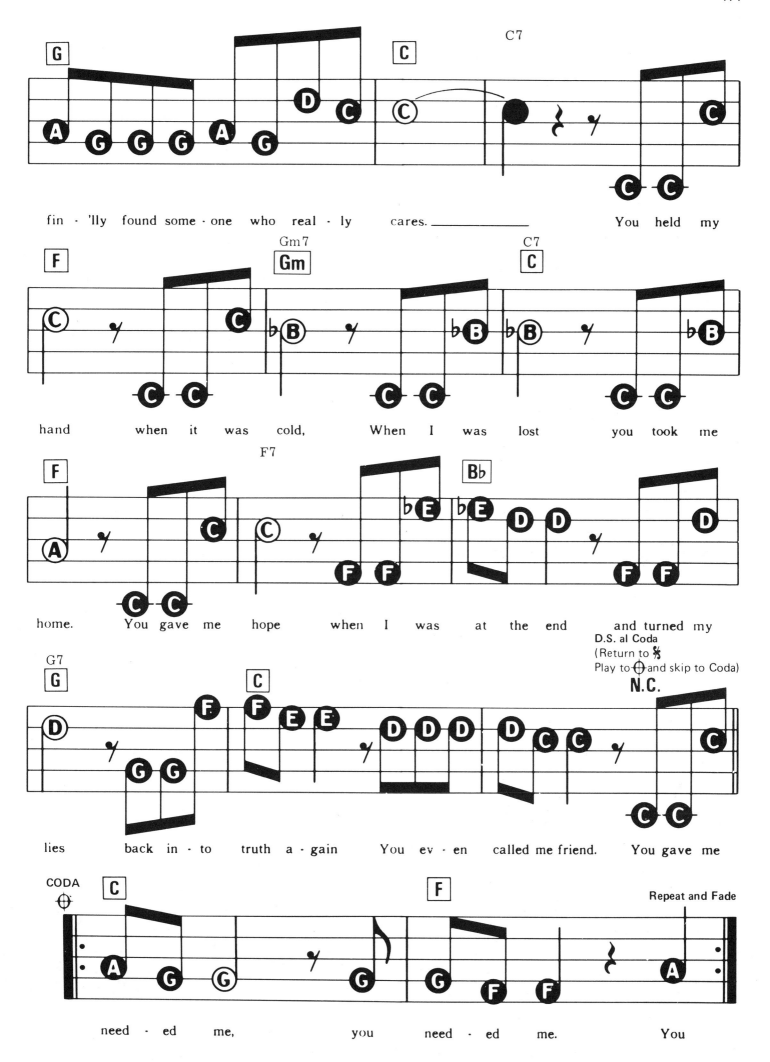

Your Song

Registration 3
Rhythm: Rock or Jazz Rock

Words and Music by Elton John
and Bernie Taupin

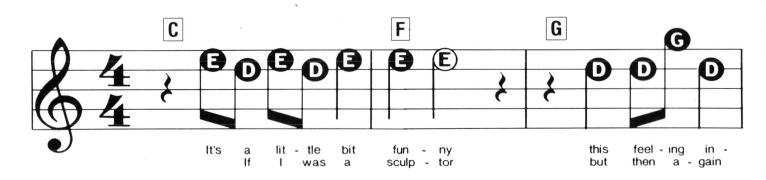

It's a lit - tle bit fun - ny this feel - ing in -
If I was a sculp - tor but then a - gain

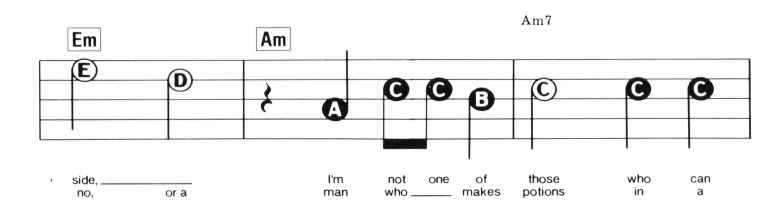

side, _____ I'm not one of those who can
no, or a man who _____ makes those potions in a

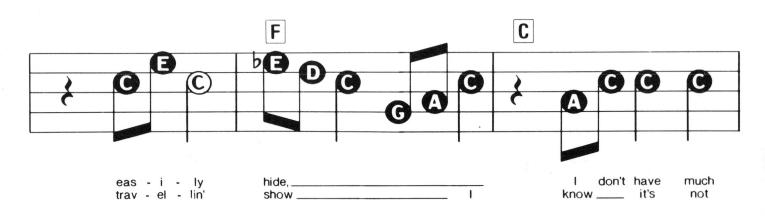

eas - i - ly hide, _____ I don't have much
trav - el - lin' show _____ I know _____ it's not

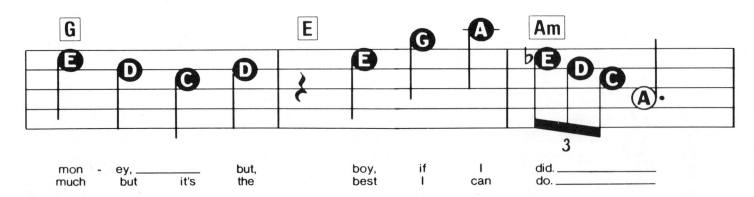

mon - ey, _____ but, boy, if I did. _____
much but it's the best I can do. _____

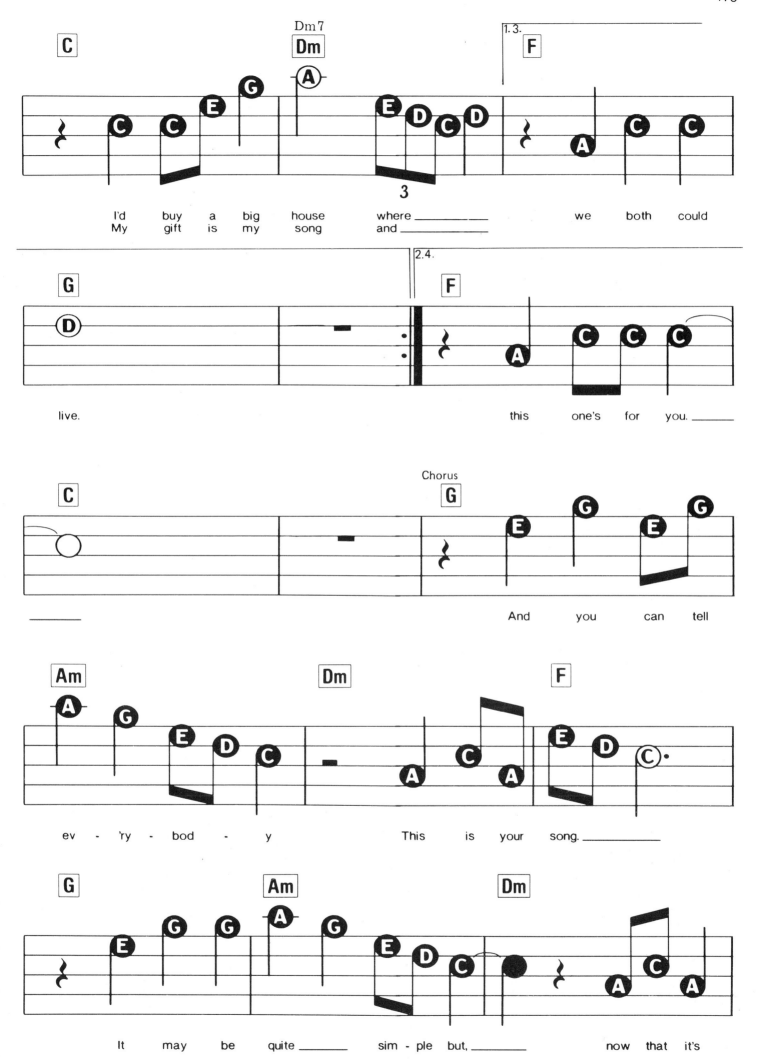

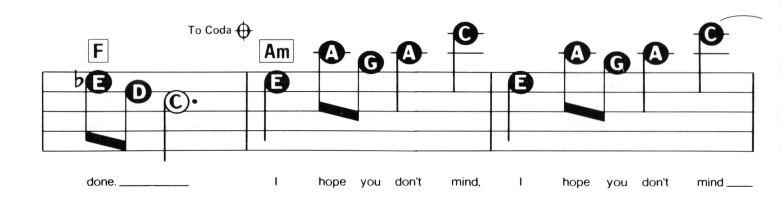

done. _____ I hope you don't mind, I hope you don't mind ____

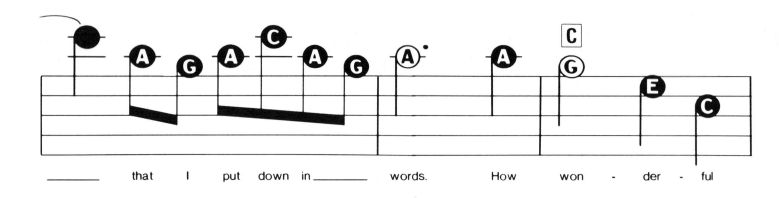

_____ that I put down in _____ words. How won - der - ful

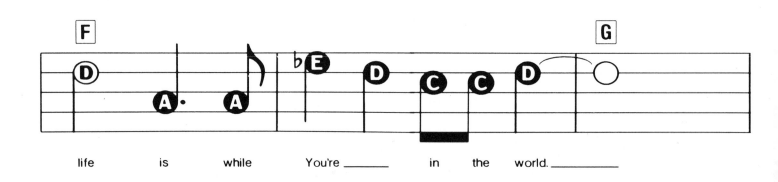

life is while You're _____ in the world. _____

D.C. al Coda
(Return to beginning, take 3rd & 4th endings, Play till ⊕ and skip to Coda)

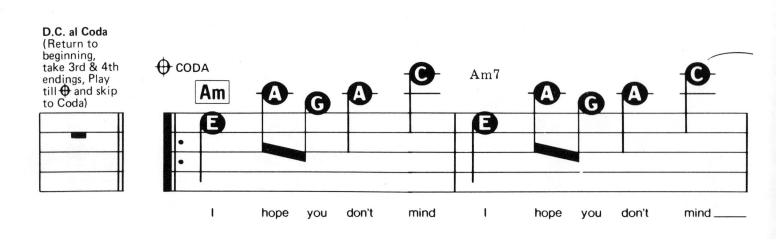

I hope you don't mind I hope you don't mind ____

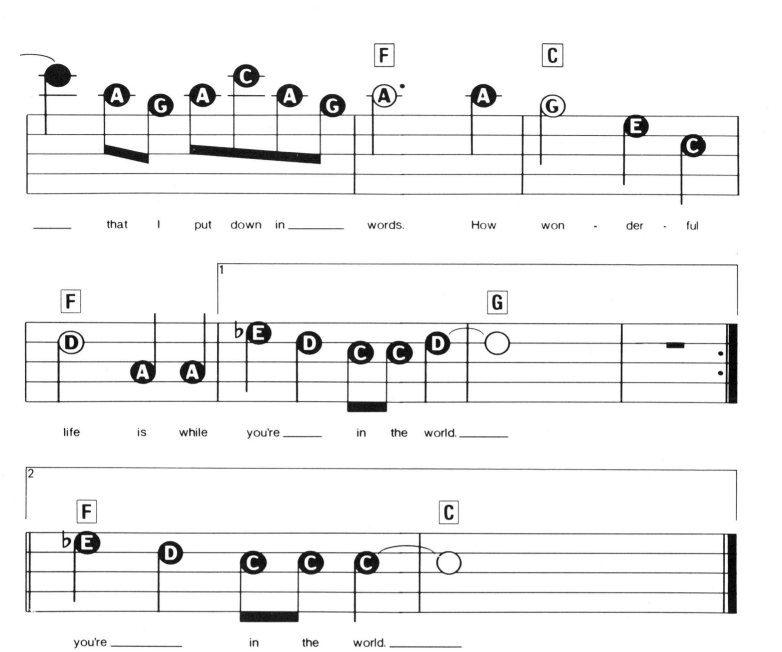

that I put down in _____ words. How won - der - ful

life is while you're _____ in the world. _____

you're _____ in the world. _____

3. I sat on the roof and kicked off the moss.
   well a few of the verses, well they've got me quite cross,
   But the sun's been quite kind while I wrote this song,
   It's for people like you that keep it turned on.

4. So excuse me forgetting but these things I do
   You see I've forgotten if they're green or they're blue,
   Anyway the thing is what I really mean
   Yours are the sweetest eyes I've ever seen.

E-Z Play® TODAY Registration Guide For All Organs

On the following chart are 10 numbered registrations for both tonebar (TB) and electronic tab organs. The numbers correspond to the registration numbers on the E-Z Play TODAY songs. Set up as many voices and controls listed for each specific number as you have available on your instrument. For more detailed registrations, ask your dealer for the E-Z Play TODAY Registration Guide for your particular organ model.

REG. NO.		UPPER (SOLO)	LOWER (ACCOMPANIMENT)	PEDAL	GENERALS
1	Tab	Flute 16', 2'	Diapason 8' Flute 4'	Flute 16', 8'	Tremolo/Leslie – Fast
	TB	80 0808 000	(00) 7600 000	46, Sustain	Tremolo/Leslie – Fast (Upper/Lower)
2	Tab	Flute 16', 8', 4', 2', 1'	Diapason 8' Flute 8', 4'	Flute 16' String 8'	Tremolo/Leslie – Fast
	TB	80 7806 004	(00) 7503 000	46, Sustain	Tremolo/Leslie – Fast (Upper/Lower)
3	Tab	Flute 8', 4', 2⅔', 2' String 8', 4'	Diapason 8' Flute 4' String 8'	Flute 16', 8'	Tremolo/Leslie – Fast
	TB	40 4555 554	(00) 7503 333	46, Sustain	Tremolo/Leslie – Fast (Upper/Lower)
4	Tab	Flute 16', 8', 4' Reed 16', 8'	Flute 8', (4) Reed 8'	Flute 8' String 8'	Tremolo/Leslie – Fast
	TB	80 7766 008	(00) 7540 000	54, Sustain	Tremolo/Leslie – Fast (Upper/Lower)
5	Tab	Flute 16', 4', 2' Reed 16', 8' String 8', 4'	Diapason 8' Reed 8' String 4'	Flute 16', 8' String 8'	Tremolo/Leslie
	TB	40 4555 554 Add all 4', 2' voices	(00) 7503 333	57, Sustain	
6	Tab	Flute 16', 8', 4' Diapason 8' String 8'	Diapason 8' Flute 8' String 4'	Diapason 8' Flute 8'	Tremolo/Leslie – Slow (Chorale)
	TB	45 6777 643	(00) 6604 020	64, Sustain	Tremolo/Leslie – Slow (Chorale)
7	Tab	Flute 16', 8', 5⅓', 2⅔', 1'	Flute 8', 4' Reed 8'	Flute 8' String 8'	Chorus (optional) Perc Attack
	TB	88 0088 000	(00) 4333 000	45, Sustain	Tremolo/Leslie – Slow (Chorale)
8	Tab	Piano Preset or Flute 8' or Diapason 8'	Diapason 8'	Flute 8'	
	TB	00 8421 000	(00) 4302 010	43, Sustain	Perc Piano
9	Tab	Clarinet Preset or Flute 8' Reed 16', 8'	Flute 8' Reed 8'	Flute 16', 8'	Vibrato
	TB	00 8080 840	(00) 5442 000	43, Sustain	Vibrato
10	Tab	String (Violin) Preset or Flute 16' String 8', 4'	Flute 8' Reed 8'	Flute 16', 8'	Vibrato or Delayed Vibrato
	TB	00 7888 888	(00) 7765 443	57, Sustain	Vibrato or Delayed Vibrato

NOTE: TIBIAS may be used in place of FLUTES. VIBRATO may be used in place of LESLIE.